Is there a Gospel for the rich?

The Christian in a capitalist world

RICHARD HARRIES
Bishop of Oxford

MOWBRAY

Mowbray
A Cassell imprint
Villiers House, 41/47 Strand, London WC2N 5JE, England
387 Park Avenue South, New York, NY 10016–8810, USA

First published 1992

British Library Cataloguing-in-Publication Data
A catalogue record for this book is available from the British Library.

Library of Congress Cataloging-in-Publication Data
Available from the Library of Congress.

ISBN 0–264–67276–3

Phototypeset by Intype, London
Printed and bound in Great Britain by Biddles Ltd, Guildford and Kings's Lynn

Contents

Acknowledgements

Biblical quotations are mostly from the Revised Standard Version of the Bible, copyright 1946, 1952, © 1971, 1973 The Division of Christian Education of the National Council of Churches of the USA.

*In memory of Jim Bottomley (1914–1969)
who lived out many of the concerns in this book
and for those who respected and loved him*

Preface

The themes of this book have been with me for many years. The foundation for my thinking on some of them was laid when I lectured in Christian ethics at Wells Theological College. In recent years some of the subjects have had preliminary outings in lectures at universities, churches and to general audiences. The spur to produce a book, however, was provided by the invitation to deliver the Hughes-Cheong (St Peter's) lectures in Melbourne during August 1991. I am grateful to the Trustees and also to those who provided warm hospitality both in Melbourne and in other parts of Australia.

I am also grateful to a wide range of people who have shared their thoughts with me and made detailed comments on earlier drafts of this book.

Richard Oxon,
October 1991

AND as he was setting out on his journey, a man ran up and knelt before him, and asked him, 'Good Teacher, what must I do to inherit eternal life?' And Jesus said to him 'Why do you call me good? No one is good but God alone. You know the commandments: "Do not kill, Do not commit adultery, Do not steal, Do not bear false witness, Do not defraud, Honour your father and mother".' And he said to him, 'Teacher, all these I have observed from my youth.' And Jesus looking upon him loved him, and said to him, 'You lack one thing; go, sell what you have, and give to the poor, and you will have treasure in heaven; and come, follow me.' At that saying his countenance fell, and he went away sorrowful; for he had great possessions.

And Jesus looked around and said to his disciples, 'How hard it will be for those who have riches to enter the kingdom of God!' And the disciples were amazed at his words. But Jesus said to them again, 'Children, how hard it is to enter the kingdom of God! It is easier for a camel to go through the eye of a needle than for a rich man to enter the kingdom of God.' And they were exceedingly astonished.

(Mark 10.17–27 from the Revised Standard Version. See also Matthew 19.16–30 and Luke 18.18–30)

1

Who Then Can Be Saved?

Alexandria was one of the richest and most sophisticated cities in the ancient world. When Christianity established itself there it is not surprising that in due course a good number of wealthy men and women were drawn to the Church. However, understandably, they were shocked by the challenge which Jesus made to people with money. They read the story with which this book begins and, like Christians in every age, felt profoundly uncomfortable. Did it really mean that they had to divest themselves of all their wealth before they could be a follower of the Lord Jesus Christ? Or was there some other way, whereby they could retain their possessions but use them in accordance with God's will? It was in response to this situation that the Alexandrian theologian, Clement, in the second century wrote his famous treatise *Who then is the rich man that shall be saved?* What Clement taught will be discussed in more detail in Chapter 3. The point now is to face squarely that challenge, 'Who then can be saved?' According to Jesus it is easier for a camel to go through the eye of a needle than for a rich man to enter the Kingdom of God. Even allowing for what the scholars like to call 'oriental hyperbole', the thrust of Christ's teaching is clear and disturbing.

But who are the rich? When, in Australia, I gave some lectures under the title 'Is there a Gospel for the rich?', a number of people came up to me and said, 'I must ring my wealthy friends and persuade them to come.' It was always assumed that the wealthy were other people. One of the most curious and slightly perverted features of riches is that very few people will actually admit that they are rich. The rich are always other people, the multi-millionaires as opposed to the ordinary millionaires. The average person from the professional classes or the person in the higher realms of management probably do not think of themselves as rich. Indeed, they sometimes cry poverty. But they are of course extraordinarily rich compared to most people in Great Britain. And everybody in Great Britain is rich compared with the millions in the world who are starving. There has deliberately been no attempt in this book to define the rich. We can each of us decide for ourselves, on our own definition, whether we think we count as rich or not. What is required, however, is honesty. With whom are we comparing ourselves? The average gross weekly wage in Great Britain in 1989 was £269 for a man and £182 for a woman. That is one line we could draw, so that at least we know whether we are above or below the average. There are dangers, however we define ourselves. To define ourselves as poor because we are only earning £30,000 a year compared with the neighbour's £90,000 per year, and to use this as an excuse for giving very little away, is hypocrisy. On the other hand, to be racked with unproductive guilt because we are earning £30,000 a year and another neighbour has only a pension of £4,000 per annum to live on is equally useless.

In 1985 the World Bank defined the poverty line as £216 (US$370) a year. One billion people were living at or below that level. When Paul Vallely went to Africa he said he felt neither rich nor poor, but

> In Africa I realised that in global terms I occupied no such midway point and returned to England with trepidation and thought of rich men and camels. . . . When so many people lived in such abject poverty there could be no neutral ground and there was no possibility of absenteeism. You are either with the poor, as Christ was, or against them. We in the West are against them, whether we know it or not.[1]

Clearly, compared to most of the world, the majority of us would probably have to define ourselves as well off.

This raises the whole question of our feelings of guilt. These had better be dealt with at the outset because half-acknowledged feelings of guilt are usually both unhealthy and unproductive. One Christian friend who operates both successfully and as a force for good in the financial world tells me that, although he tries to make the world a tiny bit better place for the poor of all descriptions,

> I do so in a remarkably comfortable way, . . . so I feel guilty. Part of me says that there is nothing wrong in good food, good wine, good things provided they are not an end in themselves and that 'give your goods to the poor' could mean 'use your talents for the poor' but . . .

Many of us will echo that sigh. Two extremes need to be avoided. First, some people are so guilt-ridden that they are emotionally crippled themselves and are of no use to anyone else. The Christian faith should come as a healing power for such guilt. Secondly, however, few of us would want to be people who are so released from feelings of guilt that we are totally blind to the contrast between Christ's ideal and our own lives.

In the trenches of the First World War, Wilfred Owen wrote a poem apparently envying all those who could lose imagination and shut out of their minds the terrible things that were happening around them. Yet in the end he repudiates this insensibility.

> Wretched are they, and mean
> With paucity that never was simplicity.
> By choice they made themselves immune
> To pity and whatever mourns in man.[2]

Guilt about money can be unhealthy and unproductive. For what is required of us first of all is not guilt but gratitude. God has set us on a good earth and bestowed many blessings upon us. He wants us to enjoy these, not be riddled by *Angst* about them. The rabbis have a saying that at the last judgement we will be called to account not only for the wrong we have done but for the pleasures put in our way which we failed to enjoy. There is still an unhealthy, puritanical element in many forms of Christianity, which spoils people's pleasure in things while failing to lead them to do anything really constructive about the ills of the world. On the other hand an element of unease, a sense that things are askew, which leads us to want to change this state of affairs, is not only a healthy but also an essential element in the Christian faith. If there is one attitude worse than useless guilt it is insensitive smugness and complacency.

'The religion of gratitude cannot mislead us', wrote Wordsworth.[3] It is where the religion of most people begins and in which it should continue to be grounded. For the rich this will include many of the good things of life which are denied to other people. Because they are denied to other people this will be a sadness, and in the case of the necessities of life, an outrage. But gratitude, rather than self-righteousness or smugness, is still in order for what we enjoy.

Feelings of guilt which simply spoil a person's enjoyment of what they have, while failing to prod them to do anything about the debilitating conditions of those who have nothing, are pathological and need to be cured. On the other hand, a genuine gratitude can and should co-exist with a determination to relieve the plight of those in misery.

Lord Runcie of Cuddesdon often uses a grace which contains the following phrases:

> Deepen our gratitude,
> Enlarge our sympathies
> And order our affections in generous and unselfish lives.

This, I think, gets it right. For any sensitive Christian there is bound to be a continuing unease. This arises not simply because of the contrast between our own comfortable lives and the abject misery of so many millions but also because many of the attitudes of the capitalist world seem to strike at the heart of our understanding of the Christian faith. A market economy takes it for granted that self-interest, competition and success in worldly matters are essential features of life. As will be argued later in this book, these need not be wholly bad; indeed, there is a basic congruity

between the Christian faith and a free market. Nevertheless, certain characteristics of the capitalist system as we know it in practice are certainly
inimical to Christian faith, and it is quite right that we should be sensitive
to this and alive to the contradiction that it presents to our value system.
Christians will take comfort from the Pauline doctrine of justification by
grace through God's faith. As Luther put it, we are always at once sinful
and justified (*simul iustus et peccator*). I do not think this means that all our
feelings of unease ought to disappear. On the contrary, in many ways they
may become intensified. But it should enable us to live with ourselves,
with joyous gratitude to God for the many blessings he bestows upon us
and a heartfelt determination to channel our unease into constructive
action to change things for the better.

This book begins with the invitation of Jesus to the rich man to give
away his possessions and follow him. It is an invitation that is characteristic
of the absolute nature and total claim that the teaching of Jesus makes
upon people. The Church has never known how to handle this teaching,
for it lies uneasily with the considerations of ordinary prudence which are
necessary for day-to-day living. For most of Christian history, the Church
taught that there are two standards, one exalted and one ordinary. Eusebius in the fourth century put it in these words:

> Two ways of life were thus given by the law of Christ to his Church. The
> one is above nature and common living. It admits not marriage, child-bearing,
> property or the possession of wealth, but wholly and permanently separate
> from the customary life of man, devotes itself to the service of God
> alone. . . . The other life, more humble and more human, permits men to unite
> in marriage, and to have children, to undertake office, to command soldiers
> who are fighting in a good cause . . . a kind of secondary piety is attributed
> to them, giving them such help as their lives require.[4]

The reformers in the sixteenth century found this distinction untenable.
In the New Testament they saw a single law, the law of Christ, which
bears on all Christians. The New Testament knows nothing of two classes
of Christians. Nevertheless, the reformers were hardly more successful than
their forebears in doing justice to the absolute nature of the teaching of
Jesus. They too had to adopt various forms of dualism, standards applicable to everyday conduct and higher ideals applicable under certain
circumstances for the individual.

Some kind of dualism is inescapable for most Christians. It is not usually
practical for them to give away all their own money. It is not appropriate,
indeed it would usually be wrong, for them to give away the assets of a
company that they were serving. Nevertheless, one of the features of Christian history is the way the Word of God keeps breaking through into
people's lives, unsettling them and refusing to allow them to be content
with things as they are. About the year AD 269 a young man called
Anthony went into the Church and heard the gospel with which this book

began being read. As the great Athanasius, who wrote Anthony's life, put it:

> Anthony, as though God had put him in mind of the saints, and the passage had been read on his account, went out immediately from the church, and gave the possessions of his forefathers to the village.[5]

Anthony heard the Word of God speaking to him personally through that gospel. The invitation of Christ to the young man in the gospel story became an invitation to him in the present. This example of Anthony was to have a decisive influence. From it sprang the great movement of Christian monasticism and it was to have a crucial role in St Augustine's conversion. He wrote:

> For I had heard the story of Anthony, and I remembered how he had happened to go into a church while the Gospel was being read and had taken as a counsel addressed to himself when he heard the words 'Go home and sell all that belongs to you. Give it to the poor, and so the treasure shall be in heaven: then come back and follow me.'[6]

The call of Anthony helped Augustine hear the Word of God to him in his situation and gave him inspiration to become an obedient follower of Christ. That Word still comes to people today. Sometimes it leads them to become monks or nuns. Sometimes the call is to do something creative with their wealth. If Christians in the past had not been touched by a certain 'holy extravagance' the cathedrals which are so much admired today would never have been built, and many of the great works of art would not have been painted or sculpted.

The Byzantine emperors would no doubt be accused of conspicuous consumption. They kept a vast retinue, including at some periods more than 500 clergy on the staff of Hagia Sophia in Constantinople. They had a centre for mosaics and other works of art, from which artists went out all over the empire. They lavished money on gifts for foreign rulers and on diplomacy generally. All this was done partly to reveal the glory of God, in particular the glory of God through his ruler on earth, and partly to maintain political harmony both within the empire and with potentially hostile states. They believed that lavish expenditure was a creative use of our God-given resources, and provided valuable employment for others.

One clergyman who was left a great deal of money did not simply give it away or invest it in the ordinary way. He used it to finance a series of ventures in the theatre, publishing and politics. Some of these failed. But it was an attempt to use the money in a bold and free way to further the work of the kingdom. Of course, because we are human, there is usually a very human motivation present in such ventures, whether among the Byzantine emperors or wealthy philanthropists. But our motives are always mixed and this holy extravagance seems much more admirable than an unholy hoarding.

For most of the time we are caught up with the claims of family, friends and work. Our life is guided by considerations of ordinary prudence. Such prudence is perfectly proper. But to be a Christian is to be open to the call of God as it comes to us through the scriptures and the conditions of life. Anthony heard Christ speaking to him personally; so did Augustine and so have millions of others. We may not be able to or it may not be right to respond literally to Christ's call to give away everything that we have. Nevertheless, the story remains haunting. As Leslie Houlden puts it, commenting on the story of Christ and the rich man,

> For we are bound to feel that it is very close to the heart of what Christian commitment involves. We cannot cheerfully relegate it to the scrap-heap of outmoded imperatives. . . . It would be a strange Christian (though they exist) who said straight out that the story of Jesus and the rich man had now no force at all. Such a one would seem to have given up the whole moral identity of the Gospel. The story haunts us.[7]

In previous generations the Church reminded human beings of their essential poverty before God by the *memento mori*, the sign of our mortality, the skull and crossbones on memorials. The Venetians, who ruled a great mercantile empire for nearly 900 years, used, in old age, to give away or pass on all their wealth and enter a monastery. Despite their terrible brutality, rapacity and greed the Venetians knew that in the end we have to appear before God with empty hands. Today, we cannot rest content with the Venetian solution to this problem. We cannot delay our response until after we have made our pile, and we cannot separate the way we make our pile from the way we intend to end our life. We are called to be obedient to Christ in our career as much as in our retirement. We are called to obedience in the world of business as much as in the world of the monastery. The worlds of commerce, trade, banking and finance all stand under the judgement of God and the claim of Christ. The Venetians were often personally generous to the poor as well as lavish in spending on the arts. But they were ruthless in the pursuit of profit, even to the extent of totally devastating the world's greatest Christian city, Constantinople, in 1204. We cannot tolerate today such double standards. The political and economic system itself has to be made to serve humane ends.

There are a number of reasons why Christian obedience in a capitalist world raises fresh urgent questions. First, with the dramatic collapse of communism in the former Soviet Union and Eastern Europe, capitalism holds the field. No longer is the debate between capitalism and communism, for the latter has been discredited and discarded. Yet the millions of poor in the developing world constantly tell us their experience of capitalism is a bad one. They are desperately worried that the collapse of communism in Eastern Europe and the old Soviet Union will serve as a pretext for underwriting the capitalisms that they themselves experience as oppressive.

Secondly, there emerged a new Christian right whose economic standpoint was close to that of President Reagan and Mrs Thatcher during their terms of office. Associated in Great Britain with Brian Griffiths, now Lord Griffiths, formerly an adviser of Mrs Thatcher, and in the USA with the Roman Catholic layman Michael Novak, these thinkers have challenged the Christian consensus which has prevailed for nearly seventy years. This consensus worked on the assumption that all right-minded, right-thinking Christians concerned to relate their faith to the economic order would be politically left of centre. They have held the moral and theological high ground. Whatever the validity of the arguments which challenge this consensus, and these arguments will be considered in some detail, the challenge itself can only be welcomed as giving new impetus to a vital debate.

Thirdly, there has in recent years emerged an evangelical social ethic, sometimes quite radical. For the past hundred years in Britain, Christian thinking on these issues has been dominated by Christian socialists of an Anglo-Catholic or liberal outlook. Again, the challenge to this way of thinking, whatever its validity, which again will be considered in more detail later, can only be welcomed. This approach, which seeks to be more definitely biblically based, and which is exhibited for example in the work of the Oxford economist Donald Hay, is very far from being identical with a new Christian right. In one manifestation it takes the concept of the transformation of the social order as seriously as liberation theologians take the notion of its liberation.

The result of all this has been a lively intellectual debate. The Social Affairs Unit has produced a number of booklets critical of various aspects of the consensus which existed on social, economic and political policies. Many of them make important points which need to be addressed, even if they are not finally persuasive. In 1991 there was a major academic conference on 'Religion and the Resurgence of Capitalism' at Lancaster University, with an underlying question of how the tiger of capitalism is to be ridden. Meanwhile, in London a number of major consultations on the morality of wealth creation and allied subjects were mounted by the Institute of Economic Affairs and the Institute of Directors, in which I took part together with people like Peter Morgan, Michael Novak, the Roman Catholic Bishop John Jukes of Strathearn and the former Chief Rabbi Lord Jakobovits. The doyen of Christian ethicists who have written on economic matters, Professor Ronald Preston, produced *Religion and the Ambiguity of Capitalism*, standing firmly in the tradition of *Religion and the Rise of Capitalism* by R. H. Tawney, *Religion and the Decline of Capitalism* by V. A. Demant and his own *Religion and the Persistence of Capitalism*.

The concept of ambiguity which Preston uses in his latest book is a thoroughly Niebuhrian term. It springs out of a Christian understanding of human nature as at once made in the image of God and flawed, and examines the implications of this in the economic and political spheres. In relation to democracy Niebuhr wrote, in what is still the best Christian defence of liberal democracy, 'Man's capacity for justice makes democracy possible; but man's inclination to injustice makes democracy necessary.'[8] It is this spirit that should also guide our approach to capitalism.

Ronald Preston uses the word ambiguity

> to refer to the analysis of a phenomenon which has an important and valid aspect but which at the same time has aspects, inseparable from what is valuable, which are undesirable. . . . In respect to particular social institutions like capitalism, it is possible at least in theory to benefit from the positive side and direct a counter balance to the negative side.[9]

Is There a Gospel for the Rich? is written in the conviction that this positive side must be emphasized. In short, instead of Christians blocking out any serious thought of the capitalist world because of their guilt and confusion about it, the market and all it entails must be entered positively. However, the necessity of erecting a strong counterbalance to the negative side must be taken no less seriously. The concept of ambiguity can lead to indecision and indifference. In contrast to this, what is urged here is action of a double kind, on the one hand in favour of the market and on the other hand in support of policies which correct its inevitable biases in favour of the rich and powerful.

The good news of God's love in Jesus Christ always comes with the possibility of transformation now, by that presence and power who in the end will transfigure and irradiate all things. It is that possibility of transformation which is one of the main themes of this book, transformation of both ourselves and the wider socio-economic order. This includes the rich and the sphere in which they operate.

The rich are people too, and so they share many of the ills to which flesh is heir. These include sickness, handicapped children, problems of relationships, divorce, death and all the pressures of striving to compete in a competitive world. Children of a wealthy home who are emotionally rejected by their parents and who grow up to become drug addicts are indeed to be pitied. It is of course true, as the cynic has often observed, that if one is going to be unhappy, it is far better to be unhappy on a comfortable income. Nevertheless, the unhappiness of the rich is still unhappiness. From this can spring a desire for help and a new life of a different quality. It is usually our own personal need, whether we are poor or rich, powerful or powerless, that turns us to God and enlists us in the ranks of the poor who are blessed.

This does not mean that a person has to be bludgeoned into discovering some inner need or weakness as a pre-condition for becoming a religious believer. Dietrich Bonhoeffer quite rightly rejected this approach as pointless, ignoble and un-Christian.[10] We are called to stand on our own two feet, assuming responsibility for our lives. Nevertheless, unless a person is open to the anguish of the world and in some way feels the needs of others, it is difficult to see how he or she can hear the Gospel. For the good news of the presence of God's Kingdom is only good news to those who are looking and longing for it.

The rich have souls and there is only one Gospel. The question, however, is whether we are capable of hearing that Gospel or whether our own sense of self-sufficiency, smugness and superiority makes us deaf. There is also the question of whether it is possible to hear the good news of the Gospel without at the same time in some way trying to respond to the challenge it presents.

A long debate has taken place down the ages about the relationship between the good news of God's grace and the ethical challenge presented by the teaching of Jesus.[11] It is quite clear in the New Testament, for example, that Jesus teaches about and shows forth God's unreserved love for every one of his creatures and at the same time calls us to respond to ethical standards presented without limit or qualification. My own view is that these are two aspects of the one love of God. We can see this by reflecting on the fact that other people's expectations of us are integrally bound up with the kind of people they are. For example, musical parents want their children to develop all the musical ability they have within them. A person who spends his or her whole time drinking in a pub wants little more of a friend than that they be an agreeable drinking partner. If God's love for us is without limit then at the same time he wants us to grow into the fullness of that we have within us to be, and that includes coming to love as God himself loves us, for we are made in his image. We cannot therefore experience God's love for us without at the same time being conscious of the claim to reflect and express love in our own person. Jesus who puts before us the boundless love of God at the same time presents us with the absolute claims of that love. So this book is not only about the good news for the rich but about what Christian obedience actually involves in the capitalist world of today. We cannot truly hear the Gospel without a sincere willingness to be responsive to it and the more faithfully we grapple with what obedience to it might mean in the capitalist world the more we make ourselves able to hear the good news.

After some background chapters, I seek to address those in the business of creating wealth, those operating in a market economy, those of us who own things, shareholders and employees, and those with money to invest. I then consider the question of desperate poverty before exploring the possibility of transformation not only for ourselves but for the whole world.

This book is written not simply for people like myself, who in the light of world poverty must be regarded as rich, but more specifically for Christian lay men and women who work out their vocation in the industrial and commercial world. One of the great insights of the Reformation was the importance of secular work. Martin Luther argued that if a job is necessary to the working of human society then it is an honourable Christian vocation. From this point of view it is as Christian to be a banker as a bishop, as religious to be a stockbroker as a monk. Among Christians working in the financial world there is, I know, a great deal of goodwill. The City of London has traditionally been a place of great personal integrity. It has produced about a hundred guilds or livery companies who have done great charitable work. But the overwhelming question with which the world of today is faced is how the charitable impulse can make an impact on the system itself. How can the vastly complex, intricate network of financial transactions and regulations be made to serve rather than crush the poorest of the poor? For millions, this is, literally, a question of life and death. For the believer it is a matter of Christian obedience to the Lord who invites us to deny ourselves, take up our cross and follow him into the exchanges and markets of the world. If it turns out that there is a Gospel for the rich, then hearing that Gospel is inseparable from a willingness to hear the call of Christ to follow him where it is most difficult.

First it is necessary to ask, 'Who are the poor and why are they blessed?' for it is quite clear, according to the New Testament, that the Church belongs to the poor. Does this mean that those of us who are materially rich are excluded from the outset?

NOTES

1 Paul Vallely, *Bad Samaritans?* (Hodder & Stoughton, 1990), p. 7.
2 Wilfred Owen, 'Insensibility' in *War Poems and Others*, ed. Dominic Hibberd (Chatto & Windus, 1975), p. 89.
3 William Wordsworth, Letter to Sir George Beaumont (28 May 1825).
4 Eusebius.
5 Athanasius, *Vita S. Antoni: The Nicene and Post-Nicene Fathers*, Vol. IV, p. 196.
6 Augustine, *Confessions*, translated R. Pine-Coffin (Penguin, 1961), p. 177.
7 Leslie Houlden, *Truth Untold* (SPCK, 1991), p. 55.
8 Reinhold Niebuhr, *The Children of Light and the Children of Darkness* (Nisbet, 1945), p. vi.
9 Ronald Preston, *Religion and the Ambiguity of Capitalism* (SCM, 1991), p. 123.
10 Dietrich Bonhoeffer, *Letters and Papers from Prison* (Collins Fontana, 1959), pp. 106–8.
11 A. E. Harvey, *Strenuous Commands* (SCM, 1990). Anthony Harvey places the teaching of Jesus in the context of wisdom literature. He provides the best modern account of the ethics of Jesus and illuminates many areas.

2

Who Are the Poor and Why Are They Blessed?

Someone who was strongly drawn to the teaching of Jesus but who had a sharp nose for hypocrisy was D. H. Lawrence. In *The Rainbow*, Ursula Brangwen tries to relate her Sunday world to her weekday world:

> 'Sell all thou hast, and give to the poor', she heard on Sunday morning. That was plain enough for Monday morning too. As she went down the hill to the station, going to school, she took the saying with her. 'Sell all thou hast, and give to the poor'. Did she want to do that? Did she want to sell her pearl-backed brush and mirror, her silver candlestick, her pendant, her lovely little necklace, and go dressed in drab like the Wherrys: the unlovely, uncombed Wherrys, who were the 'poor' to her? She did not.
>
> She walked this Monday morning on the verge of misery. For she did want to do what was right. And she didn't want to do what the Gospel said. She didn't want to be poor – really poor. The thought was a horror to her: to live like the Wherrys, so ugly, to be at the mercy of everybody.[1]

In this passage Lawrence presents the challenge of our Lord's words and strips away any false romanticism about poverty. Another person who saw this quite clearly was Dr Johnson. He wrote

> It is impossible to pass a day or an hour in the confluxes of man without seeing how much indigence is exposed to contumely, neglect and insult.[2]

He knew that poverty leaves a person powerless and therefore open to the neglect and contempt of others.

Forced poverty is an evil. As during this chapter I will be considering not only forced poverty but voluntary poverty, nothing that is said must be allowed to contradict or undermine this first basic statement. Forced or involuntary poverty is an evil. It renders a person powerless and it brings suffering and death. The poor suffer more and die sooner. This conclusion has been borne out by countless studies in this country and it stares us in the face when we try to contemplate the one billion (one thousand million) people in the world living at or below starvation level, who are prone to numerous diseases and whose life expectancy is so short by our standards. This suffering and early death is contrary to the will of God. As Jon Sobrino, the Spanish-born theologian, stresses, the God of the Bible is the God of life. By contrast, poverty is that which brings death, as the 50 million people a year who die of hunger shows so starkly.

Nevertheless, we cannot escape the sayings in the New Testament about the blessedness of the poor.

> Blessed are you poor, for yours is the Kingdom of God. (Luke 6.20)

> Blessed are the poor in spirit, for theirs is the Kingdom of heaven. (Matthew 5.3)

It is clear from those two texts that the Kingdom of God belongs to a category of person described as poor or poor in spirit. Personally, or existentially, it raises the question of whether I am one of those poor to whom the Kingdom of God belongs. It is a life or death question. It is therefore crucially important to try to discover to what characteristics it is that the gospels are referring. Is it material poverty as Luke's version suggests? Whatever the spiritual dimension of this poverty it is clear that for Luke the reference is integrally linked to material deprivation. For a few verses further on Jesus is reported as saying, 'But woe to you that are rich, for you have received your consolation' (Luke 6.20, 24).

In the synoptic gospels the normal reference of the Greek word for poor (*ptōchos*) is to material poverty. The rich man is told to sell his possessions and give to the poor (Matthew 19.21). The widow was poor because her only possessions were the two coins which she gave to the temple treasury (Mark 12.44). Zaccheus, as a result of his transforming encounter with Jesus, promised to give half of his goods to the poor (Luke 19.8).

The reason that these poor are blessed is that they are one of the categories of people who are specially privileged in the new age that is being ushered in through the ministry of Jesus. When the disciples of John the Baptist came to enquire of Jesus whether he was the one who was expected they were sent back with the message:

> Go and tell John what you have seen and heard: the blind receive their sight, the lame walk, lepers are cleansed, and the deaf hear, the dead are raised up, the poor have good news preached to them. (Luke 7.22 and Matthew 11.5).

There is here a clear reference to Isaiah 61.1–2:

> The spirit of the Lord God is upon me, because the Lord has anointed me to bring good tidings to the poor; he has sent me to bind up the brokenhearted, to proclaim liberty to the captives, and the opening of the prison to those who are bound; to proclaim the year of the Lord's favour.

According to Luke it was this passage which Jesus read out in the synagogue and about which he said 'Today the scripture has been fulfilled in your hearing.' The Isaiah passage is a reference to the new age, to that rule of God when all that is wrong will be put right, when the whole earth will be transparent to the glory of God.

So one of the signs of the presence of the new age is that good news is proclaimed to the poor. The good news is that though they have lost out in this age, in the new, changed order they will be specially blessed. They will be at home and feel at home in God's Kingdom. It is all part of what has been called the great reversal, the first shall be last and the last shall be first. Lazarus is enclosed within the bosom of Abraham while Dives is far off and cut off from the blessings of the life to come. This is not because poverty is in itself good. On the contrary, the Hebrew mind thought of prosperity and flourishing as signs of God's blessing. Poverty was not something to be sought for its own sake. As G. B. Caird has written in relation to the Beatitudes in Luke:

> They are not a general benediction upon misfortune, as though poverty, hunger, grief, and public resentment were in themselves guarantees of eternal bliss. It is only in the presence of a magnificent banquet that the hungry man is more blessed than the well fed; and it is because Jesus has proclaimed the presence of the Kingdom that the advantage belongs to those who approach it with the greatest need and capacity for its inexhaustible riches, undistracted by the spurious consolations of the world.[3]

Matthew's version of the Beatitude reads 'Blessed are the poor in spirit', which the New English Bible translates as 'How blessed are those who know their need of God'. The emphasis here on a particular spiritual attitude seems very different from that of the Beatitude in Luke's version. However, if we regard the psalms as the main background for these texts and therefore, for Christ's own statement, the contradiction is more apparent than real. The Greek word *ptōchos*, which is used in the New Testament and in the Septuagint, the Greek version of the Hebrew scriptures, translates the Hebrew word *anawim* or its singular *ani*, the poor person. In the psalms there are many references to the poor, or the poor person. Indeed it could be argued that the whole of the Psalter is the prayer of 'the poor person'.

An analysis of the Psalter, in particular those psalms that contain a reference to the poor person, reveals the following points. First, these psalms are a prayer, or rather an anguished cry to God, out of suffering and distress. Secondly, they are expressions of continuing trust in God despite adverse circumstances. Thirdly, they express the hope that God is indeed righteous and will soon act to put right all that is wrong and, in particular, to vindicate his servant, the poor person. The poverty that is referred to in the psalms is not only material poverty but affliction in the widest sense. The one who prays has to suffer the machinations of evil people, oppression, brutality, scorn and these psalms are a cry to God on behalf of all those who are in this situation.

A further point about these psalms is that it is not always possible to be certain whether the person uttering them is a poor individual Israelite, suffering at the hands of his fellow countrymen, or the people as a whole oppressed by the surrounding nations. Sometimes in a particular psalm the meaning oscillates between the two. Sometimes both seem to be intended, as when a psalm begins in a very personal manner, referring to suffering which is individual and local, but ends on a triumphant note that God will vindicate his people Israel. This uncertainty about the subject of the psalms need not lead to lack of clarity. For anyone who, out of his or her suffering, puts trust in God is likely to have an imaginative sympathy with all those in a desperate situation, and will make prayer an act of solidarity with others in a similar plight. The individual who is suffering at the hands of his or her fellows will at the same time be conscious of the nation, itself vulnerable to oppressive surrounding powers.

A few examples will suffice to substantiate these general conclusions. Psalm 9, for example, is an act of praise and thanks to God, who judges the world righteously, and a prayer that he will not forget the cry of the afflicted but will act on their behalf. 'For the needy shall not always be forgotten, and the hope of the poor shall not perish for ever.' The psalm includes a reference to those who are oppressed and in trouble; it is about what 'I' suffer yet it ends on the theme 'Let the nations be judged before thee'. In Psalm 10, 'The wicked hotly pursue the poor . . . he lurks that he may seize the poor . . . he seizes the poor when he draws him into his net.' God is asked to arise and break the arm of the wicked. The reference is personal and local, for the wicked person is a man greedy for gain, he sits in ambush in the villages, and in hiding places he murders the innocent. But no less emphatic is the universal reference, 'The Lord is King for ever and ever; the nations shall perish from his land.'

There are a number of psalms that specifically describe the subject as poor and needy (Psalms 40, 69, 70, 86 and 109). 'As for me, I am poor and needy; but the Lord takes thought for me. Thou art my help and my deliverer; do not tarry, O my God' (Psalm 40.17). Psalm 69, one of the psalms where the subject is described as poor and needy, details personal experience of suffering: 'I am the talk of those who sit at the gate.' But this too ends, 'For God will save Sion and rebuild the cities of Judah'. Psalm 72, which is on the role of the king, describes him as defending the cause of the poor, giving deliverance to the needy and crushing the oppressors.

The importance of these psalms in shaping the Jewish and Christian mind, then and now, cannot be underestimated. Sabbath by Sabbath they were recited and meditated upon in the synagogue. In short, the poor who are blessed are the poor of the psalms. Their poverty includes material deprivation but it also includes any form of affliction and oppression. The poor are those who lose out before the powers that rule this world, political, economic and social. The rapacious individual, the exploiter, the tyrant and the imperial power are all those who in one way or another bring suffering to God's poor. But it is equally clear from the psalms that the poor are not those who are simply afflicted but those who out of their affliction continue to trust in God and look for his deliverance.[4]

The other fact to be borne in mind is that there was not such a sharp contrast in biblical times as there is today between the materially poor and at least some religious leaders. Many of the scribes, for example, lived entirely on charity. Some were artisans and combined their religious calling with a trade, as did Paul. But in the main they lived on subsidies. What we learn from the gospels about the way of life of Jesus is no less applicable to the majority of scribes at the time. He carried no money; for example, he had to ask for a denarius to be brought to him. He himself accepted hospitality in Bethany and elsewhere, and taught his disciples to do the same during their work of evangelism. Some better-off women among Jesus's followers put their financial resources at his disposal. Although there were some scribes who drew a regular income from the temple or through some other means became wealthy the majority belonged to the poorer classes. Examples from the second century include that of the teacher of the law R. Aqiba and his wife, who had to sleep in straw in the winter. R. Judah B. Eli, who is quoted in the Mishnah over 600 times, more than any other scholar, had only one cloak which he and his wife had to wear in turn when they went out, and six of his pupils had only one cloak between them. The most famous story concerns that of Hillel, who worked as a day labourer, earning half a denarius out of which he had to pay the school caretaker, leaving only a quarter of a denarius for the maintenance of himself and his family. On one occasion he could not find work and so was unable to pay the entrance fee for the school. Despite the winter weather he stayed outside and listened through the window and was later found there half frozen.[5] So the poor were not just those who were crushed by poverty but those who combined their poverty with a profound trust in God.

In the light of this background in the psalms and the experience of religious teachers some scholars want to translate *anawim* primarily as the 'pious ones', rather than 'the poor ones'. Indeed, the term 'poor' seems to have become a self-designation of certain Jews in the period after the Old Testament, for example in the Psalms of Solomon and the Dead Sea Scrolls.

In the accounts of Christ's passion in the gospels it is remarkable how the psalms which have influenced the story, and which may very well have been on the mouth of Jesus, are psalms of the poor person, the righteous sufferer. According to Luke, Jesus ends his life with the words 'Father, into thy hands I commit my spirit.' This was a prayer which every Jewish mother taught her children to say as they went to sleep. It is a quotation of Psalm 31, v. 5. Psalm 31 is about a subject who seeks refuge in God, and who trusts in his steadfast love even though he is the object of scorn and horror and all manner of affliction. Despite all this, 'I trust in thee,

O Lord, I say, Thou art my God' (Psalm 31.14). Psalm 69 has already been referred to. This may very well lie behind the words in John's gospel, 'I thirst', for in this psalm of the righteous sufferer who is drowning in the waters of death we have the verse: 'I am weary with my crying; my throat is parched. My eyes grow dim with waiting for my God.' Verse 29 reads, 'But I am poor and needy; let thy salvation, O God, set me on high.' Above all, there is Psalm 22, which underlies so many of the references in the Passion account, the piercing of the hands and feet, the dividing of the garments and casting lots for them, the scorn of all those around and so on. According to Mark the opening words of Psalm 22 were uttered by Jesus on the cross: 'My God, my God, why hast thou forsaken me?' Verse 24 of Psalm 22 reads, in the Prayer Book version: 'For he hath not despised, nor abhor'd, the low estate of the poor' (the Greek of the Septuagint is *ptōchos*; the Hebrew text uses *ani*). Verse 26 says that the poor shall eat and be satisfied; again it is the *anawim*, sometimes translated in the Revised Standard Version as 'afflicted'. Christ in his dying on the cross is seen as the poor person *par excellence*, the devout afflicted one who puts his trust totally in God. Jesus focuses in himself the cry of the psalms that those who suffer because of the wickedness of this world but who continue to trust in God and look for his deliverance may indeed be delivered.

It is clear from this analysis of the Beatitudes against the background of the psalms that 'the poor' cannot be neatly classified as either a social or a religious category. It includes elements of both. The poor exhibit faith, for their cry is to God and they continue to hope and trust in him. On the other hand, the poor person is definitely someone who is losing out in some way because he or she is up against the world as it is. This understanding of the meaning of 'the poor' finds support from recent Vatican documents on liberation theology.

The Vatican, or more precisely the Congregation for the Doctrine of the Faith, has responded to liberation theology with two documents. First there was the *Instruction on Certain Aspects of the 'Theology of Liberation'*, published in 1984. This focuses on the psalms and in particular on the sufferings of the poor of the Lord who are faithful to the God of the Covenant. The Instruction emphasizes that it is not simply material poverty that is referred to but all kinds of hostility and injustice. Salvation comes from God alone and the poor live in total confidence in him and in hope of the liberation he will bring. It also stresses the Old Testament denunciation of those who oppress the poor and emphasizes God's role as the defender and liberator. These Old Testament requirements are found in the New Testament in a more radicalized form in the Beatitudes and the command of fraternal love to everyone, with no discrimination or limitation.

And in the figure of the poor, we are led to recognise the mysterious presence of the Son of Man who became poor himself for love of us. This is the foundation of the inexhaustible words of Jesus on the judgement in Matthew 25.31–46. Our Lord is one with all in distress; every distress is marked by his presence.

It is in the light of the Christian vocation to fraternal love that the rich are forcefully reminded of their duty, as in James, and as 1 Corinthians 11.17–34 indicates, there is a bond which exists between participation in the sacrament of love and sharing with the brother in need.

The document goes on to affirm unambiguously the preferential option for the poor but in section 9 criticizes the way that Marxist presuppositions and assumptions have permeated some liberation theology. There has, according to the instruction, been a disastrous confusion between the *poor* of the scriptures and the *proletariat* of Marx. The Church of the poor has been identified with a particular class which has become aware of the requirements of the revolutionary struggle. This is a distortion. Christianity is not primarily about the class struggle nor are the rich primarily a class enemy to be fought. On the contrary,

> The Church of the *poor* signifies the preference given to the poor, without exclusion, whatever the form of their poverty, because they are preferred by God. The expression also refers to the Church of our time, as communion and institution and on the part of her members, becoming more fully conscious of the requirement of evangelical poverty.

The second document, *Instruction on Christian Freedom and Liberation*, published in 1986, takes up similar themes. The prophets are God's spokesmen for the poor. God is the supreme refuge for the little ones and oppressed and the Messiah will have the mission of taking up their defence. The poor of the psalms put their trust in God, to whom they commend their cause, and they know that communion with him is the most precious of all treasures. In the New Testament the poor of God make up the first fruits of a people humble and lowly who live in hope of the liberation of Israel. Mary personifies this hope and to her the people of the poor turn spontaneously and confidently. Jesus both proclaimed the good news to the poor and himself became poor for love of us. He wishes to be recognized in the poor and in those who suffer or are persecuted.

Although the Vatican documents had an unfavourable reception from supporters of liberation theology they are in fact highly sympathetic to many of its major themes. What they do is seek to expunge, surely rightly, alien Marxist elements that have infiltrated into the proclamation. The approach of the Vatican to liberation theology seems to reflect changes taking place within liberation theology itself. In Gutiérrez the poor were primarily seen in Marxist terms. In Sobrino, however, the poor are regarded as the authentic theological source for understanding Christian truth. One survey of liberation theology concludes that the perception of the poor in essentially theological rather than sociological categories 'is the most profound change taking place in the thinking of liberation theologians at this time'.[6]

Given the arresting nature of the statement that the poor are blessed and its significance as part of the central thrust of Jesus' teaching about the dawning of God's reign on earth, it is disappointing not to find more on this theme outside the synoptic gospels. On the other hand, the fact that this was not a major preoccupation of the early Church can be seen as a sign of the authenticity of this theme as part of the genuine teaching of Jesus. It is not difficult to understand why the blessedness of the poor was not taken up more strongly in the early Church. With the resurrection the focus was on Jesus rather than his teaching about the Kingdom. He became the message, for in him the Kingdom had in some decisive sense already come. Furthermore, the first Christians were overwhelmed by a sense of their own place in the new order, either as Jews who had had their understanding radically altered or as Gentiles who had come to faith in the God of Abraham, Isaac, Jacob and Jesus. Although modern scholarship suggests that the social make-up of the New Testament Church was not on the whole drawn from the poorest classes and there was relatively little persecution, it is still likely that the first Christians identified themselves as the poor who are blessed. The Beatitudes were included in the gospels of Matthew and Luke because the first Christians felt that they above all were the people to whom the beatitudes applied.

Nevertheless, there are one or two interesting hints that the wider reference of Jesus' teaching on material poverty was not entirely forgotten. In his letter to the Galatians Paul looked back to the time when he first became a follower of Jesus and a member of the Church. He remembers how fourteen years after his conversion he went to consult the Church leaders in Jerusalem, who agreed to his being an apostle to the Gentiles but urged him to remember the poor. It is this that lies behind Paul's major efforts to raise money which we read about in his second letter to the Corinthians. In addition there is the fierce denunciation of the rich in James 5, with its clear echoes of the early Church described in the second chapter of the Acts of the Apostles. When there was need, goods were sold and a general distribution was made. No doubt a number of influences lie behind this, not least Jewish traditions of charity. However, the Kingdom of God in the teaching of Jesus was over and again depicted as a feast, a feast to which the poor were bidden to come. In one parable the Kingdom of God is likened to a banquet to which people are invited. When one after another gives an excuse for not coming the host says, 'Go out quickly to the streets and lanes of the city, and bring in the poor and maimed and blind and lame' (Luke 14.21). Furthermore, Jesus taught that 'when you give a feast, invite the poor, the maimed, the lame, the blind, and you will be blessed' (Luke 14.13). The attempt to build a Christian community characterized by mutual giving and receiving, of sharing of this world's goods with those in need, which we have in the Acts of the Apostles, is a sign of the Kingdom to which Jesus pointed.

A study of the Beatitudes, from the standpoint of an African theologian, is subtitled *The Beatitudes as a Call to Community*.[7] The early Church, both in the radical sharing of goods in Jerusalem in the first days and later in the financial support given to the Jerusalem Church by congregations in Asia Minor, correctly drew the implication of *koinōnia*, or true community, from the Beatitudes. Rich and poor are called to a fresh relationship with God and a re-orientated relationship with one another.

In addition to oppressive material poverty there is voluntary poverty, or evangelical poverty as it is sometimes called, which came into its own at the end of the third and beginning of the fourth century. A good number of Christians, dissatisfied with how easy it was to become a Christian in a Roman empire that had adopted the Christian religion, and appalled by the laxity and luxury of many Christian lives, wanted to recapture the first fresh commitment of early Christianity. Previous generations of Christians had shown their love of the Lord by dying as martyrs. How now, in this new, more comfortable world, could they show a similar love? In answer to that question significant numbers went off to live in the deserts of Palestine and, above all, of Egypt. There, on the frontiers, they felt themselves to be battling with the forces of wickedness not only within themselves and for themselves but on behalf of the world. From these first Desert Fathers sprang the whole tradition of Christian monasticism. We know something of how they lived because spiritual tourists, voyeurs of the spiritual life, used to seek them out and record answers to their questions. From the sayings of the Desert Fathers we can discern something of their thinking on poverty.[8] They were not, like the early Franciscans, total beggars. They earned enough to live on by making simple goods from rushes or linen and selling them. Work was regarded as good and one monk borrowed a shilling to buy linen. Begging was regarded as an extra act of humility, not essential to the life. What was objected to was any kind of saving or storing up for the future. This was regarded as a lack of trust in God and was fiercely condemned. They refused to accept money for future needs, not even to make provision for illness. In the same spirit they got rid of all their possessions, including books, and even copies of the Gospel were sold for the poor. Total renunciation was demanded, there was to be absolutely no holding back of any kind. Anything held back would be attacked by demons. It is a style of life, except for the reference to demons, very much in the spirit of the Sermon on the Mount where we are exhorted to trust God totally, not to be anxious about what to wear or eat and to make no provision for the morrow. There is to be complete trust and confidence in God. I quote one example because it exhibits a surprisingly modern understanding of counselling techniques.

A brother asked an old man: 'Would you have me save two shillings for myself, in case I fall ill?' The old man, seeing into his heart that he wanted to save them, said: 'Yes.' And the brother went into his cell, and was worn down by his thoughts: 'Do you think the old man spoke the truth to me or not?' So he went back to the old man again who said: 'I told you to save them because I saw you intended to save them. But it is not good to save more than the body needs. If you keep two shillings, you will put your hope in them. And if by chance they are destroyed, God is then no longer thinking of our needs. Let us cast our thought upon the Lord: it is for him to care for us.'[9]

The spirit of the Desert Fathers is well caught by the Taizé rule in a way which is even closer to the spirit of the Sermon on the Mount. The Taizé rule reads:

> Poverty is not a virtue in itself. According to the Gospel, the poor learn to live without assurance of the morrow, in joyous confidence that they will lack nothing. The spirit of poverty does not consist in pursuing misery, but in setting everything in the simple beauty of creation. The spirit of poverty is to live in the gladness of today.[10]

The spirit of poverty is to live in the gladness of today, in simple, total trust upon God, and not building elaborate plans or dreaming escapist dreams for the future. The best-known and best-loved advocate of voluntary poverty is, of course, St Francis of Assisi, who carried his quest for total renunciation to unbelievable extremes. He did not simply live out a life of poverty, he sought to make his life conform in every possible way to the spirit of poverty, with all the energy and drive that other people pursue riches. This was done in no grim spirit but with a romantic embrace of Lady Poverty, whom he conceived to have been Christ's only companion during his ministry. In the spirit of the Sermon on the Mount and the Desert Fathers Francis saw poverty as a way of becoming more and more dependent upon God rather than his own resources. This enabled him to embrace the true joy and riches of God himself. As the Franciscan poet, Jacopone of Todi, wrote in later years:

> Poverty is to have nothing,
> And to desire nothing;
> And yet to possess everything,
> In the spirit of liberty.

Francis's embrace of poverty was also a form of sacrifice, a life offered to God. But first and foremost, it was a way of life chosen by Christ himself and therefore the highest and noblest of all professions. As St Francis described it, 'Naked to follow the naked Christ'.[11]

Nearer our own time one person who has approached voluntary poverty with a similar commitment is Charles de Foucauld. Born into an aristocratic family in 1858, he joined the French army and gained a reputation for himself as an explorer in Morocco, about which he wrote a weighty book. At this time he had no religious faith and lived a scandalous life, for which he was thrown out of the army. Then, quite surprisingly and suddenly at the age of 28, he discovered the reality of God. 'As soon as I came to believe there was a God', he wrote, 'I saw I could not do anything except live for him.' What Charles de Foucauld did, whether in search of pleasure or of God, he took to extremes. He joined the Trappist Order and sought out its most isolated and uncomfortable of monasteries. But all the time he felt a call to Nazareth. For he was fascinated by the fact that whereas the public ministry of Jesus was only three years long he had lived a hidden life for 30 years. So Charles de Foucauld went to Nazareth, where a monument exists to him today, dressed like a beggar, and obtained work as a handyman at the Convent of the Poor Clares. In one of his meditations at that time he imagines God saying to him these words:

> How well I have treated you! You are living at Nazareth, unknown, inordinately poor, lowly in smock and sandals, a poor servant to poor nuns. Some take you for a labourer of the lowest kind; others think you are an outcast; some think you are perhaps the son of a criminal. Most – nearly all in fact – take you for a fool. You obey the nuns and porteresses as I obeyed my parents. You give orders to nobody, absolutely no one. You work doing what you are told sometimes by one person, sometimes by another, never doing anything for yourself, nothing you yourself choose to do.[12]

All the time he sought to make this humble way of life, hidden from the world, an unbroken union with Jesus. The same was true when he went into the Sahara to minister to tribespeople. Eventually he was killed by a marauding gang and his life ended in apparent total failure.

Charles de Foucauld saw his poverty, which was not just material poverty, but powerlessness, ignominy and total obscurity, as a way of following Jesus and as a mystical identification with the unknown years of Nazareth, witnessing silently through humility and hiddenness. Very different, though still on the theme of spiritual poverty, are the reflections of Father Harry Williams. Spiritual poverty, which is to be sharply distinguished from penury, is a mental and spiritual state in which we enjoy the world to the full without wanting to possess it. Most of us, for example, do not worry about the fact that we do not possess great works of art. We enjoy looking at them and appreciating them for their own sake. This spiritual poverty is a concentration on the present, without trying either to hold on to the past or to grasp the future before it has come. It is rooted in God, who did not grasp and clutch but let go and emptied. In short:

> Poverty as a positive quality means the recognition that in the most real sense the world is mine, whoever owns it in the narrow technical sense. Poverty is thus the ability to enjoy the world to the full because I am not anxious about losing a bit of it or acquiring a bit of it. Poverty takes pleasure in a thing because it is, and not because it can be possessed. Poverty is thus able to taste the flavour of life to the full.[13]

This is a passage which reminds us of St Paul's words: 'as having nothing, and yet possessing all things' (2 Corinthians 6.10).

Such an outlook is admirable and much needed in a society characterized by consumerism. Nevertheless, there is a need to be slightly wary about exalting such an outlook while at the same time having every physical comfort. If one is protected from all the insecurity and harshness of physical poverty it is of course better to have an attitude of spiritual poverty than one of possessiveness. But such spiritual poverty should not lead to any sense of superiority over those who are oppressed by poverty and are trying to improve their lot. Nor should we totally identify such inner spiritual poverty with the poverty of the poor who are blessed, which seems to have a very much closer relationship to actual lack of possessions and losing out to hostile forces in the world. It is also important not so to romanticize poverty in general that we blur the distinction between forced poverty and voluntary poverty. Voluntary poverty, however extreme, remains a chosen way of life. Forced poverty is an imposition, an oppression, a destructive force.

Few people have written more realistically and sanely on the subject of poverty than Dr Johnson. No doubt this was because it was rooted in his own experience. His father's failing business had led to his own withdrawal from Oxford for lack of funds and he had to struggle for many years as a freelance writer in order to earn enough to live on. This family humiliation and personal hardship gave him a great tenderness to the poor. Not only did he give away substantial sums when he himself had barely enough to live on, he opened his house to those who were indigent. As Mrs Thrale records, 'Mr Johnson has more tenderness for poverty than any other man I ever knew. In consequence of these principles he has now in his house whole nests of people who would, if he did not support them, be starving.'[14] Johnson bitterly attacked those philosophers and poets who seemed to him to romanticize poverty:

> He that wishes to become a philosopher at a cheap rate, easily gratifies his ambition by submitting to poverty when he does not feel it, and by boasting his contempt of riches, when he has already more than he enjoys.[15]

The religious orders did not escape his strictures. Monks and nuns have all they want, pleasant surroundings, agreeable companions, security, freedom from worry and enjoyment of the world's esteem.

> Poverty may easily be endured, while associated with dignity and reputation, but will always be shunned and dreaded, when it is accompanied with ignominy and contempt.[16]

So far it has been argued that material poverty is an evil that needs to be eliminated. And it is important not falsely to romanticize crushing, involuntary poverty. Furthermore, the poor who are blessed in the Beatitudes are not those who are materially poor *per se* but those who, losing out in this world in a variety of ways (including being materially poor), continue to hope that God will put right all that is wrong and who therefore continue to trust in him. Nevertheless, many Christians since the third century have deliberately chosen a way of life that includes material poverty in order to live closer to Christ in an utter dependence upon God. Some of the Church's greatest saints have walked this path.

Without denying what has already been emphasized about the evil of enforced poverty, it is also noticeable that many people who are materially poor have exhibited the most remarkable human and spiritual character-istics. The situation is similar to that of suffering in general. Suffering is contrary to the will of God. Nevertheless, we all know people who have used their suffering in a positive way. This does not mean that God has designed the suffering in order to bring good qualities out of it. Suffering remains contrary to the will of God. For suffering often crushes. Yet also we cannot deny the fact that many people have developed the most remarkable qualities through it. As far as poverty is concerned the following character-istics have been fairly widely observed.

First, those who have little are likely to be much closer to the grain of life. They know what really matters and what is simply superficial. Their values tend to be truer because less misled by spurious consolations. Secondly, those with little are often remarkably generous. The first time my son travelled abroad across Turkey he was amazed to discover that the further east he went and the poorer people were, the more generous he found them. The solidarity of the poor in sharing is an aspect of this. A story is told from the Philippines of a group of a hundred or so farmers who came together to demand the land they wanted from the government. It was Christmas and at the Midnight Mass as they shared their rice cakes they reflected on the meaning of what they were doing. One emphasized the sharing. Another more profound observation followed this one. It was:

> Even if there is not enough, we will not follow the development economists who say 'let's first increase the GNP. Then if there is not enough, we will make sure that we will first feed those who will be strong enough to work. Others can take their chance after them.' No! We won't postpone the sharing, even if there is not enough. There will not be enough for everyone but no one will have nothing.

So, as Haddon Wilmer puts it:

> The Church is the community of people who listen to these words, and who are open to their criticism and invitation. 'Jesus Christ calls us to the freedom of sharing even while we are poor' (II Corinthians 8.9).[17]

Thirdly, the poor are more likely than the rich to have real faith in God. For the poor face life as it is and they know their need. They do not have the resources to disguise the true character of existence and they have no motive to cover up their own need of God. The media magnate Rupert Murdoch has suggested that now the developed world has a reasonable level of prosperity there is likely to be a religious revival. Alas, all human experience contradicts this pious optimism. Prosperity tends to lead to complacency and indifference. So often it is the poor of the world who have had the most heartfelt faith in God. For they have been most conscious of their need.

This chapter has suggested that the answer to the question, 'Who are the poor and why are they blessed?' is not an easy one. 'The poor' is not exclusively either a religious or a social category. The tension between the emphases in Matthew's version of the Beatitudes and Luke's is one that reflects the reality. Nevertheless, it can be said with some confidence that whatever else 'the poor' includes and refers to, it is certainly a religious category. This is borne out not only by Matthew's understanding of the Beatitude and the fact that *anawim* had become something of a technical religious term by the first century, but also because the prime background in the Hebrew scriptures for understanding the meaning of the poor is in the psalms, with their longing hope directed towards God. It is therefore understandable that the New English Bible should translate Matthew's Beatitude as 'How blessed are those who know their need of God' and that the Scots version should read 'How happie the puir as is humle afore God'. This said, and it is a theme which will emerge later in the book, the poor in this sense are *almost bound to be people who in one way or another come up against the powers that rule the world and who lose out as a result.*

Although this book is concerned with large questions such as the whole relationship between Christianity and the economic order, it is concerned with them not in an abstract way but from the standpoint of Christian discipleship. What am I expected to believe and do as a person who seeks to be obedient to Christ in the world of wealth and poverty? The Beatitudes are quite uncompromising in saying that I must first be one of 'the poor'. How do I become such a person?

The starting point is a recognition of our own needs. When I was a student at theological college a friend once said to me, 'our needs are angels'. Our needs are messengers from God and open us up to him. We all have needs. The needs of a highly pressured managing director in a competitive business environment are not entirely the same as those of a day labourer in the forests of Brazil. Nevertheless, they are his needs and God relates to us as the person we are, not as someone else whom we feel we would either like to be or ought to be. Those needs are of various kinds, sometimes mainly spiritual, for peace of mind or forgiveness. At other times the spiritual and the emotional overlap, as in our need for understanding and reassurance. But it is certainly not only through our so-called spiritual needs that we are meant to relate to God. He wants us to come to him as the person we are, honest, that is to say, real. Not pretending that we are someone else or more pious than we are but frankly and humbly.

This approach lays itself open to two charges. It could be argued that this is a religion of immaturity. We should not hunt around for inner weaknesses as a way into faith in God. But if moment by moment all things are held in existence by a source beyond us, a sense of ultimate dependence is not immaturity but acknowledgement of reality, like the air we breathe and the ground upon which we walk. When in our need, whether material, emotional or spiritual, we turn away from ourselves to receive from the fount from whom our being flows, we are acknowledging reality. We are in harmony with the way things are. It is the defiant assertion of a false autonomy that is immature.

The second charge is that to focus on our inner needs in this kind of way is very bourgeois and comfortable. It is a million miles away from the struggles of the exploited. Nevertheless, we have to start somewhere. Furthermore, unless we are also aware of our own need our attempt to meet the needs of others is likely to have a built-in flaw from the beginning. An awareness of our own personal needs is certainly not the end of religion. But for many people it is a legitimate starting point, a way into faith in God.[18]

As I come before God conscious of my own emptiness, my own emotional or spiritual bankruptcy, and look to him, I am one of those whom Christ pronounces blessed. I have come under the Kingship of Christ, into his Kingdom.

In answer to the question, 'Who are the poor?' it has been argued that 'the poor' is certainly a religious category though not that alone. The poor are those who put their whole trust in God, making themselves freely available for his service and looking to him for the world's salvation. This is in itself good news for the rich. If the poor referred exclusively to the destitute, then the rich would be excluded by definition. So it is in principle possible for the rich to become part of the poor who are blessed. Yet it is also clear that, on a biblical understanding, the poor lose out in this world. They come up against the forces of self-interest, both personal and organized, which tend to ignore or brush aside anyone who does not immediately serve their purpose. The poor stand against things as they are and suffer for things as they could become. When Christians first went into the desert in the third and fourth centuries, they did so not only in order to live moment by moment in dependence on God alone but also in order to engage in a spiritual fight against the powers of darkness that rule this world. They knew that they had to stand against the Roman world as it then was. Their way of taking a stand may only be the vocation of a few, but a stand of some kind has to be taken by all who would count themselves among the poor who are blessed.

The poor are blessed because their emptiness allows the fullness of God to dwell within them, his presence of peace and joy. It is not a form of self-punishment but of true riches, as Harry Williams reminds us. The tradition of voluntary poverty, from Francis to the Taizé community, brings before us the sheer delight of trusting fully in God. It is not a deprivation but an enrichment. Nevertheless, in order to avoid all forms of self-deception, hypocrisy and cant, Dr Johnson's warnings need to be heeded. Forced poverty, oppression and humiliation are evils. The rich person who wishes to be one of the poor who are blessed must at all costs avoid the self-deception of thinking that his or her situation can be compared to that of those whose actual powerlessness allows them to be treated as of little or no account.

The Vatican study of liberation theology and recent surveys of it suggest support for the understanding of the poor outlined in this chapter. The poor do indeed have a special place in the Church but this is to be understood first of all in theological rather than Marxist terms.

The radical inner freedom bestowed by a consciousness of our poverty in relation to God brings about also the possibility of radical sharing. 'Jesus Christ calls us to the freedom of sharing even while we are poor.' The community of Christians is built up of people who listen to the judgement and invitation of those words. So often, in practice, it has been the materially poor who have been able to live out the truth of those words. For material poverty, despite its manifest ill-effects, has also so often led people to profound faith in God and a generous sharing with others, which the rich, in contrast, often find so difficult. But we, the rich, are not by definition excluded. The invitation includes us too, as we come before God conscious of our own personal needs. For to us too Christ says:

> Come to me, all who labour and are heavy laden, and I will give you rest. Take my yoke upon you, and learn from me; for I am gentle and lowly in heart, and you will find rest for your souls. For my yoke is easy, and my burden is light. (Matthew 11.28–30)

We too are offered the freedom of sharing. The next chapter looks at the remarkable tradition of mutual giving and receiving that characterized the Church in the early centuries.

NOTES

1 D. H. Lawrence, *The Rainbow* (Heinemann, 1955), p. 282.
2 From an essay in *The Rambler*: Yale edition of *The Works of Samuel Johnson*, Vol. 3 (1969), p. 284.
3 G. B. Caird, *St Luke* (Penguin, 1963), p. 102.
4 This interpretation of the Psalms is supported by, for example, Dr Sue Gillingham, *Expository Times*, 100 (1988), pp. 15–19.
5 Joachim Jeremias, *Jerusalem in the Time of Jesus* (SCM, 1969), pp. 111–19.
6 E. Weir, 'Liberation theology comes of age', *Expository Times*, 98 (1986–87), p. 6.
7 John Pobee, *Who Are the Poor?* (WCC, 1988).
8 Helen Waddell, *The Desert Fathers* (Collins Fontana, 1962).

9 'The sayings of the Fathers' in *Western Asceticism*, ed. Owen Chadwick. Library of Christian Classics, Vol. XII (SCM, 1958), p. 82.

10 *The Rule of Taizé* (Les Presses de Taizé), 1968, p. 93.

11 John Moorman, *Richest of Poor Men* (Darton, Longman & Todd, 1977), p. 83.

12 Charles de Foucauld, *Spiritual Autobiography*, ed. Jean-François Six (Dimension Books, Denville, NJ, 1964), p. 47.

13 H. A. Williams, *Poverty, Chastity and Obedience* (Mitchell Beazley, 1975), p. 40.

14 Richard Ingrams, *Dr Johnson by Mrs Thrale* (Chatto and Windus, 1984), pp. 39–40.

15 Johnson, Yale *Works*, Vol. 5 (1969), p. 289.

16 Ibid., Vol. 5, p. 291.

17 Haddon Wilmer, 'Theological questions in the poverty debate' in *Poverty* (British Council of Church Working Party Report, 1982).

18 Richard Harries, *Turning to Prayer* (Mowbray, 1984). See especially chapter 1, 'Calling out'.

3

Coming to Terms with Riches: The Early Tradition of Sharing

Jews in the time of Jesus looked on wealth as a sign of divine blessing. God wants our lives to flourish in every aspect and wealth is a means of achieving this. So it is not surprising that the early Church remembered the teaching of Jesus on this subject, for it was radically different. Wealth could become a direct rival to God himself. Jesus taught his disciples to put their trust in Abba but Mammona also seeks our allegiance.

> No one can serve two masters; for either he will hate the one and love the other, or he will be devoted to the one and despise the other. You cannot serve God and Mammon. (Matthew 6.24)

No less familiar is the theme:

> Do not lay up for yourselves treasures on earth, where moth and rust consume and where thieves break in and steal, but lay up for yourselves treasures in heaven, where neither moth nor rust consumes and where thieves do not break in and steal. For where your treasure is, there will your heart be also. (Matthew 6.19–21)

Jesus practised what he preached. The birds of the air had nests, foxes holes in the ground but the Son of Man nowhere to lay his head. He moved about from place to place with no fixed abode and no permanent possessions, and invited his followers to do the same. He taught people not to be anxious about what they should eat or drink or wear. Nature revealed God's prodigality. They were to trust the creator of nature, to seek his Kingdom first and they would receive all that they would need as well (Matthew 6.25–33).

The Church in the last quarter of the first century remembered this teaching, and like us felt both drawn and challenged by it. They also remembered that in the first months after the resurrection of Jesus and the coming of the Holy Spirit the Christian community had responded to this teaching in a remarkable way.

> And all who believed were together and had all things in common; and they

sold their possessions and goods and distributed them to all, as any had need. (Acts 2.44–45)

Now the company of those who believed were one heart and soul, and no one said that any of the things which he possessed was his own, but they had everything in common . . . there was not a needy person among them, for as many as were possessors of lands or houses sold them, and brought the proceeds of what was sold, and laid it at the apostles' feet; and distribution was made to each as any had need. (Acts 4.32, 34–35)

This picture of the early Church, with what Troeltsch described as its 'love communism',[1] has been both much admired and much discussed. Although some of Luke's terminology, in particular the phrase 'all things in common' (*panta koina*), may echo Greek ideals of community living,[2] the description in Acts is not simply Luke's idealized picture of the early Church. It is rooted in history.

This community of sharing was not a regularized, legalized community of goods like that of the Essenes. Christianity had a much more spontaneous character. The following factors lie behind it. First is the remembered, radical teaching of Jesus about possessions in its two main aspects. Giving to the poor, that is, in love doing all that is possible to meet the needs of the needy, and personally living detached from possessions with total, anxiety-free trust in the Heavenly Father. Second is the closeness of the end. The Kingdom of God, God's rule on earth, had already broken into human affairs through the death and resurrection of Jesus Christ. Its glorious consummation was very soon. In the light of this, all ordinary human calculations, legalities and probabilities faded into insignificance. It was possible to sit light to many of the considerations that long-established civilizations have to worry about.

People have sometimes seen a contradiction in Luke's description of the early Church. On the one hand, everything was said to have been held in common. This might imply that there was no private property but simply a common pool out of which everyone drew as they needed. On the other hand, it is clear that members of the community did retain their own property. Barnabas had a field which he sold when a particular need arose. The notorious Ananias and Sapphira were told that they had been free not to sell their property. Furthermore, they were also free when they had sold it to retain the proceeds. Their offence was that they had tried to deceive the Church and deceive God by secretly retaining part of the proceeds for themselves. Later in Acts we read that Peter visited the house of Mark's mother where many were gathered together in prayer (Acts 12.12). In other words, she did not sell her house and donate the proceeds to a common pool but retained it as a place for common assembly. The phrase 'everything in common' must, therefore, refer primarily to a radical attitude of mind and spirit rather than a common pool in which everything was held. But this attitude of mind, this spirit, continually expressed itself in practical terms. When there was a need people really did sell their property and donate the proceeds for distribution to those in want. The emphasis was on ensuring that the needs of all were met and it was the spirit of having all things in common which made this possible in a spontaneous way. According to the rule of the Qumran community, every novice who entered the order had to leave his possessions with the overseer. If after a year he was accepted, he had to make them over to the order. All the needs of the members of the community were met from these resources and as a result of their own work in agriculture or crafts. The early Christian community did not have anything as compulsory and well organized as this. Rather, all was done in the spirit of Jesus and with a sense that the last days were upon them. There may also have been a sense of fulfilling the promise of Deuteronomy 15.4, which describes the seventh year, the year of release when 'there will be no poor among you'. But the decisive factor was *koinōnia* or fellowship, not organization.

It was inevitable that with the passing of time the eschatological enthusiasm of the early Church should fade. Moreover, the kind of community life that was possible in Jerusalem was impractical on a large scale as the Church spread out into the Roman world. Nevertheless, the spirit and motives behind the sense of having all things in common of the Church in its earliest stages continued to be present and to express itself in other forms. As mentioned in Chapter 2, we can see this in Paul in his efforts to raise money in the dispersed churches for the impoverished church in Jerusalem. In Galatians Paul tells us that fourteen years after his conversion he went up to Jerusalem to confer with the leaders of the Christian community. He was commissioned to go to the Gentiles: 'Only they would have us remember the poor, which very thing I was eager to do' (Galatians 2.10). Paul carried out what he intended: 'Now after some years I came to bring to my nation alms and offerings' (Acts 24.17). This collection involved a great deal of worry, exhortation and organization, which we see reflected in 2 Corinthians 8 and 9.

The main reason for the poverty of the Jerusalem church was the famine of AD 44 (Acts 11.27–30 and 12.25). According to Acts it was because of this that the disciples determined to send relief to the brethren who lived in Judea. The effects of the famine were accentuated by unrest in the country as a whole and persecution of the Christian Church. But even before 44 and the controversy over distribution to those in need (Acts 6.1) the Jerusalem church may have had special needs. For many Jews came to Jerusalem to die and be buried. There was a sizeable population of people there who may have had some savings but who had no regular employment.

Paul found the church in Macedonia exceedingly generous but he had more difficulty with the church in Corinth. He first of all urged them to put something by every Sunday so that when he visited them there would be a substantial contribution already available (1 Corinthians 16.1–4). But because of various troubles it did not work out quite as he hoped and he had to exhort them by the example of the Macedonian church.

The collection for the church in Jerusalem was important to Paul personally as a sign of his goodwill towards them. More generally and more significantly, however, it was the result of his Christian understanding of love that the needs of the poor should be met by those who had something, however little, to spare. The Jews levied a half-shekel temple tax, and it has been suggested that Paul's collection took this as a model. But the two forms of raising money were very different. The tax was highly organized whereas Paul made only *ad hoc* local arrangements; the tax was collected annually at set dates whereas Paul's was an isolated project which took some years to put into effect. The temple tax called for the payment of a prescribed sum but Paul left each subscriber free to contribute what he or she would.

Behind Paul's teaching on Christian giving lies his sense that everything in this age is passing. Jesus taught his followers not to be anxious but to put their full trust in God. Paul, with his sense that the Lord is near and that the end of the ages is at hand, teaches a similar detachment from the structures of this life. More positively, however, he directs people to the generosity of God in Christ, 'For you know the grace of our Lord Jesus Christ, that though he was rich, yet for your sake he became poor, so that by his poverty you might become rich' (2 Corinthians 8.8–9).

He then goes on to say that God will supply all that we need in our giving to others. He also lays stress upon the spiritual quality and the spiritual benefits of giving. God loves a cheerful giver and this giving will overflow in many thanksgivings to God by which he will be glorified. Of particular interest too is the verse:

> I do not mean that others should be eased and you burdened, but that as a matter of equality your abundance at the present time should supply their want, so that their abundance may supply your want, that there may be equality. (2 Corinthians 8.13–14)

Actually what Paul seems to have in mind here is not strict equality, or egalitarianism, but mutual giving and receiving.[3] This is a distinctive feature of the common life in the body of Christ, the *koinōnia* that he associates with the collection.

To sum up this theme we may say that although Paul does not quote the teaching of Jesus on money and possessions, he exhibits his spirit in the circumstances of his time. He sits light to possessions; indeed he himself travelled from place to place earning his living where he could as a tentmaker. Helping the poor was an essential aspect of his ministry and took up a great deal of his emotional energy, for arranging a collection among such widely dispersed communities, when communications were so slow and you never knew who could or could not be trusted, was a major undertaking. Furthermore, this giving not only expressed the spirit of Jesus but was a sign of the true life or *koinōnia* of the Church. The Church was no longer a single local community living its intense life of close sharing, as in the early chapters of the Acts of the Apostles. Nevertheless, among the widely dispersed churches of the Mediterranean world Paul was seeking to encourage, and not without success, that same spirit under those different conditions.

In the second century there is much evidence that the Church corresponded in deed as well as in word with the ideal of a community that cared for those in need. Writing in about AD 125, Aristides pointed out to the emperor Hadrian that the Christian Church looked after strangers, provided for the burial of the poor, took food to Christians in prison, and if necessary fasted in order to meet the needs of the poor and needy.

If at all possible work was provided for the unemployed and if someone had to give up his job on becoming a Christian, as one actor did in North Africa, he was supported by the community. By about AD 250 the Roman community was regularly looking after about 1,500 people in distress, and they had a reputation for charity which extended far beyond the boundaries of Rome. At times of catastrophe huge collections were made to help those who suffered as a result of invasion or epidemic. In the fourth century the pagan emperor Julian contrasted the failure of pagan religions to help the poor with the high example set by Christian communities, who had not only abolished penury among their own members, but cared for those outside their own number. All this was unique in antiquity.[4]

In the New Testament we see that a number of attitudes towards wealth existed together, not altogether without tension. In addition to this prime theme of sharing with the needy, there was a generally negative attitude towards riches, sharpened by an apocalyptic perspective. This appears in James:

> Has not God chosen those who are poor in the world to be rich in faith and heir to the Kingdom which he has promised to those who love him? . . . Is it not the rich who oppress you, is it not they who drag you into court? Is it not they who blaspheme that honourable name by which you are called? (James 2.5–7)

> Come now, you rich, weep and howl for the miseries that are coming upon you. . . . Behold the wages of the labourers who mowed your fields, which you kept back by fraud, cry out; and cries of the harvesters have reached the ears of the Lord of Hosts. (James 5.1, 4)

A hostile attitude is also seen in the book of Revelation. The godless Roman empire, which persecuted the Christians, would be overthrown. With this would be overthrown all its ill-gotten gain.

> The merchants of these wares, who gained wealth from her, will stand far off, in fear of her torment, weeping and mourning aloud. 'Alas, alas, for the great city . . . in one hour all this wealth has been laid waste.' (Revelation 18.15–17)

However crude some of this might be it does express, if sometimes in vitriolic form, the theme of the Hebrew scriptures which came to a focus in Christ, namely that the poor who put their trust in God will be vindicated. To the poor belongs the Kingdom, the power and the glory. They will be first and those who are first in this world's terms will be last.

In the second century, the motive of asceticism comes clearly to the fore in the rejection of riches. Origen, for example, lived in extreme personal poverty. There were wandering ascetics in Syria as early as the second century AD who had no possessions and about whom we read in the *Didache*. As discussed in Chapter 2, Christian monasticism began to develop in Palestine and Egypt from the third century.

Another aspect of the background which formed the Christian attitude to riches in the early Church was the Greek idea of self-sufficiency leading to inner contentment (*autarkeia*). Paul wrote:

> I have learned, in whatever state I am, to be content. I know how to be abased, and I know how to abound; in any and all circumstances I have learnt the secret of facing plenty and hunger, abundance and want. (Philippians 4.11–12)

In Paul this ideal takes a Christian form but it echoes the idea of Socrates and the Stoics as well as some Jewish wisdom literature. In the pastoral epistles the theme of self-sufficiency is less ascetic than it is *petit bourgeois*.

> There is gain in godliness with contentment; for we brought nothing into the world and we cannot take anything out of the world; but if we have food and clothing, with these we shall be content. (1 Timothy 6.6–8)

The individual is allowed the necessities of life, enough to live on. In the *Shepherd of Hermas*, a writing of the second century, the demand is for Christians to be aliens in the world and to be content with 'a sufficient competence'.

Recruits to early Christianity did not come primarily from either the wealthy or the lowest ranks of the proletariat. The early Christians tended to be manual workers and craftsmen, small businessmen and workers on the land, all of whom had a great respect for honest labour. So, from Paul on, there is a stress upon Christians earning their living in legitimate ways, earning money to support themselves and giving away the rest. Of course in time more members of the upper classes became members of the Church and we see this even in Luke. Their money and the regular savings of those who earned their living provided resources for the Church's comprehensive care of those in need. For, as already described, in Rome, Carthage and elsewhere the Church provided a comprehensive charity to those in need of various kinds.

All the various threads came together in the teaching of Clement of Alexandria at the end of the second and beginning of the third centuries in his famous work, 'Who is the Rich Man that shall be saved?'[5] At that time Alexandria was not only the largest city in the Greek-speaking East but the richest in the whole empire, the trade centre for India, the Orient and the Mediterranean, a city which had both a unique educational position and a luxurious style of life second to none. Clement, in his extended discussion on the story of the rich man called by Jesus to give away all, sought to say something at once sensible and challenging to the educated and well-to-do groups in Alexandria. Clement lays all his stress upon the right inward attitude. What Christ gives is:

> Not the outward act which others have done, but something else indicated by it, greater, more godlike, more perfect, the stripping off of the passions from the soul itself and from the disposition, and the cutting up by the roots and casting out of what is alien to the mind. . . . For one, after ridding himself of the burden of wealth, may nonetheless have still the lust and desire for money innate and living; and may have abandoned the use of it, but being at once destitute of and desiring what he spent, may doubly grieve both on account of the absence of attendance, and the presence of regret. For it is impossible and inconceivable that those in want of the necessaries of life should not be harassed in mind, and hindered from better things in the endeavour to provide them somehow, and from some source. And how much more beneficial the opposite case, for a man, through possessing a competency, both not himself to be in straits about money, and also to give assistance to those to whom it is requisite so to do. For if no one had anything, what room would be left among men for giving? (12 and 13)

Riches are neither good nor bad in themselves. But they can be used by those who have the right attitude towards them, to do good to others. This right attitude, this inner freedom, enables a person to use wealth for others.

The rich person is not automatically excluded from the company of the saved. It is not riches that make it so difficult to enter the Kingdom of Heaven but the difficulty of eradicating inordinate passion and possessiveness from the soul. But with the grace of God this can be done, for the rich person as much as anyone else.

> For he who holds possessions, and gold, and silver, and houses as the gifts of God; and ministers from them to the God who gives them for the salvation of men; and knows that he possesses them more for the sake of the brethren than his own; and is superior to the possession of them, not the slave of the things he possesses; and does not carry them about in his soul, nor bind and circumscribe his life with them, but is ever labouring at some good and divine work, even should he be necessarily sometime or other deprived of them, is able with cheerful mind to bear their removal equally with their abundance. This is he who is blessed by the Lord, and called poor in spirit, a meet heir of the Kingdom of God, not one who could not live rich. (16)

The answer given by Clement is, more or less, the one for which most Christians in most denominations in most ages have settled. It is not ignoble; it is certainly characterized by realism and common sense. It can be regarded as a legitimate development of the teaching of Jesus. Only it is not what Jesus, in his own time, meant. He clearly called some people, at least, not simply to an inward detachment from riches, but to an outward sundering from them. Moreover, as was argued in Chapter 2, there is a closer relationship between poverty of spirit and material poverty than Clement is willing to concede.

There is in Clement another theme which has not been given so much prominence by subsequent theologians. In fact it antedates Clement and can be found in the Christian writer of the second century, Hermas (already referred to). This is the partnership of the rich and the poor and what the rich have to receive from the poor as well as to give to them.

Hermas tells the parable of an elm and a vine. The elm by itself does not bear fruit. It needs the vine to yield grapes. On the other hand, the vine needs something to support it. Otherwise it simply lies upon the ground and the fruit becomes rotten. Twined round the elm it is able to yield fruit abundantly. In a similar way, says Hermas, the rich and the poor need each other. It is the duty of the rich man to relieve the needs of the poor. But being rich he is likely to be distracted by his riches and spiritually weak. The poor, on the other hand, are likely to be rich in intercession and confession. This spiritual wealth in turn helps the rich person.

> Poor men interceding with the Lord on behalf of the rich, increase their riches; and the rich, again, aiding the poor in their necessities, satisfy their souls. Both, therefore, are partners in the righteous work.[6]

It is not necessary to agree with all these sentiments in detail to recognize that here there is a vital principle, that the rich have something to receive from the poor.

Clement, after quoting sayings from the gospels to the effect that in meeting the needs of others we are serving Christ himself, urges us not to look upon the outward appearance or make judgements about the people who need our help. However ragged or ugly or feeble the people are whom we help, there dwells within them the hidden Father and his Son. And by helping them we win for ourselves spiritual friends who will act as our protectors.

> Collect for thyself an unarmed, an unwarlike, a bloodless, a passionless, a stainless host, pious old men, orphans dear to God, widows armed with meekness, men adorned with love. Obtain with thy money such guards, for body and for soul, for whose sake a sinking ship is made buoyant when steered by the prayers of the saints alone; and disease at its height is subdued, put to flight by the laying on of hands; and the attack of robbers is disarmed, spoiled by pious prayers; and the might of demons is crushed, put to shame in its operations by strenuous commands. All these warriors and guards are trusty. No one is idle, no one is useless. One can obtain your pardon from God, another comfort you when sick, another weep and groan in sympathy for you to the Lord of all, another teach some of the things useful for salvation, another admonish with confidence, another counsel with kindness. (34)

Clement quotes the text:

> Make to you friends of the Mammon of unrighteousness, that, when ye fail, they may receive you into everlasting habitation. (Luke 16.9)

> We are to seek out such friends, indeed, friends of friends, all in need and not just on the one occasion. (34 and 35)

> A friend proves himself such not by one gift, but by long intimacy. (32)

Those whom the rich help with their money turn out to be their spiritual friends who will protect them in this life and receive them into everlasting habitations. Again, we need not go along with all the details to recognize here a profound mutuality, what Charles Williams described as 'the way of exchange'.[7]

Before Christianity became the official religion of the Roman empire the main thrust of Christian teaching on wealth and poverty was directed towards individual Christian generosity and building up the Church as a community of mutual sharing. In the last half of the fourth century, however, the scope for Christian influence was greater. First of all, far more well-connected and wealthy people came into the Church. Secondly, far from being hidden, the Church was now able to found institutions to help the poor and sick. It was during this time that the Church Fathers, both Eastern, such as John Chrysostom and Basil, and Western, like Ambrose and Augustine, developed a much more radical approach towards possessions, which contained criticisms, implicit or explicit, of the whole institution of private property. Behind this radical criticism there lay some nostalgia for an innocent paradise before the fall in which all things were held in common. This was not a distinctively Christian idea. In Stoic and much other teaching there was the idea of a golden age, a primal childhood of the human race. It was present in Ovid and Virgil, Strabo, Seneca and others. Chrysostom, Basil, Ambrose, Augustine and the other great Fathers of the fourth century all had a classical education and were steeped in the philosophy and myths of the Greek and Roman world. So the idea of a golden age would have been part of their background too. Nevertheless, in their Christian teaching, romantic longing and nostalgia were turned into sharp denunciation and practical teaching. The purpose of loosening men's minds from thoughts of the inalienable right of private property to things held in common was to get the haves to share with the have-nots.

Chrysostom asks the rich man why he is rich. He probably inherited much of his wealth from his father and his grandfather.

> But canst thou, ascending through many generations, show the acquisition just? It cannot be. The root and origin of it must have been injustice. Why? Because God in the beginning made not one man rich, and another poor.... He left the earth free to all alike. However, the person who is rich now with inherited wealth is not to blame for the sins of his forebears. His duty is to share with others with a sense of common ownership. If then our possessions belong to one common Lord, they belong also to our fellow serv-

ants. The possessions of one Lord are all common. Do we not see this a settled rule in great houses? . . . Mark the wise dispensation of God. That he might put mankind to shame, he hath made certain things common, as the sun, air, earth, and water, the heaven, the sea, the light, the stars; whose benefits are dispensed equally to all as brethren. . . . Other things he hath made common, as baths, cities, market places, walks.

The trouble is that the spirit of possessiveness has entered into human life. And

When one attempts to possess himself with anything, to make it his own, then contention is introduced, as if nature herself were indignant, that when God brings us together in every way, we are eager to divide and separate ourselves by appropriating things, by using those cold words 'Mine' and 'Thine'. Then there is contention and uneasiness, but where this is not, no strife or contention is bred. This state, therefore, is rather our inheritance, and more agreeable to nature. Why is it, that there is never a dispute about a market place? Is it not because it is common to all? But about a house, and about property, men are always disputing. Things necessary are set before us in common; but even in the least things we do not observe a community. Yet those greater things he hath opened freely to all, that we might then be instructed to have these inferior things in common.[8]

Chrysippus, head of the school of Stoic philosophers in the third century BC, wanted to defend the right to private property by reference to a seat at the theatre which is occupied by the first arrival if it does not militate against the state or the universe, which are common to all. Basil took the opposite point of view.

It is as if one has taken a seat in the theatre and then drives out all who come later, thinking that what is for everyone is only for him. Which people are like that. For having pre-empted what is common to all, they make it their own by virtue of this prior possession.[9]

Gregory Nazianzen argued that poverty and superfluity, so-called freedom and slavery, are a consequence of the Fall: 'In the beginning it was not so.' God created man 'free and independent'. Ambrose wrote:

Nature has poured forth all things for men for common use. God has ordered all things to be produced, so that there should be food in common to all, and that the earth should be a common possession for all. Nature, therefore, has produced a common right for all, but greed [*usurpatio*] has made it a right for a few.[10]

This was not just a haunting theological idea. By their personal example, their teaching and their practical organization, the early Fathers sought in every way possible to relieve the rich of their goods by relieving the needs of the poor. Chrysostom sold plate and furniture from the palace at Constantinople to give to the poor and to found hospitals. He himself lived austerely. He realized that people laughed at him and thought him mad for his constant exhortation of the rich. He rejoiced that the poor were present in the narthex of the church, ready to receive from those who could afford to give. He argued that if a tenth of the population are poor and a tenth rich, the most being middling, the needs of the poor could easily be met by distribution. Basil, as bishop of Caesarea in Cappadocia, set up a large welfare centre at the gates of the city for the poor, the old and the sick, together with a hospice for penniless travellers. Refuges of this kind also came into being in other cities in his diocese. He himself came from a family of rich landowners in Asia Minor, but after his studies distributed all his possessions among the poor.

One important theme in the thought of the fourth-century Fathers is the value of having the poor in the church and the benefit this brings to others. The poor were present in the inner narthex of the church, where they used to beg. 'What is meaner than those who beg?', asks Chrysostom.

> And yet even these fulfil a most important office in the church, clinging to the doors of the sanctuary and supplying one of its greatest ornaments: without these there would be no perfecting the fullness of the church. Their piety is a lesson to all, and though you give but a penny, they give thanks and implore ten thousand blessings on the giver; and if thou give nothing they do not complain, but even so they bless, and think themselves happy to enjoy their daily food. . . . For no physician stretching out the hand to apply the knife, works so effectually to cut out the corruption from our wounds, as doth a poor man stretching out his right hand and receiving alms, to take away the scars which the wounds have left.[11]

There is here as in Hermas a sense that the poor and the rich benefit one another. Developing 2 Corinthians 8.7, where this thought is also present, Chrysostom summarizes Paul with the words:

> Ye are flourishing in money; they in life [i.e. holiness of life] and in boldness towards God. Give ye to them, therefore, of the money which ye abound in but they have not; that ye may receive of that boldness wherein they are rich and ye are lacking.[12]

In a vivid image, Chrysostom compares the poor to an altar. A stone altar becomes holy because it receives Christ's body. The poor are Christ's body and the altar on which they lie is everywhere:

> This altar mayest thou everywhere see lying, both in lanes and in market places, and mayest sacrifice upon it every hour; but on this too is sacrifice performed. . . . When then thou seest a poor believer, think that thou beholdest an altar: when thou seest such a beggar, not only insult him not, but even reverence him, and if thou seest another insulting him, prevent, repel it.[13]

Christ told his followers to invite the poor and the lame and the maimed to their meals. By this we win the eternal friendship and gratitude of God.

> What squeamishness is this, pray, that thou canst not sit down in company with the poor? What sayest thou? He is unclean and filthy? Then wash him, and lead him up to thy table. But he hath filthy garments? Then change them, and give him clean apparel. Seest thou not how great the gain is? Christ

cometh unto thee through him, and dost thou make petty calculations of such things? When thou art inviting the king to thy table, dost thou fear because of such things as these?[14]

When we enter human palaces we do not see the poor in pride of place but when we enter the real palace, the church, the poor are there, serving us in various ways, drawing our pride from us by reminding us of our common human mortality and frailty and enabling us to be compassionate and so enter more fully into the loving kindness of God.

If God is not ashamed of them, but has set them in his vestibules, much less be thou ashamed.

Similarly, when we give a meal and invite the poor we invite Christ himself:

For if we are ashamed of those whom Christ is not ashamed, we are ashamed of Christ, being ashamed of his friends. Let thy table be filled with the maimed and the lame. Through them Christ comes, not through the rich.[15]

The poor do us a service by receiving our gifts:

So that you are rather indebted to the poor man for receiving your kindness. For if there were no poor, the greater part of your sins would not be removed. They are the healers of your wounds, their hands are medicinal to you. The physician, extending his hand to apply a remedy, does not exercise the healing art more than the poor man, who stretches out his hand to receive your alms, and thus becomes a cure for your ills. You give your money, and with it your sins pass away.

For this reason we should not simply give our money to some administrator to deliver but be personally involved in giving our own gifts, especially if we can search out poor holy men to give to.[16]

We might ask what a poor person can do for us. Far more than any slave.

For he will stand by thee in the day of judgement, and will deliver thee from the fire.[17]

Arising from the sense of common ownership of the goods of the earth there is the salutary point that when the rich give to the poor this is a matter of just restitution rather than charity. Ambrose asks:

Who is avaricious? One who is not content with those things which are sufficient. Who is a robber? One who takes the goods of another. Are you not avaricious, are you not a robber, you who make your own the things which you have received to distribute? Will not one be called a thief who steals the garment of one already clothed, and is one deserving of any other title who will not clothe the naked if he is able to do so?

Basil made the same point:

That bread which you keep, belongs to the hungry; that coat which you preserve in your wardrobe, to the naked; those shoes which are rotting in your possession, to the shoeless; that gold which you have hidden in the ground, to the needy. Wherefore, as often as you are able to help others, and refuse, so often did you do them wrong.[18]

Ambrose again:

Not from your own do you bestow upon the poor man, if you make return from what is his. For what has been given is common for the use of all, you appropriate yourself alone. The earth belongs to all, not to the rich; but fewer are they who do not use what belongs to all than those who do. Therefore you are paying a debt, you are not bestowing what is due.[19]

Chrysostom wrote:

This is robbery: not to share one's resources. . . . Because you have not made the accustomed offerings, the prophet says. Therefore you have robbed the things that belong to the poor. This, he says, by way of showing the rich that they are in possession of the property of the poor, even if it is a patrimony that they have received, even if they have gathered their money elsewhere. . . . Therefore those who have something more than necessity demands and spend it on themselves instead of distributing it to their needy fellow servants, they will be meted out terrible punishments. For what they possess is not personal property; it belongs to their fellow servants.[20]

Augustine makes the same point:

The superfluous things of the wealthy are the necessities of the poor. When superfluous things are possessed, others' property is possessed.[21]

This is a powerful theme of great relevance to contemporary debate. For some of the New Right maintain that helping the needy is always an act of voluntary charity: there is no obligation to do so. For the Fathers of the Church, on the contrary, it is a matter of justice and therefore duty.

The teaching of the Christian Church in the first four centuries provides a remarkable witness to a radical and challenging stance on wealth. Against the background of a Jewish view that prosperity is a sign of God's blessing, the first Christians remembered the teaching of Jesus to be distinctive and very different from this in its main thrust. The early Church did not simply hold this as a pious and romantic remembrance, however. They sought to realize the ideal of a sharing community in which the needs of all were met, first of all in the local church in Jerusalem and then, under very different circumstances, in the Mediterranean world. As the Church gained adherents and strength, it at the same time gained a reputation for well-organized and generous welfare.

In the second century, however, a crisis came with the number of wealthy who began to be attracted by the faith. In response to this, Clement taught that it was the inner disposition of a person that really mattered. If this inner attitude was right, the person would use his or her wealth in the service of God and others. If it was wrong, everything would be wrong even if the person was materially poor. This was encouraged by another strand of Christian teaching, whose origin lies in the New Testament, namely that of living modestly, content with enough for the necessities of life.

One of the strongest themes that emerges in this period, and is present not only in the second-century Fathers, Clement and the Shepherd of Hermas, but in the great Fathers of the fourth century, is the interdependence of the poor and the rich within the Church. More than this, they make it clear that the rich have far more to receive from the poor than the poor have to receive from the rich. Though the terms in which they develop this theme would not be used by us today and though it could encourage a social and political complacency, there is a vital truth here. For it wards off any sense of largesse from on high, and cuts out all patronizing. It is also highly relevant today, as will be outlined in Chapter 12.

Together with this, in the fourth century there emerged some very radical teaching on ownership. God intended the goods of the earth to be held in common, to meet the needs of all. It is as a result of sin that private property has entered in. This sin may not be personal, but the riches we inherit will have been obtained through some injustice somewhere along the line. There is, to use the modern jargon, structural injustice, as a result of which there are now appalling divisions between the poor and the rich. The consequence of this view is that when we meet the needs of the poor we are simply rendering them their due. It is a matter of obligation, giving them their rights, rather than bounty or charity.

Most of us today would tend to nod blandly in the direction of Clement of Alexandria. What matters is our inner disposition. There is a vital truth here. Unless our heart and mind are right, everything else will indeed be wrong. But Clement of Alexandria's attitude, taken by itself, can encourage complacency and a too easy acceptance of things as they are. We also need to allow ourselves to be questioned by other strands of early Christian teaching. First, the Christian Church is a community or fellowship in which the needs of all are to be met. This theme, deeply embedded in the New Testament, was prominent throughout this period. After this period, the ideal of Christian community came to be focused in monastic communities and was largely lost sight of in civil society. But there is no suggestion in the New Testament or the early Fathers that the sense of *koinōnia* is to be confined to monks and nuns. It is meant to be a characteristic of the Church as a whole. Secondly, the rich have more to receive than to give. The poor have a crucial role to play in the salvation of the rich. Thirdly, meeting the needs of the poor is a matter of fundamental obligation. This stress is a vital counterbalance to the ideas of the absolute rights of private property which grew up in the seventeenth century and which still permeate so much Christian thinking. The implications of this for Christian discipleship in the modern world have still to be worked out. But Christian discipleship involves, at the least, listening to this tradition and allowing oneself to be questioned by it.

NOTES

1 Ernst Troeltsch, *The Social Teaching of the Christian Churches* (George Allen & Unwin, 1931), Vol. 1, p. 63.
2 Ernst Haenchen, *The Acts of the Apostles* (Blackwell, 1982), p. 232.
3 C. K. Barrett, *A Commentary on the Second Epistle to the Corinthians* (Adam & Charles Black, 1982), p. 226.
4 Martin Hengel, 'Property and riches in the early Church' in *Earliest Christianity* (SCM, 1986), p. 190.
5 Clement of Alexandria, 'Who is the rich man that shall be saved?' in *The Ante-Nicene Fathers* (reprinted Eerdmans/T. & T. Clark), Vol. II (1986), pp. 591ff.
6 The Pastor of Hermas, Similitude II, ibid., p. 32. For the whole subject see J. A. McGuckin, 'The vine and the elm tree: the patristic interpretation of Jesus's teachings on wealth' in *The Church and Wealth*, ed. W. J. Sheils and Diana Wood (Blackwell, 1987), p. 1.
7 Charles Williams, 'The way of exchange' in *The Image of the City and Other Essays*, ed. Anne Ridler (OUP, 1958), pp. 147ff.
8 St Chrysostom, 'Homily XII on 1 Timothy 4.1–3: *The Nicene and Post-Nicene Fathers* (reprinted Eerdmans, 1983), Vol. XIII, pp. 447–8.
9 Quoted by Hengel, p. 150.
10 Ibid., p. 152.
11 Chrysostom, Homily XXX on 1 Corinthians 12.12: *The Nicene and Post-Nicene Fathers*, Vol. XII, p. 179.
12 Homily XVII on 2 Corinthians 8.7: ibid., p. 361.
13 Homily XX on 1 Corinthians 9.10: ibid., p. 374.
14 Homily I on Colossians 1.1 and 2: *The Nicene and Post-Nicene Fathers*, Vol. XIII, p. 260.
15 Homily XI on 1 Thessalonians 5.19–22: ibid., p. 274.
16 Homily XIV on 1 Timothy 5.8: ibid., p. 455.
17 Homily XI on Hebrews 6.13–16: *The Nicene and Post-Nicene Fathers*, Vol. XIV, pp. 14–20.
18 Sermon by Basil the Great on Luke 12.18, quoted by Charles Avila, *Ownership: Early Christian Teaching* (Sheed & Ward, 1983), p. 50.
19 Sermon on Naboth of Jezreel, quoted by Avila, ibid., p. 66.
20 Sermon on the Parable of Lazarus and the Rich Man, quoted by Avila, ibid., pp. 83–4.
21 Quoted by Avila, ibid., p. 113.

4

Christianity and the Economic Order

For most of Christian history believers have tried to follow Christ by acts of personal charity to individuals and by founding institutions devoted to meeting human need. Poverty has elicited personal generosity, which has been given directly to the person in need or channelled through some foundation. So all Churches, Eastern and Western, have founded orphanages, hospitals, hospices and schools and raised money for distribution. The example of Chrysostom, quoted in Chapter 3, was repeated innumerable times in many different ways.

Now, however, the situation is different. For many of the traditional spheres of operation of the Church, such as the provision of social welfare, health care and education, have been taken over by the state. So, as Dr Edward Norman has put it, 'These incursions make it very difficult for the Church *not* to be politically involved, for politics has actually moved into its own sphere.'[1]

For good and ill, the state now controls much of our life. The late Professor A. J. P. Taylor wrote:

Until August 1914, a sensible law abiding Englishman could pass through life and hardly notice the existence of the State, beyond the post office and policeman. All this was changed by the impact of the Great War.[2]

All this was changed. The result is that if a person is genuinely concerned about human well-being, that concern can no longer be limited to individual acts of charity or contributions to some charitable foundation. These are still, of course, essential. Nevertheless, it is the legislation of the modern state which more than anything else affects human well-being. The idea that people can be anxious to alleviate poverty, in their own country or abroad, while being indifferent to the legislation, economic arrangements and trade agreements which, one way or another, radically affect the position of people in poverty, is a pious fraud.

This, it must be emphasized, is not a left-wing, still less a party political, point. Dr Edward Norman, the scourge of Christian left-wing politics, has been quoted to support the point made here. Again, he has written:

> In the world, the Christian seeks to apply the great love of God as well as he can in contemporary terms. And that will actually involve corporate social and political action.[3]

What kind of social and political action remains to be seen. But that there must be such a corporate dimension to Christian discipleship today is inescapable.

There are many different ways in which the Churches relate to the economic order, depending upon their basic theology and position in relation to the state. However, the most basic distinction is between the Church approach and the sect approach. A sect will seek at least some degree of withdrawal from the wider society and will set its members distinctive standards. One of the best known examples is that of the Amish branch of the Mennonites. In the United States and Canada, on their extensive farms, they separate themselves as far as possible from modern society, eschewing telephones in the house, television, motor cars and so on. This is not just a question of quaint old-fashioned dress and horse-drawn buggies. They refuse to serve in the police or the armed services. Those who take this attitude believe that Christ's teaching is for Christian believers, who are expected to obey it without qualification. This means separation from the rest of society.

Such an approach, like Christian pacifism in other forms or monastic communities, serves an essential purpose within the spectrum of Christian truth. It witnesses to the perfect standard that Christ set before us. For various reasons, that is not the approach followed here. The main reason is that the central concept of Christianity, as of Judaism, is the rule or Kingdom of God. This rule embraces the whole of human existence. The leading theme in the Hebrew scriptures is of God's Kingdom. This was the heart of the message of Jesus. It is the consummation of that Kingdom to which Judaism and the Christian Church look forward, and for which they work and pray. One of the great shifts in modern theology, particularly in the Roman Catholic Church, has been the recovery of the centrality of the Kingdom of God. No longer is it identified with the Church. The Church is a sign and witness to that Kingdom.

Some Christians today, while recognizing that the Church had a responsibility to speak to society as a whole in the past, argue that we are now in a post-Constantinian world. Now, whether we like it or not, all Churches in the West are much more in the position of sects, and instead of trying to speak to society as a whole they should be cultivating distinctive, higher standards among their own membership. Some people who argue along these lines regard the establishment of the Christian Church under Constantine in the Roman empire in the fourth century as the great 'sell-out' and believe that now is the time for the Church to recover its own soul.

The late Professor Paul Ramsey gave a characteristically sharp critique of this attitude:

> I never cease to wonder why there are so many 'post-Constantinians' in our so-called 'liberal' churches who (1) proclaim with joy the end of that era, yet (2) never hesitate to issue advice to states as if they were Christian Kingdoms, and (3) continue to applaud the destruction of the remaining 'social space' that sustains the independence of educational and other church institutions – which will be needed if the church is to be even an effective *sect* in today's world.[4]

Ramsey argued that we may indeed be called to be a sect again, in which case we must have the high standards and the discipline of a sect. But at the moment we reject such discipline and 'speak like sectarians speaking like churches'. In our present situation we should not give up what influence we have but seek to use it, while recognizing that it is also to the world we speak, not only to professed Christian believers.

> The Church should not *of itself* cease to influence public policy, having grave moral import for its own members and for the community at large. It ought not to *seek* to have such influence no longer, nor should it *avoid* what little it may still have or *avoid* what it may yet regain in God's afflictive and over-ruling providence.[5]

An approach along the lines indicated by Paul Ramsey rests on three assumptions. First, all human beings, whatever their beliefs or lack of them, have a moral awareness, a capacity for distinguishing right from wrong, even if they do not agree in every instance about what is actually right or wrong. Secondly, this moral capacity is only partially effective. Because of human wilfulness we are not always able to see clearly what is right and because of human limitations generally we are not able to comprehend all the good that God has in mind for us. So, thirdly, Christ comes both to correct our errors and to give us the full vision of God's glory in human beings.

In traditional Christian thinking, at least in its Roman Catholic and Anglican forms, this approach would be categorized as an example of natural law thinking. The concept of natural law was a controversial one at the time of the Reformation, where it was often argued that human beings were so blinded that without the grace of Christ they were incapable of either seeing or doing the good. More recently the concept has come under attack philosophically. Certainly in its traditional form it cannot be fully maintained any longer. Nevertheless, in the more restricted sense described here, all human beings have a moral capacity, so that even when two cultures disagree about the morality of a particular custom, they are at least able to engage in common discourse about it and this discourse assumes some commonality of understanding about morality. The more restricted sense accepted here also seeks to incorporate the Reformation and Augustinian emphasis upon human sinfulness.

This means that, corresponding to the understanding of natural law outlined above, there is, first, something in every culture to which we can say 'yes'. Secondly, there is therefore something in every culture which answers to Christ and finds its fulfilment in him. Thirdly, however, there is something in every culture which is challenged by Christ and which can only find its fulfilment as a result of repentance and correction in the light of that challenge.[6] Various examples of what this might mean in relation to, say, the cultures of the Indian sub-continent or Papua New Guinea might be given. But Western industrialized society also provides a particular culture. It has its own assumptions and norms. As the economic order that we live in today is integrally bound up with our developed industrialized society, it is important to look at that culture in the light of Christ's 'yes' and 'no'.

Modern industrial society, based as it is upon science and technology, a technology which is increasingly computer-based, has as its foundation the idea that human beings can take control. The essence of scientific method is that on the basis of observed regularities from the past we can make reliable predictions about the future. In the light of these predictions we can invent, design and control so that what occurs is a result of human choices. As has been argued many times, this foundation for the success of modern society has been made possible by a Christian, de-sacralized approach to nature.

Although there has been a tendency among Christians to try to turn the clock back and reject this 'coming of age', such attempts must be firmly rejected, as Bonhoeffer argued in his letters from prison. The movement which began in the sixteenth century, which put more and more power into the hands of human beings, and which has reached such dizzying heights today, needs to be embraced as part of God's gift to us and an essential aspect of our God-given responsibility.

Economists argue that economics, though not always very precise, counts as one of the sciences. 'Economics is the science which studies human behaviour as a relationship between ends and scarce means which have alternative uses.' Or 'Economics is a study of the implications of human choice and fields coming under the measuring rod of money.' For the present purpose, whether economics is precise or imprecise, the economic order as we know it is an essential aspect of the developed world, whose basic presupposition is that human beings can predict and to some extent control what happens.

In the light of the general approach sketched out above, namely that there is something in every culture to which Christ says 'yes', we can and must say a resounding 'yes' to this God-given human advance. We do so from a theological point of view, for it is God's will that we should stand on our own feet even more than it is the will of human parents that their children should do so. But this decisive human movement also needs to be affirmed from the point of view of its consequences. It is easy for well-off Christians to lament the loss of green fields or to hanker back to some over-romanticized agrarian society. The fact is that it is the Industrial Revolution, with its scientific and technological base, which has been responsible for alleviating so much poverty, hardship and suffering. We hardly need to be reminded of the dark satanic mills, sweated child labour in factories, deaths in mines and so on. Nevertheless, with all this taken into account and not forgetting the often disastrous ecological effects of industrialization, the gain has been great. Those who romanticize the past forget the extent of rural poverty and the way in which human livelihood and life was dependent upon the season-by-season vagaries of the weather. And it is almost impossible to imagine what human suffering must have been before the advent of modern scientific medicine, not least the invention of anaesthetics and painkillers.

This leads on to the second point, that the present economic order has its proper completion and fulfilment in Christ. The ability of human beings to take control of the earth and utilize its resources will find its proper goal when there are adequate resources made available for every single human being. Until then, however, and this is the third point, there is something in our present system to which Christ says no, and which must be challenged. There is the effect of pollution and widespread damage to the environment. The fact that this may be even worse in countries that were until recently under communist rule underlines the fact that for the present we are not talking about a particular economic system, capitalist or communist, but the whole process of industrialization, shared by wealthy countries and rapidly being acquired by many parts of the underdeveloped world. There is exploitation. There is the break-up of traditional human communities, from the family to the village. There are the many casualties, from executives whose family life collapses under stress to those killed in industrial accidents on oil rigs or in tunnels. More specifically to do with the international economic system, there is the great load of debt which weighs down so many developing countries, the low prices paid for their commodities and often their inability to obtain markets in the developed world. There is so much that needs to be corrected before our present relatively advanced culture can find its proper fulfilment.

Christ's 'yes' and 'no' to the economic order that we have at the moment gives a basic attitude but nothing in the way of guidance on particulars. Although such guidance is frequently offered by Church leaders or Church bodies the mass of people remain unconvinced that there is any integral connection between the Christian faith and a particular set of economic policies. The difficulties can hardly be exaggerated. Enoch Powell has written that 'The Gospel has three fundamental characteristics which defeat any "Christian approach to politics": it is pacifist; it is eschatological; and it is individualist.' Pacifism or, as it is more aptly termed in the economic sphere, the rejection of aggressive self-interest will be considered in a later chapter. The question of how we derive a social ethic from an individual ethic is already being considered in this chapter and will continue to be in subsequent ones. The eschatological nature of Christianity does indeed pose major problems. For Christ sets before people the absolute standards of the Kingdom of God, which he taught was breaking into the world through his mission and which would shortly come to its climax. The standards and values of the Kingdom of God, though they always bear upon this world, cannot easily be translated into day-by-day practice. If the Kingdom were here in its fullness, we could happily give away everything we possess and trust moment-by-moment for God to provide. But as that state has not yet been reached it is perfectly proper to be prudent, to take our own interests and the interests of our families into account. There is a continuing tension between the two claims upon us, which will be here until the end of time, for Christians live between Christ's rising and his coming again.[7] This means that every set of economic principles is provisional, standing under judgement and challenged to conform to higher, more humane values. This is true of economic systems as a whole, both capitalist and communist. It is also true of particular principles or so-called economic laws within a system.

The Calvinist tradition of social ethics works on the assumption that God has disclosed his will for economic life in the scriptures, particularly the Hebrew scriptures which deal with communal life, in contrast to the New Testament which on the whole deals with person-to-person relationships. Recently there has been a revival of this approach within Anglicanism. Two Anglican laymen, Brian Griffiths,[8] a former adviser to Mrs Thatcher, and Donald Hay,[9] a lecturer in Economics at Oxford University, have tried to set out a distinctively Christian approach to the economic order. Although they reach rather different conclusions they both draw on the Old Testament. Donald Hay, for example, sets out eight guiding principles. These will not be discussed in detail at this point but one is selected to indicate the kind of difficulties of this approach. Hay's fourth principle is that man has a right and obligation to work. It is a principle with which the vast majority of Christians would be thoroughly in sympathy and it can certainly be grounded in the biblical witness, both old and new. However, I suspect that the reasons that we judge work important are somewhat different from those adduced at different times in the biblical period. Then, as now, there would have been the sheer necessity of earning a living, of keeping alive, but now we would also look to work as a form of fulfilment, an activity in which many of our creative impulses can find expression. No less importantly, work is the way in which most people relate to the community and through which they find their dignity and status. The humiliation of unemployment is notorious. So too is the difficulty many experience on retirement. From a theological point of view, particularly in the light of evolution, we more and more see work as a way of sharing in the continuing creative work of God. So there is much today in our general evaluation of work that comes not directly from the Bible but from theological reflection on contemporary experience.

The biblical principle that human beings have a right and obligation to work, fine sounding though it is, seems to offer little help on one of the most intractable problems of the twentieth century, namely endemic unemployment in capitalist societies. In Marxist societies there is in principle no unemployment. Everyone is found a job. But as they now move to Western-style free markets, major unemployment is already in evidence. Western economies during this century have had to battle with the twin claims of keeping inflation down and keeping unemployment down. Very often we have had full employment only at the expense of unacceptably high inflation or low inflation at the expense of unacceptably high unemployment. Hard choices have to be made. It is true that in stressing the right and obligation to work, Hay does not just mean paid employment. He also includes those who work without pay, such as housewives. Nevertheless, the availability of paid work is vital. People who are seeking paid employment usually find schemes of unpaid work highly unsatisfying.

If a Christian places the right and obligation to work as a principle overriding every other consideration, then he or she must opt for a socialist and perhaps even a Marxist model. Hay suggests this, though at the same time indicating the difficulties of making such a system work properly. If the Marxist model is rejected, then within the capitalist framework hard choices will often have to be made. Nor can it be assumed that maximum employment must always be chosen in preference to low inflation. For continuing high inflation can undermine a whole society. The effect of runaway inflation in Germany between the wars was devastating and helped prepare the way for the Nazis. When money loses its value in a rapid and unpredictable manner, the very foundations of society are undermined. A stable currency is part of the trustworthy order of things, without which there can be no human community. God wills a stable order, as a pre-condition for genuine human community. So, however painful and undesirable it is, it may be necessary for a society to experience substantial unemployment, at least for a period. The Bible offers no direct guidance here, as Hay concedes. Two fundamental principles are in conflict. All a Christian can do is insist that extensive unemployment cannot be tolerated indefinitely. The ideal, which continually calls for its implementation, is a society in which paid employment is available for all who need and want it.

Both Ronald Preston and Donald Hay emphasize the importance of certain technical aspects of economics. However, they are both no less emphatic in drawing attention to the way that values drawn from elsewhere can come to permeate an economic theory, and therefore, to the importance of fully considering the political, ethical and theological dimensions. As Preston writes:

> The conclusion is that economists by themselves have little to say about policy, but the little they do say is important. Beyond that, politics, sociology and the other social sciences are involved, and so is ethics. Behind ethics is some view of the nature and significance of human persons, and so on that religion and philosophies have much to say.[10]

There remains the perennial question of how we reach an assured understanding of what it is to be a human being in society and how we draw the right economic and political conclusions from this understanding. I do not think it is possible to draw a two line answer from the Bible or Christian tradition. Christians will want to look at both the Hebrew scriptures and the New Testament, taking their insights and warnings seriously. We will want to examine the long tradition of Christian thinking on this subject, not least where it is misguided or plain wrong. We will also take into account contemporary experience and reflection. All this means that there is not likely to be a distinctively Christian position, nor is one necessarily desirable. The long-established Christian tradition of natural law thinking worked on the assumption that there are certain basic insights about human behaviour which it is possible for all people, whatever their religion or lack of it, to see and in part respond to. This book seeks to stand within that tradition. In other words, although they have been inspired and shaped by our Christian inheritance the arguments set forward claim to be able to persuade all people of good will, even though there is a particular call to obedience for those of us who regard ourselves as followers of the Lord Jesus Christ.

So the approach in this study, while rooted in the biblical witness, will also take into account the teaching of the Church on economic questions down the ages, and our own contemporary experience as we reflect on it in the light of the view of humanity revealed in Christ. It is not possible to draw a sharp line between what society as a whole is thinking and what Christians judge should be the case, for in every age the Church has been embedded in a wider society, both contributing to it and in its turn being influenced by it. So Christians have no monopoly of wisdom and they certainly have no simplistic answers to complex questions. What they hope to do is contribute to the debate, giving a particular emphasis to certain points or principles.

During the mediaeval period the Christian Church taught both a concept of the just price and a just wage. Economics, as R. H. Tawney observed, was regarded as a branch of theology and ethics.[11] However, with the rise of capitalism, particularly in the seventeenth century, the Church's traditional economic teaching had become very out-of-date and Christian thinking had failed to relate itself realistically to the new situation. For example, all through the seventeenth century the Church went on repeating its traditional condemnation of usury, just when lending money on interest was basic to the new capitalism, encouraging people both to save and to invest in new ventures.

During the nineteenth and twentieth centuries many individual Christian thinkers tried to establish a new Christian approach to economics and various movements and groups sprang up. The fruits of this thinking can be seen in the statements of the World Council of Churches and in papal encyclicals over the period. In 1925 there was a major 'Life and Work' conference in Stockholm. This rejected atomistic individualism. It opposed any view of original sin that ruled out all possibility of change. It stressed the influence of the environment on individual life and the necessity of state action to ensure that the common good was being served. It argued for equality of opportunity as a vital element in the Christian understanding of man. In general it can be said to have blessed the social movement and overcome the Protestant hostility to democratic socialism. The conference at Oxford in 1937 was the most comprehensive review of economic problems that the Church has ever undertaken. No doubt partly through the influence of Reinhold Niebuhr in the preceding years, it corrected the somewhat uncritical acceptance of the social Gospel that had been gaining ground in the Churches. There was greater realism and a more profound theological base. This work was taken up again at a conference in Amsterdam in 1948, which tried to formulate a Christian ethic of justice derived from the love commandment. It emphasized the prophetic mission of the Church in relation to the state and the economic sphere generally. Against Lutherans, it held that the state was not just a dike against sin, but that 'forms of production and methods of co-operation may serve the cause of human brotherhood by serving and extending the principle of love beyond the sphere of purely personal relationships'. At Amsterdam, when the World Council of Churches formally came into being, there was a fierce clash between advocates of a free enterprise system and those who saw socialism as the true expression of the Christian Gospel. Both extremes were rejected. Property rights were upheld but it was maintained that they are not absolute and they can be curtailed in accordance with the requirements of justice. The conference at Amsterdam advocated a mixed economy in which both private initiative and state direction would have a place. The key theological concept was that of 'the responsible society', which is one 'where freedom is the freedom of men who acknowledge responsibility to justice and public order, and where those who hold political authority or economic power are responsible for its exercise to God and to the people whose welfare is affected by it'.

The WCC conference at Evanston in 1954 continued the exploration in more detail of how a mixed economy should operate. However, it also continued criticism which had by then begun of the concept of the 'responsible society' as too Western an idea and one that did not do justice to the rapid social changes taking place in the underdeveloped world. At Evanston attention was switched to this developing world, a trend which was continued in New Delhi in 1961 and in the conference on 'Church and Society' at Geneva in 1966. It was during the 1960s that many

Christians became attracted to Marxism, and theologies of hope and liberation theology emerged as powerful shapers of Christian consciousness. Liberation theology will be considered more fully in a separate chapter. However, this brief survey is enough to show that the witness of the non-Roman-Catholic Churches in the economic sphere during this period has had a certain consistency and that, while not distinctively Christian, it is a teaching that the Churches can still own as expressing Christian values and making a contribution to the debate in society as a whole. It firmly rejected Marxism. No less did it reject a purely individualistic approach. For it asserted the necessity of state action in order to achieve the justice that is the political expression of love. Quite properly, the Churches in the United States and Europe have taken on board the concerns of the developing world, which in recent years have been very much to the forefront of thinking in the World Council of Churches. This may not appear a very exciting record but it is one of which the Churches need not be ashamed. In a time of very rapid social change the Churches have made real efforts to grow out of positions that had been ingrained for centuries.

Even more important has been the parallel development in the Roman Catholic Church, as expressed in papal encyclicals and the teaching of the Second Vatican Council. *Rerum Novarum* of Leo XIII in 1891 was concerned to find remedies to what it called 'the misery and wretchedness which presses so heavily at this moment on the large majority of the very poor'. While rejecting a false socialism and asserting the right to private property, it urged the traditional teaching of the Church that material goods were for the common use of humanity. Wealth should be distributed in such a way that the poor in particular were protected. It affirmed the right to a just wage and the right of workers to join or form unions. *Quadragesimo Anno* of Pius XI in 1931 reaffirmed these principles. Asserting that capitalism was not itself evil, it rejected an individualistic, every man for himself, outlook and urged the necessity of state action for the common good. *Divini Redemptoris* of Pius XI in 1937 strongly rejected communism. At the same time, it stressed the necessity of social justice whereby common action was taken to remedy social ills, individual action by itself not being enough. This theme was stressed again in *Mater et Magistra* of John XXIII in 1961, which began to focus on the plight of the poor in underdeveloped countries, a theme which was taken further in his *Pacem in Terris* in 1963 and *Populorum Progressio* of Paul VI.[12]

In May 1991 Pope John Paul II brought out *Centesimus Annus*, to mark the centenary of the first major social encyclical, *Rerum Novarum*. *Centesimus Annus* has been widely praised by people of differing theological viewpoints. It stands within the tradition of previous encyclicals in preferring capitalism to communism but goes into somewhat more detail on the advantages of the capitalist system. Asking whether capitalism should be the goal of the countries now making efforts to rebuild their economy and society, the encyclical says:

If by 'capitalism' is meant an economic system which recognises the fundamental and positive role of business, the market, private property and the resulting responsibility for the means of production, as well as free human creativity in the economic sphere, then the answer is certainly in the affirmative.

One of the burdens of the past from which the Churches, both Reformed and Catholic, have been trying to struggle free in the past 150 years is the excessive individualism of so much Christian thinking at the expense of any social ethic. One of the ways in which the tension over this issue has surfaced is in the alleged contradiction between the claims of justice and the offer of love. When Sammy Davis Jr became a Jew he said 'As I see it the difference is that the Christian religion preaches love thy neighbour and the Jewish religion preaches justice, and I think justice is the big thing we need.' But although love and justice have often been set in opposition to one another, for example by Tolstoy, who thought they were incompatible, or the Lutherans, whose tradition suggests that they are radically different, modern Church teaching brings them much closer together. As F. R. Barry put it: 'the political expression of love is justice'. Or again, we can say that justice is an instrument of love, an essential instrument. Justice is concerned with the needs that human beings have in common. Love goes beyond this only in that it is also concerned with the unique needs of each individual as well. Both justice and love are concerned with the fulfilment of individual need, although they approach this differently. Love meets individual need directly. Justice meets it indirectly by aiming for the good of a particular group to which individuals belong.[13] When legislation is enacted which meets the just demands of, for example, farm workers, or teachers or migrant workers, the good of each individual member of those groups is being served. But it is being served in an indirect manner. The contrast is not between love and justice as such but between ideal justice and justice as we know it. For every actual system of justice reflects the interests of those in power. It needs, therefore, to be subjected to the scrutiny of absolute justice.

Since the time of Plato, justice has been seen in terms of rendering to every person their due. But what is their due? Is it the reward they should receive for working hard? Or the reward they should receive through doing jobs which nobody else would choose to do? There is scope for endless debate. A Christian idea of what is due cannot be separated from that which a person needs and from God's understanding of our needs. For God knows our needs and is concerned to meet them in such a way that our fulfilment is fostered. In the Hebrew scriptures the care of the poor, immigrants, slaves and so on is held to be a matter of justice. They have particular needs and trying to respond to those needs is what God wants of us. Justice, we might say, is using whatever abilities and goods we have for those in need.

Quotations from Church Fathers of the fourth century in Chapter 3 showed how strong is the idea in Christian tradition that God has given the goods of the earth to humanity as a whole. Everyone, without exception, has a need for them and a claim upon them.

Aid agencies are sometimes accused of being too political. They campaign on such issues as world debt and commodity prices, which, in their judgement, vitally affect the material well-being of the poorest people on earth. In contrast, they know that what will set alight the imagination and arouse the sympathy of potential supporters is a specific project, such as digging a well in an Indian village or financially adopting a particular child. The two approaches are complementary, not contradictory. Both are expressions of love. The latter approach seeks to meet the needs of individuals directly. It might also be able to meet the particular needs of those who are helped. For example, a child might be not only supported through school but helped to obtain a scholarship for some form of further education. The former approach is no less an expression of love. But it is considering the poor of the world in their millions, whose standard of living can only be raised as a result of fundamental structural changes in the international economic order. Here millions of people are being considered in the category of the hungry and diseased. Yet in trying to meet their needs through appropriate political measures, we are still serving the one Christ who has said that in meeting the needs of the needy we are rendering what is due to him.

Actual justice, justice as we have it in this world, cannot be separated from considerations of power.[14] The point about the poor is that they are in human terms powerless. In the developed world this powerlessness may simply be shown in an inability to work the system, a difficulty in understanding the many forms compiled by the bureaucracies, not knowing whom to speak to or whom to influence. In the developing world this powerlessness is shown in its starkest forms when, for example, South American Indians are turned off their traditional lands because international mining companies or logging companies are working in their area. In Nadine Gordimer's novel *July's People*,[15] Johannesburg is taken over by black forces of liberation. With the help of their houseboy, called July, a liberal white family are able to flee to his traditional village. For the previous fifteen years July had been totally dependent upon 'his people'. However nice they were to him, and they were nice, this was the fundamental fact of his existence. Now they were dependent on him. Like all good novels the dilemma and tension is focused in details. Who, for example, should now keep the keys of the Land Rover in which they have fled? Indeed, to whom does the Land Rover now belong?

Perhaps the biggest failing of well-meaning people who 'want to help the poor' is a failure of the imagination in this area of power. As long as the poor are being helped they are also being controlled. So a fundamental objective of any Christian approach to the poor, that is, one which recognizes their fundamental dignity as human persons, is to achieve a proper balance or equality of power. When a giant meets a dwarf in the road there is always either a veiled threat or a scarcely hidden patronization. When two friends from the same social background meet they do so on the basis of equality and mutual respect. We cannot look for less in the relationship between the rich and the poor, the developed and the developing world.

Goodwill and benevolent intentions are essential. Nevertheless, they are by themselves not enough. The industrial classes have bettered their conditions over the past 200 years by organizing themselves. The power of capital has been balanced by the power of labour organized in unions. Often goodwill has been present as well, goodwill which has eventually been expressed in legislation recognizing certain basic rights. But for most of this period it has had to be fought for in many a bitter struggle. The fact that the power of trade unions in Great Britain has now 'been broken', and that this was necessary, as people like to think, should not blind us to the fact that the power of the unions was a decisive factor in bringing about the kind of society which we now take for granted and recognize to be in accord with certain minimum standards of social justice.

The problem of the poor in the 1990s, both within industrialized countries and in the poorest parts of the world, cannot, however, be solved so simply. For the poor have little or no leverage. Modern industry, utilizing advanced electronic skills, requires a smaller and a more highly trained workforce. Except in the service industries, there is little demand for unskilled labour. Within the world as a whole, what need has Europe for West Indian sugar cane or Indian cotton? The short answer is, not much. There is, of course, a continuing need for minerals from many parts of the world. But many of the poorest countries have no minerals and the crops they do produce, though they may be bought by developed countries, are not usually essential to them. Such crops can often be produced at home or bought from elsewhere. The poor country which produces them is at the mercy of fluctuating commodity prices and the muscle of more advanced economies.

It is here that the churches may have a contribution to make. For equality of power, though it is desirable in a fallen world, where we are always likely to exploit or patronize one another, is not the only possible basis for mutual respect. Within the one fellowship we have as much to receive from the poor as we have to give to them, even if they can exert no leverage over us. For the poor retain values, at once spiritual and human, which we desperately need. Indeed, in that kingdom in which the poor are blessed, the materially rich have more to receive than they have to give. The theme of Clement, Hermas and the fourth-century Fathers is still true. Within the one body of humanity, of which the body of Christ is a sign and a symbol, those who think they are giving often have more to receive. A recognition of this is the basis of a relationship of mutual dignity and respect.

The implications of this chapter are directly relevant to those of us who have money, power and influence in the industrialized world. For it has been argued that the expression of Christian faith today in practical terms will inevitably be political. This is because the state, for good and ill, now controls so much of our life. It is legislation which directly affects the well-being of our fellow human beings and therefore concern about their well-being necessitates concern about the legislation. This necessity for a political dimension is not contrary to Christian faith but congruous with it, for the Church exists as a sign and witness to the Kingdom of God which embraces the whole of human existence. Nor should the Church accept that it has been reduced to the status of a sect. It still has a position and influence in society and should therefore seek to use this for the benefit of society as a whole, not simply its own members.

If the Church is to speak to society as a whole it will need to appeal to values shared by the majority of human beings and speak in a language which does not depend for its validity on an acceptance of the Christian faith. This means in fact standing in the natural law tradition, which has been the dominant one down the ages for the relationship between Christianity and the economic order. This assumes that there is a basis for moral discourse and moral co-operation between people of very different beliefs. This means also that there is that in our advanced industrialized society about which Christians can say 'yes', and which finds its proper completion in Christ. Above all, there is the fact that human beings now have the expertise and the technological power radically to improve the conditions of human life for humanity as a whole. Because human existence, including the structures of the economic order, are also blighted by sin, Christ says no to the system we have at the moment. He says no to the fact that so many millions are still not sharing, even in a minimal way, in the prosperity enjoyed by a minority.

When it comes to being more specific about the economic policies which flow from Christ's yes and Christ's no to modern society, there are major difficulties. New Testament Christianity is eschatological: the first Christians were conscious of the Kingdom of God about to come to its climax. So Christians have no option but to try to do justice both to considerations of common prudence necessary for survival on earth and to the overarching absolute call and claims of the Kingdom. There is a similar difficulty posed by the New Testament view of self-interest, which will be considered in a subsequent chapter. Another difficulty is the fact that the New Testament provides an ethic for individuals rather than for society as a whole. The Hebrew scriptures do provide an ethic for the community, but it was directed towards an agrarian society and in any case there are disputes about how the Old Testament should be interpreted by Christians in relation to the New. The result is that the attempts by some recent Christian economists to derive a distinctively Christian economics direct from the Old Testament are unlikely to succeed. There are no easy answers and we need to take into account not simply the scriptures, but the long tradition of Christian thinking on this subject, even though that thinking was always marked by the age in which it was produced.

The brief examination of statements by the World Council of Churches and papal encyclicals from the end of the nineteenth century and during the twentieth century reveals a fairly clear consensus on some of the major issues: a decisive rejection of communism, an affirmation of the role of the state in capitalist societies in intervening on behalf of the poor and, in recent years, the placing of the poor of the developing world at the top of the Christian agenda.

Despite this, many individual Church people have had difficulty struggling away from the old individualism. This is partly because of a false understanding of the relationship between love and justice. Justice is an essential instrument of love, considering people as members of groups, which we all are, as well as individuals with special needs. To work for justice for groups of disadvantaged people through political action is proper, is indeed an indispensable expression of Christian love in the modern world. Christians, too, have a particular approach to the question of what is justice. If justice is rendering to all people their due, then a Christian's understanding of what is due to people will be shaped by God's approach to them. God is seeking their full development, physical, emotional and spiritual, as human beings into all the fullness that they have it within them to be. In the light of the teaching of the fourth-century Church Fathers meeting the needs for this personal growth is a matter of basic obligation, not an optional extra.

Justice cannot be separated from power. In the light of a Christian and humane understanding, there is justice when neither partner in a relationship is in a position either to exploit or to patronize the other; when they meet on a basis of equality. This is a goal towards which we must work, not only in personal relationships but in relationships between the developed and the developing world. However, there is a major problem in the modern world, in that the powerful, in many spheres, simply do not need, from an economic point of view, the contribution of the powerless. In advanced industrialized countries they do not need their labour. In the world as a whole they often do not need their goods. This brings out the absolute necessity of a moral approach, rather than a Marxist one, to the economic order. If it is not in the interests, at least the short- or medium-term interests, of the powerful to help the powerless, there remains an overriding moral obligation to do so. The Christian faith, with its emphasis upon the human family under God, and the fact that the powerful have more to receive from the powerless than to give to them, has a particular feel for and contribution to make to this point. It is not only a matter of justice that we work to change the economic order so that it actually meets the needs of the poorest one-third of the world, but within the one fellowship of humanity for which Christ died we belong together, with more to receive than to give. Yet we cannot receive unless we are giving, that is, striving to make the economic order conform to the will of Christ by meeting the needs of all his brothers and sisters. Christ calls us to that task. In responding to that call we will also begin to hear more clearly the good news as it applies to us.

NOTES

1 Edward Norman, *Christianity and the World Order* (OUP, 1979), p. 3.
2 A. J. P. Taylor, *English History 1914–1945* (OUP, 1965), p. 1.
3 Norman, ibid., p. 79.
4 Paul Ramsey, *Speak up for Just War or Pacifism* (Pennsylvania State University Press, 1988), p. 126.
5 Ibid., p. 127.
6 *For the Sake of the Kingdom* (ACC, 1986) and *Many Gifts, One Spirit*, Report of ACC 7 (1987), pp. 61ff.
7 For a development of this point see Richard Harries, *Christianity and War in a Nuclear Age* (Mowbray, 1986), ch. 2.
8 Brian Griffiths, *Morality and the Market Place* (Hodder & Stoughton, 1980).
9 Donald Hay, *Economics Today* (Apollos, 1989).
10 Ronald Preston, *Religion and the Ambiguity of Capitalism* (SCM, 1991), p. 34. The approach of this book, namely that whatever our beliefs we can come to some common understanding of what it is to be a human being, at least as far as our physical needs and our political rights are concerned, has often been criticized in recent decades. However, it is important to note that the sceptical view, namely that it is not possible to come to a common mind, has social and political implications. 'Scepticism about common values, common morality and common assumptions about human flourishing actually tend to support what might be called a new right approach to the ideas of social justice and freedom': Professor Raymond Plant in the Sarum lectures, 1991. I explore this point in more detail later in Chapter 7 when discussing the views of Michael Novak.
11 R. H. Tawney, *Religion and the Rise of Capitalism* (Penguin, 1937).
12 *Proclaiming Justice and Peace* (Documents from John XXIII to John Paul II), ed. Michael Walsh and Brian Davies (Collins, 1984).
13 Reinhold Niebuhr, *An Interpretation of Christian Ethics* (SCM, 1936).
14 Reinhold Niebuhr, *Moral Man and Immoral Society* (Scribner's, 1960).
15 Nadine Gordimer, *July's People* (Jonathan Cape, 1981).

5

The Challenge of Liberation Theology

Since its advent in the 1960s liberation theology has made a major impact on the thinking of many Christians throughout the world. It is a theology which gives courage to the poor, nerving them for action to change their lot. It also offers a particular challenge to the rich. But can it also offer courage and hope to the rich? Such challenges can sometimes leave people oscillating between guilt and romanticism, one moment feeling hopelessly guilty and inadequate, the next admiring some Latin American movement from afar. Liberation theology, to be Christian liberation theology, must bring good news to the rich as well as a challenge. Liberation theologians are now quite numerous and certainly varied in their different emphases. However, there are certain major concerns and themes which they share, which the Vatican singled out for discussion in two important documents. Because on this issue the Vatican can fairly be taken to represent the mind of mainstream, traditional thinking from the developed world, the points made in these documents will be looked at in some detail. First, however, a number of general characteristics of liberation theology will be set out.

Liberation theology directs us to the context in which theology is done. A Christian living in an ashram and working among those whom Mother Teresa called the poorest of the poor on the streets of some large Indian city and a Christian acting as managing director of a major international soft drinks firm are set in very different environments, with very different pressures upon them. Both are professed believers. Both are sincere in their desire to follow the Lord, but it would be surprising if the very different contexts in which they operate did not in some way make their mark on their thinking and understanding of obedience. An emphasis upon the context in which theology is done can take an extreme, reductionist form. It can suggest that the theology not only arises out of a particular context but is determined by it. It simply serves the interests of those from whom it emanates. Like all forms of determinism this view is logically self-defeating. For the statement that all theology is determined by a particular set of social conditions would itself be determined. So there would be no way of arriving at the truth or falsity of such an assertion. It is quite clear, however, that theology is always done by particular people in a particular environment and it would be strange to claim that their thinking did not in some way reflect that environment. It is not Marxist analysis but Christian humility which leads to such a conclusion. For we do not have a God's eye view of the universe. We are limited, finite creatures embedded in a particular social matrix in which we do our reflection. This reflection, when genuinely reflective, can transcend the limits of a particular time and place. But it is always coloured by that time and place. To recognize this is to acknowledge our creatureliness. To deny it is to be guilty of hubris.

Liberation theology also directs us to consider the social and political impact of particular kinds of theology. Some forms of Christian faith have buttressed hierarchy and the position of the ruling elite, encouraging the oppressed to feel content with their lot, looking to the next life rather than to this one for a change in their condition. Other theologies, from John Ball, who led the Peasants' Revolt in the thirteenth century with the jingle 'When Adam delved and Eve span, who was then the gentleman?', through the radical sects of the Reformation and the left-wing elements in Cromwell's army to the Christian socialists or Christian Marxists of our own time, have offered ideological support to those who have challenged the *status quo*. For theology takes on not only the colour of the environment but the interests of those who theologize within it. Marx saw behind the values of the bourgeoisie the interests of the bourgeoisie. Lenin thought that every priest was simply a *gendarme* in a cassock. For the reasons suggested in the previous paragraph this extreme view is untenable. Nevertheless, serious attention has to be paid to the social, economic and political impact of a particular way of thinking about God.

Liberation theology is concerned for action on behalf of the poor, not simply thought about them. Indeed, some liberation theologians would assert that contemplation and action come first and that theology is a second-order activity arising out of struggle for the oppressed. Above the grave of Karl Marx in Highgate Cemetery are carved his famous words, 'Philosophers have only interpreted the world, the point is, however, to change it.' For liberation theologians the crisis of the modern world is not as some theologians in North America and Europe have suggested, a crisis of meaning, but a crisis of misery. For liberation theologians theology that does not arise out of and encourage action on behalf of the poor is worse than useless, for such theology encourages passive acceptance of things as they are.

Liberation theology directs us to look to the context from which a theology arises so we can apply that principle to the debate between liberation theologians and the Vatican itself. Liberation theology springs out of a solidarity with the poor and a sense of the horrific things that are being done to them. In contrast the Vatican works in accord with its old saying, 'We think in terms of centuries here.' The primary concern of the former is to do something about the desperate plight of the poor. The Vatican, on the other hand, is concerned with what it regards as the abiding truths of the Christian revelation which have been faithfully pre-served for nearly two thousand years and which must be safeguarded for the next two thousand. The Vatican documents also express the widest possible contemporary context. They bear in mind not only the struggle of the poor in the developing world but the struggle against communism in Europe. Perhaps both these contexts have important contributions to make to the debate. As already mentioned, there have been two major Vatican responses to liberation theology. The first, entitled *Instruction on Certain Aspects of the 'Theology of Liberation' (Libertatis Nuntius)*, was published in 1984. The second, *Instruction on Christian Freedom and Liberation (Libertatis Conscientia)*, was published in March 1986.[1] The primary function of the first document was to correct certain alleged errors in liberation theology. At the same time it asserted that there could be a properly Christian liberation theology and promised a more positive statement later, which came in the second document.

The starting point for the Vatican is the truth of God revealed in Christ, witnessed to in scripture and safeguarded in the magisterium, the teaching authority of the Church. Christ himself is the liberator and through his life, death and resurrection he liberates us from sin, the power of evil and death. Sin is first of all, and fundamentally, personal, an alienation from God. This liberation has immediate ethical implications. The liberated person is driven by love of God and love of fellow human beings. Love is the key ethical concept. The documents lay little stress on the future, whether on this earth or beyond this earth. Love rather than hope is central. Love for those who suffer in the present rather than hope that a time will come when none will suffer. This Christian love is above all a love for the poor. An analysis of the Bible, particularly the life and teaching of Christ, gives a preference to the poor. Christian love is, to use the Vatican's phrase, 'A love of preference for the poor'. This love is a love for the whole person, his or her physical and material well-being as well as spiritual salvation. The Church is quite right to align itself in solidarity with the poor, to make their yearning for liberation from poverty and disease its own. This means that a Christian judgement must be brought to bear on the social and economic structures that continue to keep so many millions in poverty. Although the Church is not an expert in political and economic matters it offers a set of principles for reflection and criteria for judgement as well as directives for action, 'so that the profound changes demanded by situations of poverty and injustice may be brought about, and this in a way which serves the true good of humanity'.

Christian love leads to a full recognition of the dignity of each individual. To this foundational principle two other principles are intimately linked. First is the principle of solidarity. By virtue of this, everyone is obliged to contribute to the common good of society at all its levels. Hence the Church's doctrine is opposed to all forms of social or political individualism. The second principle, of subsidiarity, means that

> neither the State nor any society must ever substitute itself for the initiative and responsibility of individuals and of intermediate communities at the level on which they can function, nor must they take away the room necessary for their freedom. Hence the Church's social doctrine is opposed to all forms of collectivism.

On the basis of these principles the Church can make judgements on structures and on systems and give guidelines for action. There is a great work to be done, to bring about, in a fine phrase, a 'civilization of love'. This effort must begin with education: education for the civilization of work, education for solidarity and access to culture for all. Work is regarded as the key to the whole social question. The civilization of work 'will affirm the priority of work over capital and the fact that material goods are meant for all'. Every person has a right to work and the creation of jobs is a primary social task facing individuals and private enterprise, as well as the state. Furthermore, wages must be such as to enable the worker and his or her family to have access to a truly human standard of living. 'The priority of work over capital places an obligation in justice upon employers to consider the welfare of the workers before the increase of profits.' Important points are also made about solidarity and culture. Material goods are meant for all and therefore there must be a new solidarity with the poor at every level, including the international, the richer countries with the poorer ones. Everyone has a right to culture; hence the necessity of promoting and spreading education. Although it is noted that there are serious flaws in some theologies of liberation, warning against them

> must not at all be taken as some kind of approval, even indirect, of those who keep the poor in misery, who profit from that misery, who notice it while doing nothing about it, or who remain indifferent to it. The Church, guided by the Gospel of mercy and by the love of mankind, hears the cry for justice and intends to respond to it with all her might. Thus a great call goes out to all the church . . . with a love for the poor which demands sacrifice, pastors will consider the response to this call a matter of the highest priority, as many already do.

That is the positive call of the Vatican, as it bears on the central concerns of the liberation theologians. It is important to bear this in mind as much as the Vatican's warnings about deviations. Nevertheless, there have been, from the Vatican's point of view, serious errors in some liberation theology.

First is the question of the starting point for theological reflection. The thrust of much liberation theology is that true theology can only come from a solidarity with and a commitment to the poor. It is from this active commitment that the truth can be seen and from no other position. As pointed out earlier, this claim can take extreme and less extreme forms. One extreme form suggests that all ideological truth is simply a reflection of a particular socio-economic matrix; but this is self-contradictory. Linked with this extreme form of the claim is the notion that truth or falsity is to be judged by what helps or hinders the poor in their struggle in history. Such a notion is not self-contradictory but according to Vatican thinking it is difficult to see how it can be judged Christian. Christianity has always claimed to be a revealed truth. The attempt to set up the criterion of whether a theological view helps or hinders the struggle of the poor is to posit an altogether different standard.

The emphasis on the context in which theological reflection takes place may have validity in a more modified form. For Christianity has always rejected the idea that knowing the truth can be a purely intellectual matter. It always involves the heart and will as well as the mind. 'Blessed are the pure in heart for they shall see God.' There is a biblical theme about doing the truth as well as seeing it. We could certainly say therefore that it is difficult to see how anyone who is not sensitive to the plight of the poor and committed to alleviating it can come to know the God who has a preferential love of the poor. The Vatican seems prepared to take one step down this road while also making another point: membership of the Church is itself a context, an indispensable context for a true theology, and the experience of the Church itself has to be taken into account.

> Theological reflection developed from a particular experience can constitute a very positive contribution, inasmuch as it makes possible a highlighting of aspects of the Word of God, the richness of which had not yet been fully grasped. But in order that this reflection may be truly a reading of the Scripture and not a projection onto the Word of God of a meaning which it does not contain, the theologian will be careful to interpret the experience from which he begins in the light of the experience of the Church herself.

The second issue raised concerns the primary location of sin. The Vatican statements emphasize that political and economic structures can become manifestly unjust and Christians must work to change them. The two instructions are at pains to point out, however, that the root of sin lies in individual persons, not the structures themselves. Sinful structures are the result of human actions and therefore are more consequences than causes. Furthermore, even when structures are made less unjust this does not of itself lead to a change in personal life. Personal corruption is all too evident in countries that have experienced political revolution. Personal conversion is necessary and it is important to work at one and the same time for change in persons and change in structures. Without denying the validity of the Vatican's stress on personal responsibility it is doubtful if its documents go far enough in recognizing the power of the right structures to shape personal life for good and the power of wrong structures to shape personal life for ill. It is not necessary to take a materialistic or deterministic view to recognize how a community shaped in its structures by brotherhood can induce feelings of brotherhood – and vice versa. By allowing so little to the role of structures in their account of sin the documents verge on dualism. For Christianity, which affirms the creation and man as a social being, can hardly ignore the role of the outward in shaping the inward, or the mutual interaction of the personal and the social.

The third issue concerns the use made by many liberation theologians of Marxist analysis. It is the argument of the first instruction, *Libertatis Nuntius*, in particular, that it is not possible to use some Marxist analysis and ignore the rest; the use of even some leads to the importing of a wholly alien ideology and the setting up of non-Christian criteria of truth. In particular the statement objects to the notion of class struggle. Now it can be readily conceded that Marxism, taken as a whole, is incompatible with Christianity. But as was mentioned earlier, even such a right-wing historian as Edward Norman has willingly conceded that some aspects of Marxist analysis can be useful in illuminating society and its history. Moreover, Niebuhr's *Moral Man and Immoral Society* (the classic statement by a Christian of how groups relate to one another) makes good use of the idea of class struggle. But in Niebuhr this is seen as one form of the endless struggle for power between human groupings and this in turn is seen as a form of human hubris, man's attempt to put himself rather than God at the centre of things. It simply is not true that the use of some Marxist analysis commits a theologian to the whole of Marxism.

The fourth issue concerns the evaluation of liberation in European history. The second instruction, *Libertatis Conscientia*, examines secular liberation in the Renaissance, the Reformation, the Enlightenment and the French Revolution. While admitting the genuine aspirations in this movement and its real achievements, the document judges it to be deeply flawed. For it has led to a situation where technology itself now imposes a terrifying threat to mankind. In the sphere of politics, revolutions aimed at liberating man from injustice have set up new and worse tyrannies. The fundamental flaw in this whole process is an underlying sense that to be free means to be free of morality and the ultimate freedom is to be free from God himself. There is both alienation and hubris in this movement. In contrast it has to be said that true liberation, Christianly understood, has to begin with a sense of man as a creature of God, called by God to use his freedom responsibly for others.

> It is from God and in relationship with him that human freedom takes its meaning and consistency. Man's history unfolds on the basis of the nature which he has received from God and in which the inclinations of this nature and of divine grace orient and direct him.

The Vatican documents are surely right to make this point. A person who believes in the reality of God will have a different concept of liberation from an atheist for he or she will have a different understanding of maturity. Freedom involves a recognition of reality and for those who believe in God this is the supreme reality to be acknowledged. Further, human beings on this view have a nature that is made in the image of God. Freedom means working with this nature not against it. All this needs stressing, though more in relation to European thought than to what is happening in Latin America.

The fifth issue concerns the relationship between the spiritual and the material. The Church is concerned for the whole person, in the totality of our surroundings. Nevertheless, the Church is the guardian of a revealed truth, Christ himself, in relation to whom true and lasting happiness lies. The first task of the Church is evangelization and its purpose is salvific, bringing eternal salvation to people. The documents suggest that some liberation theology downplays this and encourages the view that improving the social conditions of the poor is the primary purpose of the Church. When the Church talks about justice and urges the laity to work for it, she is not going beyond the sphere of her mission.

> She is, however, concerned that this mission should not be absorbed by preoccupations concerning the temporal order or reduced to such preoccupations. Here she takes great care to maintain clearly and firmly both the unity and the distinction between evangelisation and human promotion: unity, because she seeks the good of the whole person; distinction, because these two tasks enter, in different ways, into her mission.

This is right in theory. Yet in practice, faced with terrible poverty and oppression, the priorities can seem so different, a point to which we must return.

The sixth issue raised is the relationship between human action now and the coming of the Kingdom of God in the future. Marxism sets out the visionary hope of a classless society on earth that will be achieved by human action in co-operation with the destiny of history in that direction. By contrast Christianity suggests a Kingdom beyond space and time brought about by God. Not only do the two views seem incompatible, the latter seems to undermine the former (and vice versa). For if we are waiting for God to bring in the Kingdom what is the goal of human action? *Libertatis Conscientia* argues that the Christian hope does not undermine but on the contrary strengthens and gives meaning to our efforts on this earth.

> It is of course important to make a careful distinction between earthly progress and the growth of the Kingdom, which do not belong to the same order. Nonetheless, this distinction is not a separation; for man's vocation to eternal life does not suppress but confirms his task of using the energies and means which he has received from the Creator for developing his temporal life.

Furthermore, we know that 'all the good things we work for on earth, human dignity, fraternal union and freedom will be rediscovered, illumined and transfigured when Christ hands over to the Father the eternal and universal kingdom'. Given the fact that the Christian faith is not about human action to achieve an earthly goal but an ethic of love in response to the love of God this goes far to rebut the criticism that the Christian faith undermines work for human progress. For love leads Christians to work for human dignity and fraternal union, to free mankind from the fetters of injustice. And as St Paul said, our labour in the Lord 'is not in vain'. It has a place, purified and transfigured, in the Lord's kingdom.

A seventh issue concerns the use of certain biblical material. The Vatican documents, while affirming that the Bible is very much concerned with social justice, argue that the Exodus story, for example, is not just about human liberation in general but about the bringing into existence of a people charged with a divine task. The Exodus was followed by Sinai. Similarly, the Magnificat is not just about the proud being scattered in the imagination of their hearts. It is about the Mother of God submitting herself to divine grace and her divine calling. This exegesis is in line with the general thrust of the arguments of the documents, that the Christian faith is first of all about the revealed truth of Christ and only then about politics and economics.

From the standpoint of a Christian in Western Europe the Vatican's two responses to liberation theology can look balanced and fair. How do they look to someone committed to the poor in South America? Perhaps, first, the language lacks a certain passion and urgency. To a priest in Latin America faced with a destitute child and knowing that the international economic system somehow conspires with the country's own oligarchy to keep that child destitute, there is a proper passion, an anger, even a bitterness. There are only hints of this in the Vatican documents.

More fundamentally, talk of evangelization and salvation in a world where children want bread to live can seem an affront. There is a dilemma to which there is no obvious answer. The Church has a message of eternal salvation in Christ. But the urgency of the situation calls for the means to live and an end to all that perpetuates sub-human living. Yet also, from the perspective of the poor and especially from them, there is a longing for a justice that this earth cannot give. For the poor, like the rest of us, die; but die so often with their earthly promise unfulfilled.

> For true justice must include everyone; it must bring the answer to the immense load of suffering borne by all the generations. In fact without the resurrection of the dead and the Lord's judgement, there is no justice in the full sense of the term. The promise of the resurrection is freely made to meet the desire for true justice dwelling in the human heart.

This hope is not an escape from human responsibility, nor is it the opium of the people. For it is above all those who are truly in solidarity with the poor and committed to them who will feel the need for that full justice, whose fulfilment is not limited by the bonds of space and time.

Moving away from the Vatican critique, there is a further reservation that must be expressed about liberation theology. God is indeed a liberating God, who not only frees us from inner and personal bondage but who is liberating the whole of life, including the social, economic and political orders. Indeed, it is basic to the approach of this book, as of liberation theology, that Christianity cannot be confined to the so-called spiritual sphere. Unless we are involved in God's work to liberate the whole of human existence from its shackles of sin we ourselves are not personally liberated. Nevertheless, between the theological affirmation that God is ceaselessly at work liberating his children and specific political action, there are a number of intermediate judgements that have to be made and on which there is no clear consensus.[2]

Theology cannot move straight to action; there is also required both ethical reflection and political judgement. In the former Soviet Union and Eastern Europe, God was at work liberating people from communism. In Latin America, God is at work liberating people from the worst excesses of capitalism. In both contexts serious political analysis is required on the nature of communism and the nature of capitalism in order that a judgement might be made about the political system one should be striving to change or improve. Theology informs such a debate but of itself gives no answer. Similarly, there sometimes comes the difficult decision of whether armed force should be used to overthrow a manifest and long-standing oppression. It will be necessary to draw on the long tradition of Christian thinking on the morality of force, in particular the just revolution tradition. Theology offers criteria for this debate but does not provide a solution.[3] Again, it can never be obvious simply from theology exactly what is and what is not liberating. In a country beset by anarchy and uncontrolled random violence, the first step towards liberation is the creation of ordered and stable conditions. There can be no true justice without order, that is genuine order, not the kind of repressive violence of so many dictatorships. But liberation in practice is never simply about justice, it is about the combination of *pax–ordo–iustitia* which provides the basic framework for harmonious and fruitful human community.

Since the Vatican response to liberation theology a fresh and challenging voice on the subject has been heard from India, Aloysius Pieris SJ in his book *An Asian Theology of Liberation*. What immediately marks out Pieris from his counterparts in other parts of the world is that he takes religion seriously. In India, religion is an essential part of the being of the poor, so to be with the poor and for the poor is to take their religion seriously. Therefore the religion of India cannot be dismissed in Marxist terms as simply a sop to the people, nor can it be rejected in Christian terms as not being centred on Christ. It is part of the life of the poor. More than that, religion in India is essentially soteriological, concerned with salvation, with liberation. This is the point of entry, not mysticism or philosophy or even theology. Furthermore, although this salvation is usually conceived of first of all in terms of personal liberation, the myths and rituals of

Indian religion make it quite clear that what is involved is the salvation of the whole universe, the liberation of the cosmos. There is that in Indian religion which points to the transformation of the whole of humanity.

Distinguishing voluntary poverty and forced poverty, Pieris argues that in Christian discipleship the two concerns must come together. In Christian history voluntary poverty has often been chosen by individuals but those individuals have as often as not belonged to religious communities which have been exceedingly wealthy. Forced poverty has been seen as something which must be eliminated, but this task has not always been seen in integral connection with the call to voluntary poverty. Spiritual poverty today must be seen in the closest possible alliance with the struggle of the poor to overcome forced poverty. 'We become one with God to the degree that our poverty drives us to appropriate God's concern for the poor as our own mission.'[4] Pieris sees the future of the Church as being with basic human communities, communities composed of Christians and others, living with the poor, for the poor. Working for the poor means above all struggling against Mammon. For he sees in the Bible a fundamental struggle between Abba and Mammona, God our Father and that alliance of money, power and often religion that crushes people. The good news is that God is acting through the poor to overthrow the kingdoms of this world and to establish his kingdom. 'The poor must be seen as those through whom God shapes our salvation history.' Pieris writes:

> The Asian dilemma, then, can be summed up as follows: the theologians are not (yet) poor; and the poor are not (yet) theologians! This dilemma can be resolved only in the local churches of Asia – that is, in the grass root communities where the theologians and the poor become culturally reconciled through a process of mutual evangelisation. This reciprocal exposure to the Gospel consists in this, that the theologians are awakened into the liberative dimension of poverty and the poor are conscientized into the liberative potentialities of their religiousness.[5]

> No wonder that the very sight of money polluting religion made Jesus resort to physical violence, for his mission was a prophetic mission – that is, a mission of the poor and a mission to the poor, a mission by the poor and a mission for the poor. This is the truth about evangelisation that the local churches in Asia find hardest to accept. To awaken the consciousness of the poor to their unique liberative role in the totally new order God is about to usher in – this is how I have already defined evangelisation – is the inalienable task of the poor already wakened. Jesus was the first evangeliser – poor, but fully conscious of his part in the war against Mammon with all its principalities and powers.[6]

According to Pieris, then, the poor have a special role in ushering in God's Kingdom. Their liberation begins when they awake to this. But where does this leave the rich? How do they share in this liberation? This is a question that must continue to press upon us as we explore the themes of later chapters.

One of the most encouraging developments of the Christian scene in recent years has been the development of a radical evangelical approach to the economic order and an evangelical social ethics to go with this. This is in strong contrast to the evangelicalism of a previous generation, which tended to concentrate on the inner and personal spheres while accepting a conservative political order.

A consultation of Christians from churches, missions and aid agencies meeting at Wheaton College in the United States in June 1983 agreed on a statement stressing the necessity of Christian social involvement, which took as its key concept the transformation of the whole of human life. Since the Wheaton conference, evangelical social ethics has continued to develop along the same lines. Its strength is that it seeks to combine the personal and the corporate, the spiritual and the political. 'The transformation that the Bible calls us to is a transformation of both individuals and social structures that allows us to move toward increasing harmony with God, with our fellow human beings, with our environment, and with ourselves.'[7]

A conference with the same standpoint took place in Oxford during 1990, which produced the 'Oxford Declaration on Christian Faith and Economics'. In many ways, for example in its analysis of how the burden of debt arose and in its emphasis on a particular concern for the poor, it pursues the same themes as Roman Catholic liberation theologians. Of course, here and there, there are differences in emphasis and qualifications, but not in the stress that structural as well as personal change is needed. 'We realise that ethical demands are often ineffective because they are reinforced only by individual conscience and that the proclamation of Christian values needs to be accompanied by action to encourage institutional and structural changes which would foster these values in our communities.'[8]

The theme of transformation, and the concerns it takes up, is an encouraging one. The word 'liberation' can imply, wrongly, only liberation from certain ills. The word 'transformation' conveys the idea of positive change in the light of God's purpose for the world. This too, of course, is what liberation theologians have in mind, but a transformation theology, coming from the evangelical tradition, is a welcome complement to liberation theology. Those who wrote 'The Oxford Declaration on Christian Faith and Economics' are probably too optimistic in thinking that it 'offers a significant way to bridge the hostile divisions'[9] caused by debates between liberation theologians and others. Nevertheless, it would be good if liberation theology and transformation theology could come together for the enrichment and strengthening of both. Another area where it would be good to see transformation theologians active is among Pentecostalist groups, particularly in the developing world. In Latin America Pentecostalism is mushrooming. Pentecostalism, with its traditional stress on the salvation of the individual, its other-worldly orientation and its willingness to put up with debilitating human conditions, needs to be challenged and changed by the newly revitalized evangelical social ethics of transformation.

It has sometimes been suggested in recent years that we need a liberation theology for Great Britain. However, it seems doubtful if all the factors which would make this possible are present. Kenneth Leach, who is certainly sympathetic to the idea, maintains that for a viable liberation theology to develop in Britain it would be necessary to have a clear social need, an interest in such a theology and a movement.[10] There is certainly both a need and an interest. However, there have been no signs of a real movement. This is in part because, whereas in Latin America there is still a strong predominantly Christian culture which can be mobilized, this is not so in Britain. Secondly, the groups who have been identified as potential initiators of such a movement, black congregations in inner-city areas, feminists and alienated Muslim communities, would not seem to have enough overlap to make common cause. There is also the further fact that Latin America is for the most part a pre-socialist society and Britain is a post-socialist one. Much of what needs to be achieved in terms of basic social and political rights in Latin America was achieved in this country by the struggles of the trade unions and allied groups in the nineteenth and earlier part of the twentieth centuries. What is needed in this country might be very different from what is needed in Latin America or the Soviet Union. Clifford Longley has written:

> If there is such a thing as a generic theology of liberation, applicable in Britain as well as in Latin-America, then it must also be applicable in the suburbs of Moscow or Warsaw – where there are also 'the poor awaiting liberation'. Their freedom will not come from abolishing private landlordism, however, for there is none in sight; it is more likely to come from allowing them to engage in a little free-market capitalism.[11]

This highlights the point made earlier that it is not possible to move straight from liberation theology to political action; political analysis is an essential intermediate step, and that analysis is likely to reveal different conditions and therefore different necessary remedies in different societies.

All liberation theologians emphasize that the theology they publish in books is only an indication of the true theology of liberation going on in communities committed to social and political struggle. Liberation theology is theological reflection by the poor as they seek to create genuine Christian communities engaged in the task of liberating themselves and society from the ills which beset us. What we can say, therefore, is that genuine theology today, whether we call it liberation theology, transformation theology or any other name, needs to have living contact with such people and groups. Gustavo Gutiérrez has written that:

> To be poor is to be insignificant, because one has no power economically or politically; moreover, one's values are not appreciated. The poor are the nameless, the little ones. And when the church talks about 'the preferential

option for the poor' this means really entering into the world of the insignificant.[12]

Personally, he writes: 'I am becoming more and more, in the last years, impressed by the complexity of the world of the poor. It was my most profound experience of the last ten or twelve years.' Gutiérrez argues that the preferential option for the poor is not simply a Latin American question. It is a biblical one. Everyone must find their way within this option. 'I am not able to say to you what your own way of commitment to the poor must be. Without doubt it would be different in manner to that of people living in the poor countries themselves.' Nevertheless,

> To be committed to the poor signifies taking part in the struggle for justice. It also signifies having friends among the poor. It is not only a commitment with a given social group, it is above all an expression of solidarity with concrete persons. Friendship is not an addition to our efforts for justice, it is the very meaning of these efforts. Clear friendship presupposes that we share our lives.

There is no substitute for personal experience. Members of the Archbishop of Canterbury's Commission on Urban Priority Areas which produced *Faith in the City* paid a number of extensive visits to the areas about which they were writing. They wrote:

> We have to report that we have been deeply disturbed by what we have seen and heard. We have been confronted with the human consequences of unemployment, which in some urban areas may be over 50% of the labour force and which occasionally reaches a level as high as 80% – consequences which may be compounded by the effects of racial discrimination. We have seen physical decay, whether in Victorian terraced housing or of inferior system built blocks of flats, which has in places created an environment so degrading that some people have set fire to their own homes rather than be condemned to living in them indefinitely. Social disintegration has reached a point in some areas that shop windows are boarded up, cars cannot be left on the street, residents are afraid either to go out themselves or to ask others in, and there is a pervading sense of powerlessness and despair.[13]

It was this personal experience which gave the report they wrote a passion and urgency. From this, one basic, underlying principle emerges for anyone who is concerned with Christian liberation and transformation. It is the necessity of somehow keeping in touch with, and allowing oneself to be affected by, those who are losing out in the struggles of this world. Pictures on television are not enough, books are not enough. There needs to be personal contact and experience of some kind. This is why links between parishes in the suburbs and parishes in urban priority areas are so important. This is why links between dioceses in the developed world and dioceses in the developing world are so crucial. Sometimes people sneer at these and it is certainly possible for a patronizing, do-gooder attitude to arise. What needs to be emphasized, therefore, is that these links are simply an expression of our solidarity in the one body of Christ, in which there is mutual giving and receiving. If the deprived have something to receive from the relatively prosperous, the relatively prosperous have much to receive from those who are physically deprived. The only links worth having are those which foster this sense of mutuality. From my own point of view, it is my membership of the Anglican Peace and Justice Network which has been important. Through the living experience of Anglican friends in other parts of the world I have been able to receive and to some extent retain a sense of what it is like to live in a society that is impoverished or oppressed and where church leaders will very often put their own lives at risk in the struggle for justice. For some, their point of contact has been a deprived inner-city area. For others, it will be visiting someone in a mental hospital or a hostel for the homeless.

This chapter is written in the conviction that God's liberation is for everyone. The rich need to be liberated no less than the poor. This begins when we find ourselves in genuine solidarity with a person or a group of people who are poor and powerless. This is strangely liberating. First, it puts the usual preoccupations and anxieties of bourgeois existence in their proper perspective. Suddenly one sits lighter to the daily struggle for personal power, prestige and fortune. One sees life from a very basic standpoint, perhaps that of life or death. Secondly, it is to see one's own social context, with its taken-for-granted values and outlook, not as a timeless verity, but as the product of a particular constellation of circumstances and interests. It is to be liberated from absolutizing one's own position in society. Then, as one begins to make one's own the struggle of the poor, there is an overwhelming sense of powerlessness. How can one person do anything against the systems and forces that rule in this world? But in this sense of powerlessness begins our freedom. For we are thrust upon God and his grace. Herein too, is our liberation.

Liberation theology certainly challenges us. It makes us aware of the context in which we ourselves are situated and how this inevitably affects our thinking and judgements compared with those who are relatively powerless. It offers a critique of our own personal beliefs from the point of view of their effects on the social, economic and political order. Do they reinforce the *status quo* or provide an incentive to work for change?[14] It challenges us to struggle with and for the poor, in the knowledge that as one of those who are poor, God's grace is active with and through us in a special way, ushering in his Kingdom.

Some form of personal experience and the solidarity that springs from this is the basic requirement. As the Vatican document puts it:

> Solidarity is a direct requirement of human and supernatural brotherhood. The serious socio-economic problems which occur today cannot be solved unless new fronts of solidarity are created. Solidarity of the poor among themselves, solidarity with the poor to which the rich are called, solidarity among the workers and with the workers . . . when the church appeals for

such solidarity, she is aware that she herself is concerned in a quite special way.[15]

NOTES

1 These documents are available from the Catholic Truth Society, 38/40 Ecclestone Square, London SW1V 1PD.
2 A good example of this is provided by the debate in Jewish circles on liberation theology. Mark Ellis wrote a book called *A Jewish Theology of Liberation*. But other Jewish theologians conceived liberation in very different terms with very different political implications. See *Christian–Jewish Relations*, 21, no. 1 (Spring 1988), published by the Institute of Jewish Affairs, 11 Hertford Street, London W1Y 7DX.
3 Richard Harries, *Should a Christian Support Guerillas?* (Lutterworth, 1982).
4 Aloysius Pieris, *An Asian Theology of Liberation* (T. & T. Clark, 1988), p. 23.
5 Ibid., p. 41.
6 Ibid., p. 49.
7 *The Church in Response to Human Need*, ed. Vinay Samuel and Chris Sugden (Eerdman/Regnum, 1987), pp. 254ff.
8 Ibid., p. 47.
9 *Transformation: an International Dialogue on Evangelical Social Ethics*, 7, No. 2 (April/June 1990), p. 8. Oxford Centre for Mission Studies, PO Box 70, Oxford OX2 6HB.
10 Lecture at St George's House, Windsor in 1990.
11 Clifford Longley, *The Times*, 4 November 1989.
12 Gustavo Gutiérrez, 'The Church of the poor', lecture at the Von Hügel Institute in Cambridge, published in the *Columban Contacts Newsletter*, 28 Redington Road, London NW3 7RH.
13 *Faith in the City* (Church House Publishing, 1985), p. xiv. See also *Living Faith in the City* (Church House Publishing, 1990).
14 Alistair Kee, *Domination or Liberation* (SCM, 1986) and David Nicholls, *Deity and Domination* (Routledge, 1989) explore the connection between particular pictures of God and the social and political policies that people draw from these conceptions.
15 *Instruction on Christian Freedom and Liberation*, para. 89.

6

For Those Engaged in the Creation of Wealth

The exasperation of British industry and commerce with the Church finally boiled over in 1990. Peter Morgan, Director of the Institute of Directors, strongly attacked the Church's negative attitude to industry and its hostility to wealth creation. Others followed suit. They all argued that Church pronouncements had concentrated far too much on the poor and too little on making the wealth without which the poor could not be helped.

In fact, not all Church leaders had been as negative as was implied. In October 1989 *The Director*, the house magazine of the Institute of Directors, published a long and thoughtful interview with Robert Runcie, then Archbishop of Canterbury. The national press took this up in a sensational way, focusing on the criticisms the Archbishop made of the ethos of our current economic life. In fact, he began the interview with the words, 'I believe of course in wealth creation – that's necessary if we're going to do all the things that we ought to be doing for our society in our privileged position in the world. It enables us also to give leadership in other parts of the world for good causes.' However, that strong endorsement of wealth creation went unnoticed.

For a long time the Church has had a negative attitude to industry, one shared by the educated classes in Britain as a whole, who for far too long have exuded an air of disapproval. This has nothing at all to do with Christianity, but much to do with snobbery. It is a hangover from the nineteenth century when grandfather in the West Midlands built up a small thriving firm from nothing. His son took it over and expanded it successfully but his grandsons then went off to be doctors, clergy or musicians, somewhat embarrassed about the source of the money that enabled them to receive their education and position in society. Nineteenth-century businessmen and industrialists who made money, like their counterparts in the Roman empire, loved to buy a country estate and live the life of a country gentleman. Or, if they themselves did not want to do that, their sons or grandsons did. In nineteenth-century Britain this attitude was reinforced by the great public schools. An alternative to country life was provided in administering justice at the edges of the growing Empire. Either way industry was on the whole shunned. There may also have been another reason. The romantic movement had taught people to look at nature with new eyes. Industrialization created a blot on the landscape. The dark satanic mills, blackening the fields and skies, seemed ugly, an affront. The result was that people sought an escape to the countryside and religious imagery was almost exclusively drawn from the pastoral idyll.[1]

All this needs to be corrected. There is, first, nothing wrong with making money; that is, with a person trying to provide for himself or herself and family. As Dr Johnson put it, 'There are few ways in which a man can be more innocently employed than in getting money.'[2] Secondly, the world of industry and commerce is just as much part of God's good creation as is agriculture. Indeed there is some contradiction in thanking God for harvest, that is, for successful agriculture, while being niggardly about blessing God for a flourishing economy as a whole. Thirdly, unless the whole industrial and commercial enterprise is an activity that human beings can engage in with a sense that what they are doing is morally and spiritually worthwhile, they are hardly likely to be concerned about the morality of particular parts of the system. If industry and commerce can be affirmed, then it will follow that honesty in details of the system are a matter of profound importance. If, however, it is all regarded with a sense of snobbish distaste, as a squalid activity where a quick buck is to be made, then there is no moral basis for day-by-day dealing. If the whole house stinks, putting a deodorizer into one cupboard is hardly going to be effective. If, however, the system is in principle wholesome, an essential part of the human enterprise under God, which is what the Churches should be saying, then there is some incentive to strive for integrity in the daily operations of buying, producing and selling.

> Social and moral attitudes in Britain are powerfully influenced by Christian teaching which has never found it easy to affirm and bless industry and commerce in the way that it has been able to affirm and bless farming, the police and professional services and the arts,[3]

wrote Kenneth Adams, while noting that a more positive attitude is beginning to come about.

In her speech to the General Assembly of the Church of Scotland in Edinburgh on 21 May 1988, the Prime Minister set out to give a biblical approach to the economic order. She found first that 'We must work and use our talents to create wealth.' Therefore, 'Abundance rather than poverty has a legitimacy which derives from the very nature of creation. It is not the creation of wealth that is wrong but the love of money for its own sake.' The spiritual dimension comes in deciding what one does with the wealth and we would not be able to respond to the many calls for help, invest for the future, or support the arts, which glorify God, 'unless we had first worked hard and used our talents to create the necessary wealth'. It is a view not unlike that of Clement of Alexandria, who has indeed been described as the first Thatcherite. It is a view that stands in the tradition of John Wesley's 1744 sermon 'The use of money', in which he told Christians to 'Gain all you can: save all you can: give all you can.'[4]

There is much here that is unarguable. As has often been pointed out, religion in the Hebrew scriptures is thoroughly and properly materialistic. God wants the whole of human life to flourish, the corn and wine and oil to increase. Such prosperity is seen as a sign of divine blessing. Too often Christians have read the New Testament in isolation from the Old, that God wants the whole of existence to blossom bountifully. The Jewish view, that is, the Jewish interpretation of the Hebrew scriptures, is interestingly different from the Christian one, and in some ways much better balanced.[5] What we must question, however, is the continued and unexamined use of the phrase 'wealth creation', or 'the creation of wealth'.

It would not be unfair to see in Mrs Thatcher's speech a reflection of the views of Brian Griffiths, then head of the Prime Minister's Policy Unit at No. 10 Downing Street and a professed Christian. In his book *Morality and the Market Place*, Professor (now Lord) Griffiths argues on the basis of the Genesis account that because it is part of our human vocation to work and because we have been given responsibility over the resources of the earth, 'it follows that the process of wealth creation is something intrinsic to a Christian view of the world'.[6] Indeed, the first Christian guideline for economic life is that 'there is a positive mandate to create wealth'.[7] However, to interpret the Genesis account in this way is, within the modern context, seriously misleading. Genesis 1.29 reads:

> Behold, I have given you every plant yielding seed which is upon the face of all the earth, and every tree with seed in its fruit; you shall have them for food.

In other words, the resources of the earth are there first and foremost to meet humanity's basic need for food. Secondly, Genesis 2.9 reads: 'And out of the ground the Lord God made to grow every tree that is pleasant to the sight and good for food.' Verse 15 then continues: 'The Lord God took the man and put him in the Garden of Eden to till it and keep it.' In short, God has created for us an environment which not only meets our basic needs but which is pleasant to the sight. Our responsibility is so to work that environment that it meets our needs, both physical and aesthetic. It is true that after that, to use the old terminology, Adam sins and is expelled from the Garden. Thereafter, work is also a burden and the earth brings forth thorns and thistles as well as plants to eat (Genesis 3.17–19). Nevertheless, the original purpose of God in creation, though never entirely realizable in this life, is not lost sight of.

Donald Hay, who belongs to the same evangelical tradition as Brian Griffiths, also seeks to ground the Christian approach to the economic order in the early chapters of Genesis. However, he emerges with a very different interpretation. Donald Hay's principles are that:

1 Man must use the resources of creation to provide for his existence, but he must not waste or destroy the created order.
2 Every person has a calling to exercise stewardship of resources and talents.
3 Stewardship implies responsibility to determine the disposition of resources. Each person is accountable to God for his stewardship.
4 Man has a right and an obligation to work.
5 Work is the means of exercising stewardship. In his work man should have access to resources and control over them.
6 Work is a social activity in which men co-operate as stewards of their individual talents, and as joint stewards of resources.
7 Every person has a right to share in God's provision for mankind for his or her basic needs of food, clothing and shelter. These needs are to be met primarily by productive work.
8 Personal stewardship of resources does not imply the right to consume the entire product of those resources. The rich have an obligation to help the poor who cannot provide for themselves by work.[8]

There is no mention there of wealth creation. Indeed, the only reference to wealth in Donald Hay's book is to an accumulation of goods or money, a surplus, which so often comes in for criticism by the Old Testament prophets, and in the New Testament.

Brian Griffiths is certainly not insensitive to the plight of the poor, nor does he equate capitalism and Christianity. Indeed, he is concerned sharply to distinguish them. But the flaw in his approach, which sets the creation of wealth before any other goal in the economic order, can be seen in his discussion on the Third World. He writes: 'Consider the successful economic performance of Brazil, Mexico or Hong Kong, Singapore, Korea or Taiwan, all of which have tapped the powerful resources of free enterprise.' The mention of Brazil highlights the problem, for although Brazil is the eighth wealthiest country in the world, it contains 16 million destitute children, many of them roaming the streets and obtaining their food from dustbins. Every child born in Brazil is immediately encumbered with a burden of hundreds of dollars of debt, so heavily is the country in thrall to the international economic system. This situation is considered more fully in Chapter 11. Clearly, a number of factors – the international economic order, the desperate attempts of the oil-producing countries, through Western banks, to lend money in the years of the oil boom, the unenlightened social policies of the ruling elite and so on – all play a contributory role. But if Brazil is an example of an economy which sets the creation of wealth through tapping the powerful resources of free enterprise at the top of its agenda, then on any human judgement it is clearly a lamentable failure. Nor can this be seen simply as a failure of distribution, as though Brazil is really a wealthy country that has failed to get its internal politics correct. There is something fundamentally flawed with the whole notion. It implies the individual or sectional pursuit of as much money as possible. But from a Christian and humane point of view, what matters, from the outset, is the well-being of the community as a whole. Moreover, this well-being, again from the outset, must be seen to include far more than wealth. This is not to deny the importance of prosperity, nor the applicability of certain economic policies associated with successful free market economies. Both of these can be affirmed by Christianity. It is to question the priority accorded to the notion of wealth creation, when for so many people in so many situations that means, in theory and in practice, the wealth of a tiny minority.

How we view wealth creation raises the issue of the whole relationship between means and ends. Those who stress wealth creation assume that this is a necessary means to achieve other worthwhile ends. However, on a Christian view, means and ends cannot be seen simply in instrumental terms; there is a much closer relationship between the two. The values inherent in the end must also be to some extent anticipated and expressed in the means.[9] Everyone can see this in extreme cases, when, for example, we rule out torture to obtain information, even though the cause might be totally morally justified. If the cause is one in which human beings are treated as of value in their own right then any means to promote the cause that denies this would undermine the whole enterprise.

Capitalism is founded on the assumption that there can be endless growth. During the 1960s this assumption came to be questioned. Some Christians in particular argued for a radical shift in Western economic policies together with the adoption of much simpler personal lifestyles.[10] This challenge to the idea of limitless growth has surfaced again with even greater force. First, it is quite clear that the earth has only a limited supply of non-renewable resources. There will come a time in the future when there will be no more oil, coal or other basic minerals. Secondly, it is now widely accepted that pollution is severely damaging the environment, both the ozone layer and the earth itself. The result is that if we go on producing more and more cars every year, with more and more roads and factories, the earth will be covered in concrete and the ozone layer will be thinner still, with potentially disastrous effects on the earth's climate.

In theory, it is possible to conceive of an alternative society in which we all live simpler lives and less is produced. Realism suggests, however, that the power of self-interest, particularly the power of organized self-interest in capitalist enterprises, is such that this could not be achieved except by Draconian measures, carried out by strong governments simultaneously throughout the world. This would inevitably lead to a suspension of normal human rights and democratic procedures. Is there any other way forward?

Over the years, Kenneth Adams has wrestled with the relationship between Christianity and a market economy. His starting point is, first, that human beings are unlimited in their desires. Secondly, the aim of business is not simply to meet needs but, as Peter Drucker has put it, to create a customer. Therefore business in recent years has focused on how to arouse the interest of potential customers in a new range of goods or old goods presented in a fresh way.

The market economy as we have it at the moment is based upon the assumption of continuous and unlimited growth. But this assumption is challenged by the limited resources of our planet, by the ever-increasing dangers of pollution to the environment and by the traditional Christian emphasis upon self-denial and being content with little. Kenneth Adams argues that it is possible to meet these challenges by going for growth in areas which do not involve using up scarce resources and which do not pollute the planet. Business operates in many non-material markets, such as broadcasting, entertainment, tourism, sport and the arts. It is more and more moving into education and health. Increasing demands in some of these markets can be minimally pollutive, using little in the way of material resources.

In short, then, according to this view, we should put aside Christianity's traditional emphasis upon poverty and begin with the assumption that human beings are creatures with desires and wants, that these are good because they are implanted by God and that they are potentially unlimited. Underlying the current concept of business in a market economy is a view of humanity which, as Kenneth Adams puts it, 'sees people as having limitless latent desires which can be continuously and progressively converted into felt wants while the product or service to meet that want is being invented, designed, produced and marketed'. In the face of current challenges these wants should be directed to the area of new markets in the non-material, non-pollutive areas of human potential growth. In this way the Christian vision of limitless growth in the right direction and the underlying philosophy of business can come together for mutual enrichment.

This refreshing approach challenges an underlying puritan assumption in the lives of so many Christians, that our wants are something to be overcome. This is particularly so among Protestants. But God has created us as creatures with a bundle of wants. We are not asked to get rid of our wants but to come to want what God wants and God himself. This approach is much stronger in the Roman Catholic Church, which for so long took the philosophy of Aristotle seriously. Among Anglican writers the boldest is undoubtedly Thomas Traherne, the seventeenth-century poet and mystic. He wrote: 'It is of the nobility of man's soul that he is insatiable . . . do not your inclinations tell you that the world is yours? Do you not covet all?'[11] Traherne believed that it is of the essence of human nature that we want more and more. People who want more and more money or more and more property are being true to their nature but too unambitious in what they want. For God has promised us the universe. As Traherne put it:

> Your enjoyment of the world is never right, till every morning you awake in heaven . . . look upon the skies, the earth and the air as celestial joys . . . till you perceive yourself to be the sole heir of the whole world, and more than so, because men are in it who are every one sole heirs as well as you.[12]

It has been reported that Fidel Castro has banned Monopoly in Cuba. It is not difficult to see why. When I was a child I did not rest content until I owned every property on the board, and developed them first with those little green houses and then those impressive red hotels. But that desire to own, to expand, to possess more and more will hardly be eradicated by forbidding Monopoly. When a Russian Church delegation was being conducted around London, the names Piccadilly, Pall Mall, Regent Street and so on brought an immediate warm response from our interpreter. In Moscow, when work was over she and the other interpreters would shut the door and get down to some serious Monopoly.

Moralists in every age have tried to block our acquisitiveness by preaching against it, without any luck. Communists have tried to change our nature through a more socially based political system, again with no great success. For the whole world is switching to an economic system which recognizes and seeks to harness our desire to own more and more. If Thomas Traherne is right we need not disparage this inclination. It is a proper starting point. The question is: more and more of what? More practically, can the insight of Traherne be translated into economic terms in such a way that the environment is not polluted and scarce resources are not used up?

Kenneth Adams thinks that such a shift can be made.

> Suppose that our increasing demand is for entertainment, sport, music, theatre, literature and all other areas of human growth in relationships in intellectual and aesthetic delight – these will place much smaller demands on materials and energy. Furthermore, as desire grows in those wider, richer, higher areas of human need it is likely that desire for increase in the material areas will stabilise or decline.[13]

This is an exciting thought. Only the experience of the next decades will show whether or not it is valid. For capitalism is based upon what people are actually prepared to buy. For the kind of shift indicated by Kenneth Adams actually to take place, it will require millions and millions of people the world over to exert their purchasing power in different ways from those in operation at the moment. Yet those who lead in business could affect this profound shift. As they open their eyes to see where the true growth markets are they will see that while the need for food and other basic survival necessities is physically limited because we can only eat so much, wear so much, and drink so much, human needs in the non-material areas of human desire and aspiration, such as delight in companionship, are much less physically limited. Because of that characteristic there are much larger potential markets, and therefore business, in pursuing its own drive to create customers, ought to move increasingly into these markets in developed societies. In short, as Kenneth Adams puts it:

> It is what we are persuaded to spend our money on which counts and the enormously grave environmental problem can only be solved by opening people's eyes to those huge areas of unexploited markets which lie in the higher ranges of human need. Such persuasion is what business is for – its very purpose – and therefore the lead should come from business itself.

Most Christians have an instinctive suspicion of the idea of economic growth, linked as it is with a very materialistic form of consumerism. So Donald Hay writes: 'The many New Testament warnings concerning the dangers of possessions and possessiveness need to be taken seriously. Economic growth leading to ever increasing consumption is not therefore an objective for the economy which a Christian can espouse.' This kind of sentiment sounds unexceptional from a Christian point of view. Yet we need to be on our guard against it and to subject it to searching critique. First of all, human beings have an insatiable desire for more and more which, as has been argued, is God-given. Secondly, this desire for more and more need not simply be expressed in terms of consuming more material goods, indeed it must not be. Moreover, we must certainly not despise the material improvement of society and it is economic growth which makes this possible. Many poor countries are desperately in need of economic growth, and many poor people need to benefit more than they do from continuing or enhanced economic growth in developed countries. The fact is that money matters, money gets things done. The Lighthouse Centre in West London has been founded for those who have been diagnosed as HIV positive or who are suffering from AIDS. It is a superbly designed reconstruction of an old school, light and colourful inside and with every facility for aiding the sick. It is a pleasure to enter and those associated with it feel justifiably proud that those who seek its help are offered superb standards of care down to the smallest well-designed detail. It is money that has made this possible, money for the most part voluntarily raised. Entering the Lighthouse one cannot help wishing that every old people's home, every residential centre for the handicapped and every hospital ward was characterized by a similar quality. The same point could be made about our schools and every public amenity. Too easily we accept that the badly designed, the drab, the shoddy is good enough for others. Is it possible to achieve the standard we want in our schools, hospitals and other institutions without economic growth?

Similarly, for most people who have achieved things in life, it has been money that has provided the opportunities. Of course, there are numerous exceptions. Thousands of people starting from nothing have done great things in life simply through their own talent and determination. But the majority of people who occupy the commanding heights of our economic, social and political life are those who have had chances, and these chances have been provided by the money which has purchased an education and entry to some profession or walk of life. Money does not bring happiness but money can enlarge the possibilities in people's lives, can present them with a greater range of choices. The hypocrisy of those who have had every chance in life that a well-provided home can provide, moaning about the materialism of the age or the grasping nature of people less well-off than themselves, is sickening.

There are plenty of good reasons for adopting a simpler lifestyle, not least the fact that if we ate and drank less, we would be less obese and feel fitter. But trying to slow down economic growth is not one of them. In Brecht's play about Galileo, Galileo expostulates at one point:

> Virtues don't depend on misery, my friend. If your family were well-off and happy, they'd have all the virtues being well-off and happy brings. These virtues of exhausted men come from exhausted fields and I reject them. My new water pumps work more miracles than their ridiculous drudgery.[14]

Visitors who travel in South Africa over land that is farmed by both blacks and whites cannot help contrasting the productivity of the latter with the relative barrenness of the former. Much of this has to do with the fact that the apartheid system gave the minority white population not only the vast majority of the land but also the best land. Furthermore, land allocated to the blacks, heavily over-populated and therefore over-grazed, has in many places deteriorated and crumbled into sand. But there is also the power of capital to make the desert bloom. On one white farm I visited there were several thousand avocado trees. At the cost of many thousands of pounds a pipe led to each one of them, sprinkling its roots with a gentle spray of water. Initiative and organizational skills were partly responsible for this wonderfully flourishing farm. But none of it would have been achieved without capital. Money makes things happen, brings water pumps and irrigation systems. Money improves the quality of people's lives, and that quality includes a wider range of personal possibilities.

Much of the foregoing discussion has been from the standpoint of someone in the developed world. In the developing world where the vast majority of the population are working on the land, perhaps only just surviving and living in small communities, the situation is different. What are needed are small-scale projects, utilizing minimum capital and labour-intensive. In India, for example, where more than 80 per cent of the population live in agricultural communities, the Gandhian ideal of simplicity and self-sufficiency is still highly applicable. Yet Nehru's alternative of modernization is no less necessary if a country like India is to take its place in the modern world. The challenge for a country like India is to modernize without destroying the way of life and living of the vast majority of the population for whom the benefits of modernization, such as education and health, though essential, need to come in a form that is appropriate.

There remains the problem of the resources of the earth, both renewable and non-renewable, being used up too fast. However much growth is orientated in the direction of activities which do not use up scarce resources or pollute the environment, other forms of action also need to be taken. First we need to consider the whole question of waste.

Underlying much of the discussion on environmental issues is the assumption that waste is a bad thing. For some people, who are hard up, frugality is an obvious virtue. Avoiding waste means saving money and therefore being better able to survive. For them the old adage 'waste not want not' applies literally. This is still crucially true for nearly one-third of the world's population, as it was until fairly recently true for the majority of the working class in Great Britain.

In the developing world every item is used and re-used. Some peoples, such as South American Indians, Botswana Bushmen and the Kenyan Masai, have developed the conservation of everything they can use to a fine art. Clearly this is a matter of sheer survival. But if our avoidance of waste in the developed world is to be more than a hangover from attitudes that prevailed through necessity in the depression of the 1930s and the rationing of the Second World War, the matter needs to be thought through rather carefully.

In his retirement my grandfather lived on £1 a week. He refused to accept any state pension and simply lived off his savings. His invariable diet was rice pudding, cooked in the oven at the side of the coal fire, cheese and, his one concession to luxury, fresh coffee. He was a man who saved everything, every can, every piece of string however short, every piece of paper. Nearly all of this he put to good use. For he was an inventive person, skilled with his hands. Before the days of automatic washing machines, he invented his own hand machine, made out of a wooden handle and two baking tins with holes in, joined together. This device, pushed up and down in soapy water, kept the hands dry and agitated the washing far more effectively than arms and fingers alone. He made, and gave away, hundreds of these devices, in addition to other inventions such as a hook for opening high windows. Nothing was wasted and everything was repaired. Today it presents a heroic, rather romantic ideal. But if everyone were like my grandfather it is difficult to see how the modern economy could survive, based as it is upon built-in obsolescence, with waste an inherent part of the whole system.

I once asked a vicar of Bolton whether he brewed his own beer. He replied: 'Certainly not. I don't believe in taking bread out of the mouths of the working classes.' In short, he believed in supporting the local breweries and therefore enabling people to retain their jobs. It is a legitimate point of view. Modern life depends upon specialization. Everyone has his or her own particular skill or function. If everyone made their own beer thousands of people would be put out of work and the English institution of the public house would rapidly die out. The modern economy and therefore jobs and family incomes depend upon people consuming, upon millions of people regularly purchasing a wide range of goods and services. The more goods and services that are purchased, the more money will go round and, theoretically, that is leaving aside imports and inflation, the more everyone should share in a gradually rising standard of living. Against this background, the stern injunction against waste seems rather anti-social and destructive, almost Luddite in its attitude. So if the avoidance of waste is to be endorsed, why? Donald Hay's first biblical principle for the economic order is: 'Man must use the resources of creation to provide for his existence, but he must not waste or destroy the created order.' The prohibition on waste he derives from the fact that in the Hebrew scriptures, when animals were killed, their blood was to be respected as a symbol of their life and not drunk. This seems somewhat bizarre, and would apply only to animals and not, for example, to forests.

If an item we possess would be valued and used by someone else, it is prima facie a waste to throw it away. Yet even if there is no obvious use for something we often feel a pang about discarding it. Food thrown away, for example, when everyone is full, goes against the grain. Is this feeling simply irrational? Not entirely.

It is perhaps because labour and indeed love have gone into the preparation of that meal. It has value not simply because of the calories but because, as John Locke might have put it, it is that with which a person has mixed their labour. It has that added value. A person wears out an old vest. It could be thrown away but it also makes a useful duster. Throwing it away may not be the end of the world. It is only a worn and holed piece of cloth. But human labour and human ingenuity have gone into it. It represents value. Bound up with this consideration is the understanding of human beings as rational. What they do, they do for a purpose. Prodigality can also be the expression of a purpose, as it was for the woman in the gospels who poured expensive perfume over Jesus as an expression of love. But sheer waste is a denial of rational purpose. There comes a time when, as we say, things have served their purpose. Beer cans are empty and vests are worn out. Yet they have not lost all sense of the value with which they were endowed in their making.

It would seem then that the widely shared dislike of waste is not simply a hangover of past poverty or wartime conditions. It expresses a sense that human beings are rational creatures, designed to act purposefully in the world. Furthermore, that in which they invest their ingenuity, skill and effort takes on value. Sheer waste is, literally, pointless. It is therefore an effront to the rationality of human beings and an implicit denial of rational purpose in the universe. It is, moreover, a rejection of the product of human creativity and implicitly therefore a rejection of human worth.

Given the fact that there should be a proper bias against waste, because we are rational creatures who invest the products of our minds and hands with value, each environmental issue should be strictly assessed in rational rather than sentimental terms. First, to take an example of renewable resources, why should we believe in recycling paper, if we should? Trees are a crop like any other. It could be that it was both cheaper and environmentally less damaging to keep planting and cutting new plantations of trees, rather than recycling old paper. The key point here is that recycling paper uses less than half the energy, less water and creates less pollution and waste than felling new trees and making new paper. There is also the question of whether quick-growing conifers, which are planted to make paper, are being planted at the expense of native deciduous trees and the plants and wildlife they support. Some people also find plantations of conifers aesthetically displeasing. These may be factors that have to be taken into consideration. The point being made here is a simple one, namely that each of these issues needs to be considered in a fully rational way, taking into account not only economic factors, but a whole range of environmental ones, including, if appropriate, aesthetic considerations. Two extreme positions need to be avoided. The first is the idea that human beings should not interfere with nature. But every improvement to human life has been made as a result of human action in relation to the natural order. This can improve the quality of life for millions. To take two comparatively small examples. There was a time when prawns were a luxury for the few. Now, prawn sandwiches are available at every snack bar. Similarly, there was a time when trout was a luxury food. Now, as a result of fish farms, millions enjoy trout. Sometimes people complain that the quality has decreased. If so, this is certainly a factor to be taken into consideration. Also, if the fish or animals are made to suffer, as with factory farming for hens and veal, this is unacceptable. But the Genesis account, in ascribing to human beings dominion over nature, reflects a true aspect of our vocation. What applies to food is no less true of the aesthetic side of life. The landscapes we so much admire are not simply the result of nature being left to itself, they are usually the result of hundreds if not thousands of years of interaction between human beings and the environment. The other extreme is that human beings in harnessing the resources of nature can simply do what they like. There is, however, a wisdom in going with the grain of things rather than against it. Modern ecology has shown quite clearly that the ecosystems of nature are delicately balanced and interdependent. We are continuing to damage the environment in many ways through a failure to observe and act on this.

In relation to renewable resources we have a duty to maintain them in existence and not to allow a species of animal or insects or particular kinds of plant to die out. A justification for this is sometimes made on the grounds of rare drugs or some other purpose of long-term benefit to humanity. Yet there is a more fundamental reason. We recognize the instinctive worth of the great variety and richness of creation. In relation to many species the utilitarian advantages must be minimal. Yet we all feel the conservation pull and this is an impressive witness to the value of creation in itself.

In relation to non-renewable or exhaustible resources, there is a prima facie case for going slow and preserving something for future generations. Yet there cannot be a total embargo. Here we have to trust the inventiveness and creativity of human beings to discover new forms of energy. In all these issues there are of course a number of factors to be considered. One of them, in relation to exhaustible resources, is the hideous scars left by mining and quarrying. On the other hand, many of the prized minerals in the world come from developing countries who desperately need the money engendered. Aluminium is an expensive metal made from bauxite, which is mined in huge quantities in the sub-tropics. A vast amount of energy is used and large amounts of red mud are produced in the process of extracting the aluminium from the bauxite. If aluminium is recycled 95 per cent of the energy is saved, as well as much of the landscape. So people are urged to collect aluminium cans, ring pull tops and the tops of milk bottles, yoghurt cartons and so on. The clash of interest between the economy of a developing country with mineral resources and environmental considerations may be covered over for a while but it is only sentimental to think that it can be avoided for ever.

In recent years the Church has been criticized for a negative attitude to industry and wealth creation. It is undoubtedly true that the Church has not affirmed the industrial and commercial world in a way that it ought. A much more positive attitude is needed. However, there are proper hesitations about an unqualified championing of the concept of wealth creation. The phrase itself too often implies the ruthless pursuit of self- or sectional interest. It is doubtful if the notion can be grounded in the Bible and it too easily leads to a disjunction between means and ends. It is preferable to see *the aim of business as increasing the resources of society so that the quality of life for all might be improved.*

Capitalism is built on the assumption that there can be endless growth. This has been increasingly questioned in recent years. Nevertheless, it is both sentimental and wrong to think that we can have no growth. Furthermore, not only is the idea of growth built into capitalism, it is congruous with the Christian understanding of human nature. What we need is growth that neither destroys the environment nor uses up non-renewable resources. There are some signs that business can be increasingly developed in such ways. Christians would better use their energies exploring alternative forms of economic growth rather than simply opposing the idea of growth altogether. Similarly, a rather more critical understanding of waste is needed. The bias against waste is well founded, but Christians in the developed world must nevertheless be wary of championing environmental considerations against the desperate need of poor countries for economic growth, even when that growth depends upon mining non-renewable resources. There is often a connection between issues of justice and environmental concerns as the World Council of Churches has recognized in its project on Justice, Peace and the Integrity of Creation,[15] and as the Pope has set out in a number of his statements. For example, destruction of the Amazonian forests is integrally linked to the violation of the indigenous people who dwell there and fundamental injustices in that society. Nevertheless, environmental concerns must not be allowed to blur the need to make economic growth work to the benefit of the most needy of the earth.

For Christians engaged in the wealth-creating sections of society there seem to be three cardinal principles. First, the aim is not wealth as such but increasing the resources of society so that the quality of life for all might be improved. Secondly, while affirming growth as a legitimate expression of the Christian understanding of what it is to be a human being, it is necessary to do everything possible to channel growth towards areas that do not involve the destruction of the environment or the use of non-renewable resources. Thirdly, Christians should have a particular concern for bringing about economic growth in the developing world.

NOTES

1 See David Edwards, *The Times*, 12 March 1990 and the other articles in that series by Lord Caldecote, Bishop John Jukes and Clifford Longley.

2 Boswell's *Life of Johnson*, Everyman edn, Vol. I (1958), p. 532.

3 Kenneth Adams, 'Changing British attitudes', *RSA Journal* (November 1990).

4 Discussed by Redmond Mullin, *The Wealth of Christians* (Paternoster, 1985), pp. 93–6.

5 Jonathan Sacks, *Wealth and Poverty: a Jewish Analysis* (Social Affairs Unit, 1985).

6 Brian Griffiths, *Morality and the Market Place* (Hodder & Stoughton, 1980), p. 80.

7 Ibid.

8 Donald Hay, *Economics Today* (Apollos, 1989), pp. 72ff.

9 J. L. Stocks, *Morality and Purpose* (Routledge & Kegan Paul, 1969).

10 E. F. Schumacher, *Small is Beautiful: a Study of Economics as if People Mattered* (Abacus, 1974); and John V. Taylor, *Enough Is Enough* (SCM, 1975).

11 Thomas Traherne, *Centuries, Poems and Thanksgivings*, ed. H. M. Margoliouth (OUP, 1972), Vol. I, Century 28, p. 14.

12 Ibid., Century 22.

13 Kenneth Adams, 'Changing British attitudes' and private communications.

14 Brecht, *Galileo* (Methuen, 1961).

15 *Now Is the Time*, World Convocation on Justice, Peace and the Integrity of Creation, Seoul 1990 (WCC, Geneva).

7

For Those in the Market Place

The coming to power of President Reagan in the United States and Mrs Thatcher in Great Britain brought a new emphasis upon the importance of the market economy. Backed by influential economists both politicians sought to move away from the stress on state intervention that had characterized the previous decades, at least in Britain. They sought to make the free market truly free, a place of genuine competition, with commensurate rewards for those who succeed and less of a safety net for those who failed. These policies succeeded in bringing greater prosperity to the majority in both countries. The bottom 10 per cent of the population, however, became relatively poorer during this period.[1] Then, 1989 saw the dramatic collapse of communism in the Soviet Union and Eastern Europe. What had for so long been obvious to the rest of the world, the inefficiency and failure of state-directed economies, was at last publicly recognized within the countries concerned. So the 1990s began with a much wider acceptance of the concept of a free market economy than prevailed in the 1970s. However, it is important not to overstate the change that has taken place. For within Western liberal democracies, the free market has always been accepted by the majority. A leader in *The Guardian* in 1981 argued that the market is an inescapable fact of life.

> It is the market which acts as an essential signal from consumers to firms telling them how much to produce, when to produce it, and what sort of quality to make. Consumers have never been wholly sovereign. Their judgements may indeed be clouded by advertising and other techniques. But consumers do nevertheless wield real power.

The leader then went on to argue that profits are essential: 'The profit of companies (or co-operatives) is also the market's way of signalling success: it is an essential guide to, and source of, investment.' It further argued that the dislike of profit because of its historical association with unequal income and wealth distribution was increasingly irrelevant because so much in the way of profits and dividends went into pension funds and similar institutions. There was, as the leader rightly argued, no dissenting from the view, except by a very small percentage of the Labour Party, that the free market was essential, inescapable and, for all its flaws, to be valued. It was as robust a defence as could come from any Thatcherite economist.

Although some Christian pronouncements over the period have betrayed a romantic and unrealistic longing for some alternative to capitalism, and although there have been far too few Christian reflections on the strength of a free economy, nevertheless most Christians have been happy to live, however uneasily, with the market. The quotations from pronouncements of the World Council of Churches and papal encyclicals in Chapter 5 all rejected the Marxist alternative and affirmed the free enterprise system, even though the emphasis was very often on correcting the defects of that system. Nor did it need the thinkers of the new Christian right in the 1980s to give a Christian underpinning to the free market. For the most convincing Christian defence had already come from an Oxford academic economist writing in the 1950s, Denis Munby, who died tragically young.[2]

Munby argued that the price system ensures that when you go into a shop you can, as it were, vote for what you want with your money. If the price of the goods and their cost are more or less related then you have some real freedom in this area. The price system has the further function of setting in motion a series of impulses whereby the kind of goods you vote for with your money will eventually be produced and those you do not buy will disappear from the market. It is, of course, this latter aspect of the price system that is disputed. In Western democracies what goods are produced depends upon businessmen acting as *entrepreneurs*. In communist command economies it is the state that decides what will be produced. Munby argued that if under the Western system prices really are related to costs, in other words if price fixing and monopolies are held in check and if there is real freedom for new firms to enter the market to challenge the old order, then this system really does make the consumer sovereign. To the objection that one person should not have the freedom to buy a fur coat while someone else is unable to pay the rent, he argued that this was not the fault of the price system as such but of the fact that people have unequal incomes. It is as though we had a system of proportional representation with some people having a hundred votes and others only one.

Munby argued that the free market system is fundamentally in accord with and derived from Christian principles about the freedom and responsibility of human beings. God leaves us free to make our own choices even though we often make mistakes. In this area of freedom we come to learn responsibility. Because of the high valuation of freedom in Christian thinking, people should be given the maximum degree of freedom in the economic realm. In a communist system a group of experts decides what people's needs really are and this constitutes a limitation on personal freedom. However, it is important to note that Munby maintained that the price system, in which the consumer is rightly supreme, is one which could operate as well or better in a socialist state. There could, for example, be simulated competition between state-operated organizations, and this would ensure that prices were indeed related to costs. It is interesting that in the NHS, public welfare and public services Britain is now experimenting with forms of competition in which both private and state-financed enterprises tender against one another.

In Dostoevsky's great novel *The Brothers Karamazov*, Christ is depicted returning to earth at the time of the Inquisition. He confronts the Grand Inquisitor in Seville who, however, far from being penitent about the atrocities carried out in Christ's name, turns on Christ and accuses him of having too high an estimate of human beings. Christ treated human beings as free. In fact, argued the Grand Inquisitor, human beings cannot cope with freedom and do not want it, and therefore the Church has had to correct Christ's work and once more human beings rejoiced that they were being led like sheep. Dostoevsky's insight, which in this incident is focused on Christ's temptations in the wilderness when he rejects ways of winning people's allegiance that would treat them as less than fully free persons, is unerring. We are not puppets or robots. God has created us as free beings, called to exercise responsibility. In his ministry among us Christ totally respected that freedom, and he seeks to win us to himself through the persuasive power of love alone. Quite rightly, Christians will stress the value of freedom, not only personal freedom but freedom in the political and economic spheres as well. Sometimes at the height of the cold war it was extremely distasteful when champions of the 'free enterprise' system justified the struggle in Christian terms and saw it as a crusade. Nevertheless, this need not blind us to the fact that certain Christian values, such as freedom, are genuinely better expressed in and through one system rather than another. Sadly, rampant and unashamed greed has been the creed of some.[3] Selfishness has 'come out'. The head of a major international recruitment agency wrote to *The Times* to say that the new breed are 'aggressive, restless, greedy urban technocrats . . . interested in money to the point of obsession. Let them make a million and they will strive for ten.' He concluded: 'That's the way they are, and that's the way we want them.' Ivan Boesky told some American business students before his fall: 'Greed is all right, by the way, I want you to know that. You can be greedy and still feel good about yourself.' But this is part of the moral dilemma. A market which encourages freedom entails the consequences that some will use their freedom primarily to enrich themselves.

One of the concerns of the New Right has been to wean people away from a dependency culture to one characterized by enterprise. Whether this is a fair way of putting it is for the moment left aside. But is there an adequate theological underpinning for this emphasis upon an enterprise culture? Once again, Denis Munby made a thoughtful contribution which, if it had been more widely heard and regarded, would have spared us some of the Christian polemic of recent years. For in *Christianity and Economic Problems* he has a chapter devoted to the role of the businessman in which he argues that such people have an essential task to perform in any society and that if they do not do it, other people will have to. The businessman co-ordinates all the signals that come from the consumer, in fact his prime function is that of a representative of the consumer. Furthermore, he is essentially an initiator, because under modern conditions everything that is likely to be needed has to be set up before consumers make their choice. Factories have to be built, marketing chains put into place and so on. It is only after this that the consumer says yes or no by the purchases that are made. Here is risk. The enterprise may succeed or it may fail. There is also opportunity for initiative and creativity. The initiative and creativity required by people setting up new businesses, or expanding old ones, is a reflection in human terms of the divine initiative and a sharing in the divine creativity. Furthermore, in creation, God himself takes a risk. He has created us free, free to frustrate or to further his purposes. Logically, the whole creation enterprise could fail. So the element of risk in business ventures is also in some sense a sharing in the risk which is inherent in creation.

These are some very important ways in which the market economy is congruous with the Christian faith. It expresses and safeguards freedom of choice. It allows for and encourages initiative and enterprise, with all the concomitant risks involved. However, there is no doubt that many people, including a good number of Christians, remain uneasy about a market economy for a number of reasons, first and foremost because it seems to be based on and to encourage self-interest, both in a personal and in an organized form. Or, to put it more harshly, its driving force is sheer greed. Christianity teaches us to put aside thoughts of self and to think of others and their interests. How then can this aspect of the market economy be reconciled with Christian faith and values?

Contrary to what some people have been taught, self-interest is an essential and God-given feature of human nature. Without the will to survive, the drive to look after itself, no baby or child would survive and very rapidly the human race would die out. To exist at all is to exist with a drive and dynamic to be. Often this has unfortunate consequences, for our drive to be comes up against that of other people. But it is not possible to exist without it. Nor is it in itself bad. We would, for example, far rather have an adult who was taking proper steps to provide for himself than one who was waiting for others to support him. In the spiritual life, before we come to rejoice in God for his own sake, we often come to value God for what we receive from him. There is nothing wrong in this. If we have been so made that our peace of heart and deepest well-being come from a right relationship to God, then our being will be orientated to want both God and his gifts for ourselves.

It is true that as a result of human sinfulness, self-interest often takes warped and distorted forms. It becomes, in the words of the Book of Common Prayer, inordinate. Or it is conceived in very narrow or short-sighted terms. Or, as so often happens, it exists without a proper imaginative sympathy for the self-interest of others. Nevertheless, self-interest in itself is not simply a result of the Fall. It is an essential part of our good God-given human nature. Moreover, in practice it is very difficult to distinguish self-interest from at least some degree of altruism. A man who seeks promotion and a higher salary will in all likelihood be doing so not just for his own sake but for the sake of his family, whom he is supporting. Immigrant workers in Germany and the world over are not just seeking to better themselves. They send huge quantities of money back home to support their impoverished wider families.

Capitalism appeals to self-interest. It also makes use of organized self-interest. A firm, like a nation, utilizes both people's self-interest and their wider loyalties in order to engender a dynamic for the enterprise as a whole. Organized self-interest is not always a pretty sight, particularly when it takes the form of one company trying to do another down. Nevertheless, in itself it is not wrong. It is quite proper, for example, that a school, university or hospital should want to succeed, that is, be an institution which does its job well, efficiently and in a way that people can feel proud of. We want a university, for example, to have a proper self-esteem. We want it to be able to attract the best scholars, have the best equipment, produce the best exam results. In a competitive world, in order to achieve this it is necessary for that university, or any other institution, to look after and further its own interests. A business organization, whether it is a small firm or a transnational is in no different situation. It seeks to be the best, that to which people can feel proud to belong.

Ronald Preston has written that:

> Capitalism relies explicitly far too exclusively on self-interest, ignoring the necessity of other motives on which (as we have seen) it must implicitly rely in practice but does nothing to cultivate, and indeed actually undermines.[4]

Preston of course recognizes the legitimate role of self-interest in capitalism. But as that quotation makes clear, he argues that it tends to undermine other values. Gerard Hughes, however, in a philosophical analysis of the appeal to self-interest, argues that this is not the case. He makes a distinction between motives and justifications. A company might justify what it does in terms of the interest of the organization. However, it can quite properly appeal to the altruistic motives of those who work for it.

> Once a distinction between motives and justifications is made clear . . . I see no reason why capitalists cannot, and many reasons why they should, seek to encourage genuine feelings of concern for others. . . . Evidently, egoists, and capitalists in so far as they are egoists, cannot appeal to anything other than self-interest in justifying their policies, or in justifying their view of the motives

they wish their employees to have. But that is quite a different assertion from saying that those motives themselves have to be motives of self-interest.[5]

The market economy is itself grounded in moral values, above all freedom. Moreover, as has been shown, the appeal to self-interest is not immoral. Nevertheless, nearly all Christian writers who have reflected on the market, whatever their political views, have urged the necessity for a wider moral framework and other values to be taken into account as well.

Bishop Joseph Hall, who wrote intelligently about these matters in the seventeenth century, really wanted a publicly set fair level of prices. Where the price was not fixed he argued that the conscience of the seller should be a factor, as well as the current price. Taking advantage of the rareness of a commodity or the necessity of the buyer is a breach of charity. In the case of necessities, particularly when there is shortage, sellers should strive to keep the lowest price. In general, when there was no certain price, 'conscience must be the clerk of the market'. He decisively rejected the common maxim that people should get all they could as uncharitable and unjust. 'Every man hath a bird in his bosom, that sings to him another note.' This conscience tells us that excessive pricing 'is but a better-coloured picking of purses; and what you get is but stolen goods, varnished over with the pretence of a calling; and will prove, at the last, no other than gravel in your throat'.[6]

Lest this sound too idealistic, it should be noted that many businessmen today will as a matter of integrity always go for a fair price and a reasonable profit, rather than push for all that they can get. No doubt this is partly out of self-interest: the drive for excessive profit is in the end self-defeating. Nevertheless, it is a mistake to underestimate the sense of fairness and integrity in the business community.

Adam Smith, with whom the free market will for ever be associated, was first and foremost a moralist.[7] He was highly committed to the idea that the market, to work properly, depends upon certain moral values which had to be enforced by some external agency, often the state. For example, the free market is incompatible with monopolies and cartels. Businessmen left to themselves might fix prices. As Adam Smith puts it in a famous quotation:

> People of the same trade seldom meet together, even for merriment and diversion, but the conversation ends in a conspiracy against the public, or in some contrivance to raise prices.

Although Adam Smith is well known for his view that if everybody pursues their own interest an invisible hand will bring about prosperity for the community as a whole through a million transactions, he was quite firm that the public interest needed to be safeguarded in a number of different ways.

> The interest of the dealers in any particular branch of trade or manufacturers,

is always in some respects different from, and even opposite to, that of the public. To widen the market and to narrow the competition, is always the interests of the dealers. To widen the market may frequently be agreeable enough to the interests of the public; but to narrow the competition must always be against it.

It follows, Smith added, that a proposal for any new law or regulation in commerce which came from the business community should always be looked at sceptically.

> It comes from an order of men, whose interest is never exactly the same with that of the public, who have generally an interest to deceive and even to oppress the public, and who accordingly have, upon many occasions, both deceived and oppressed it.[8]

It is not only the state that needs to intervene in the free workings of the market. Every institution needs to have its own system of regulations. For example, Peter Morgan has said that:

> A market economy had to operate within a framework designed to ensure that the market worked properly and fairly. For example, insider trading on the Stock Market cannot be permitted. It has to be regulated against, and there have to be laws. No responsible businessman or company director could ever suggest that the markets can operate without regulations.[9]

Although Brian Griffiths, the former head of Mrs Thatcher's Policy Unit, is sometimes regarded as an uncritical supporter of unfettered capitalism, he is in fact concerned to develop an approach to the free market that sets it firmly within a moral framework. Indeed, it is only within such a framework that it can work effectively. Griffiths has the usual criticisms of Marxism. But he is hardly less critical of capitalism as we know it. In particular, he criticizes the gurus of capitalism, Milton Friedman and F. A. Hayek, for putting economic freedom and that alone as the basis of our society. He maintains that freedom must be balanced by controls of various kinds. A Christian perspective is distinct from secular capitalism or Marxism. Griffiths characterizes it as: 'A market economy bounded by Biblical principles of justice'.[10] In particular, on the Hayek view that there is no proper motivation either to help the poor or to avoid pollution:

> From a Christian point of view, the concern for the poor is more than just an individual matter: it is legitimately a function of government acting on behalf of society as a whole and comparable to its mandate to maintain law and order.[11]

The necessity for a market economy being firmly set within a moral framework of justice arises not just because everything human needs to be so set but because a free market will never be entirely free. It will always reflect the interest of the most powerful and work to their advantage against the most vulnerable. Gerard Hughes argued that there is no reason why a philosophy of self-interest or egoism should not take the interests of other people into account. In the economic realm, for example, it is clearly in the interests of an organization to ensure that its workers feel that they have a stake in it. Hughes's criticism of capitalism in practice is that it has so often tried to get away with the minimum. People have been given the minimum wages that are compatible with retaining their labour and limited loyalty. In short, capitalism has in practice so often been exploitative. There is no reason in theory, according to Hughes, why an ideology of self-interest should necessarily lead to this conclusion. But in practice it has. So here other values, above all a biblical understanding of justice, will be to the fore to ensure that people do not try to get away with as little as possible, particularly when those who are exploited are the poorest and most vulnerable members of society, who have no leverage of their own. South Africa in recent years has provided a sad example, though not the only one, of this truth. It is well known, as defenders of the South African regime have consistently argued, that wages for black workers in South Africa are relatively high compared with surrounding African countries. There is also a huge pool of labour from the homelands awaiting to take up any spare jobs. So the gold and diamond mines have been able to operate fairly effectively, with a steady workforce, all of whom, out of necessity, will operate the system, with occasional periods of extreme unrest, to the satisfaction of the owners and managers. Self-interest has suggested that this system cannot go on for ever and self-interest, beginning with the business community, has been a major factor in bringing about a more hopeful atmosphere. Yet all the time, and no less powerful, there has been the conscience of so many people that the whole system is fundamentally immoral. Enlightened self-interest has been prodded and made urgent by wider considerations of basic human justice.

So the market is not morally neutral. It both expresses and needs a moral framework which is wider than the market itself. This framework can quite properly justify the basic operations of the system. But because it is a wider moral framework it will also correct and supplement those operations in the light of values to which the market itself appeals.

One of the features of the new Christian justification of capitalism is the attempt to locate the moral and religious vision behind it. This is to be welcomed. The old polarization, when socialism in one form or another claimed all the high moral ground and capitalism was written off as a system of exploited individualism, was both untrue and unfair. The new debate, in which the moral dimension inherent in capitalism is fully acknowledged, can therefore be a much more honest and searching one. As already mentioned, Brian Griffiths has always sought to set capitalism within an overall moral framework, but the person who has attempted to do this more systematically than most is the American Roman Catholic, Michael Novak.

In *Free Persons and the Common Good* he argues that the liberal tradition (that is, liberal democracy and the market economy) is not simply a system of possessive individualism. It has its own distinctive and powerful understanding of the common good. He examines the works of the founders of the American constitution, in particular articles in *The Federalist* by James Madison. These writers were concerned for the common good; in particular they sought to devise institutions that dealt realistically with human nature as it is, including the role of self-interest in life. Novak then looks at the writings of Alexis de Tocqueville, who had such an admiration for American institutions and the American way of life. Tocqueville was particularly impressed by the role of 'self-interest rightly understood' in American society. This was not simply everyone out to make all they could but people co-operating with one another in a whole range of associations both for their own benefit and for the benefit of others.

Liberalism as Novak understands it is to be sharply distinguished from tribal societies with their unified conception of the common good. It takes fully into account the multiplicity and diversity of human desires and interests. We cannot, therefore, identify the common good with the concrete good expressed in a particular state of affairs. Nor can we attribute to society as a whole a common good understood as one overall conscious intention, aim or purpose. In a liberal society, each person has his or her own purposes and aims. What society can do is establish general rules designed to bring to all the benefits of human co-operation and to nourish the habits and institutions that promote co-operation.

> A footpath along a river or up a mountainside may have been formed co-operatively by human beings over centuries, but quite apart from the intentions of any one person, any pursuit of aims as various as the multiple motives of the multitudes of person who use such a path. There are common goods apart from common intentions, aims and purposes. Were it not so, societies of free persons could not exist.[12]

The key virtue in the economic sphere for the achievement of this common good is practical intelligence. The outcome is not known in advance but millions of individual decisions made on the basis of practical intelligence will achieve an actual state of affairs that is conducive to the well-being of all.

Novak admits that liberal societies have not yet achieved all they can achieve. We have therefore to take into account not only the common good as institutional framework designed to encourage co-operative working for the benefit of all and the actual achievement of the present state of affairs, we must have a benchmark of what could be achieved in actual practice.

Three points need to be made in relation to this liberal concept of the common good. First of all, no human institution is value-free. The presuppositions and assumptions behind all human arrangements in the political and economic sphere are rooted in a particular set of values and ultimately in a religious vision. Secondly, however, human arrangements in the political and economic sphere do not just drop down from heaven ready-made according to some blueprint. They arise in history as a result of particular humans within particular human societies wrestling with the dilemmas of the present in the light of the legacy of the past and their hopes for the future. Despite Novak's appeal to history it is this historical dimension which seems to be lacking. He gives us an ideal. In reality what we have is the product of the past and the past was the expression of particular interests worked out in relation to other interests, not least the will to power and possession. Thirdly, because all human arrangements inevitably express certain value systems there is no reason why a society should not enshrine and express in its economic and political institutions a much broader and deeper vision of common good than simply the harnessing of individual self-interest.

If these points are taken together it means that we will always be on the alert for the way political and economic systems do in practice express and safeguard the interests of certain groups, working for the benefit of some and against the well-being of others. In the light of this there is no reason why we should not, and every reason why we should, have a vision of the common good which consciously seeks to counteract the dominance of the powerful and which keeps in mind the well-being of the whole; not simply in Novak's sense of allowing the self-interest of every individual free play, but with a conscious purpose to promote the well-being and interests of those unable to take advantage of the market.

One dramatic example of this is the housing policy in Hong Kong. Hong Kong is often held up as one of the prime success stories of the free market economy. One of the most remarkable features of this colony is the way that it has in a comparatively short time been able to house some six million people. But this almost miraculous achievement is not simply the result of the unfettered play of free market forces. On the contrary, the Hong Kong government has played a decisive role through its housing authority. This authority produces 40 thousand flats a year, 32 per cent of which are for sale. This is in addition to the 30 thousand flats being built by the private sector. The Government presents the land on which flats are built to the housing authority free of charge. Otherwise, the housing authority is on course to be financially self-supporting, despite the fact that flats are let at economic rents and sold at prices which people can afford. Here is a powerful example of strong government support for the common good, which does not lead to either the inefficiency or the dependent mentality so dreaded by opponents of government intervention in the market.

In *Morality, Capitalism and Democracy* Novak is primarily concerned to explore the concept of liberty and its role in capitalism. He stresses that the search for a new economic order is 'a search for an arrangement of social institutions worthy of human capacities for reflection and choice'. This stress, as was argued earlier in this book, is indeed a fundamental component of Christian faith and one of the reasons why there can be a congruity between it and some forms of capitalism. However, Novak takes four further themes from Jewish and Christian history which have a bearing on liberty, and his development of each of these is disquieting. First of all, he emphasizes the notion of human fallibility and sin. He is right to do so. One of the implications of this is that in order to maintain the liberty of reflection and choice the major spheres of human existence, political, economic, cultural and moral, will need to be separated and kept in independent hands. This is correct. Too often there has been and still is an alliance of money, political power and ideology which has worked for the interests of the powerful against the weak. It is therefore important to ask what kind of alliances are operative in our own society and what are their effects. Novak consistently fails to take into account the way the economically powerful can gain control of every other sphere of human existence. In the name of the common good, therefore, the political organs of society will need to be used, in a capitalist order, in part at least, to counteract the potentially all-encompassing dominance of the economically powerful.

Secondly, Novak stresses the role of human creativity, as a reflection of the divine creativity. This is welcome, as is its application to business life. 'This personal creativity, the very principle of economic progress, calls forth in humans to identify themselves, to cherish, and to nurture the virtue of enterprise.' The poor, in particular, must be enabled to develop their entrepreneurial skills. But there are many forms of creativity, indeed the majority, that are not directly related to commercial life and that are no less essential for society. We need only think of teachers, consistently undervalued and underpaid in capitalist societies, nurses, mothers with young children and so on. Any society that seeks to reflect the divine society, any notion of human creativity as participating in the divine creativity, will stress these as an essential aspect of our life together, even though they are only indirectly related in most cases to financial reward and economic enterprise. Novak's stress on economic enterprise also being a way of sharing in the divine creativity is to be welcomed, it is a healthy contrast to the usual snobbish denigration of commercial life in some quarters. Nevertheless, a society, a community, is composed of people who live together and relate to one another in a whole range of activities which are valuable, indeed essential for human flourishing.

Thirdly, Novak highlights the role of community. Here, quite properly, he emphasizes that there are many forms of community, what Burke called the 'little platoons' of society, voluntary associations and corporations of many different kinds. A society that is concerned to foster freedom will encourage such associations and corporations and give them legal status independent of the state. 'They are social but not statist.'

All this is important and well said but it poses a question about the proper role of the state. The objective of the New Right to achieve a minimal state has a partial moral legitimacy. People do not like to have either a big boss or a nanny always in the background telling them what to do and looking after them. The idea that we should be encouraged to stand on our own feet, accepting responsibility for our own lives and for assisting others, is conducive to maturity and is certainly at one with the Christian vision of human beings called to grow up into the full stature of Christ. Nevertheless, lurking behind the notion of a minimal state is an essentially individualistic understanding of human beings, individuals who have come together to agree on certain arrangements that will protect and foster individual desires. Even when we have taken into account man's social nature as expressed through various subsidiary communities, which the state exists to safeguard and encourage, we have not done justice to the full role. The state is not there only to foster individual and community interests. It structures our human vocation to participate in the ordering of human society according to a moral vision which carries with it a concern for that society as a whole. The size of modern democracies means that we have inevitably lost something of the vision of politics in a Greek city state, when men (not slaves or women) saw their coming together to order their common life as an essential aspect of mature human living. But that ancient Greek ideal is still worth bearing in mind. So too is the ideal of the fourth-century Christian Fathers of the good of the whole human race rather than the interests of particular sections or individuals.

Even in the minimal state, national security is the responsibility of government. The days when people could purchase commissions in the army, or even purchase whole regiments, are long gone. National security is the proper concern of government but it is not their only concern. Health, education, welfare and communications are no less the concern of government. This does not mean that all these spheres need to be totally financed and controlled by the state. It does mean, however, that the role of the state goes far beyond simply allowing a free play of market forces.

Novak's main concern is with liberty. Isaiah Berlin distinguished two concepts of liberty: one is negative, constituted by the absence of external constraints, a view usually championed in democratic societies; the other, a socialist conception of liberty, is a more positive one, constituted by a grant of the means necessary to exercise liberty, such as education or income. To these Novak wants to add a third. This is a moral concept of liberty, an internal recognition of the moral law through the exercise of conscience. As Lord Acton expressed it: 'The liberty to do not what we like but what we ought'. Novak regards this moral concept of liberty as essential to the proper working of a democratic capitalist society. No Christian will dissent from this but two questions need to be asked about Novak's understanding of this notion of liberty. The first is, does it have any content? Or is it simply a matter of each individual following the dictates of his or her own conscience, and are there sharply differing understandings of right and wrong? According to Christian tradition in its Catholic and Anglican forms there is a natural law, that is a moral law which can be recognized by all human beings whatever their religious beliefs or lack of them. The positive laws of the state will give expression to and safeguard this natural law. If this is so, however, it will mean that the institutions of the state will express an understanding of the common good which goes way beyond simply encouraging individuals to make morally correct choices.

There is another somewhat different point. Novak's vision of society is one in which the freedom of each individual to make his or her way is maximized and the cultural tradition is one in which every individual accepts the internal restraints of the moral law. In theory this might sound fine. In practice, as in Victorian Britain, such societies tend to favour the strong in the economic sphere, while reinforcing a cultural norm of hierarchy, obedience and acceptance. The early Methodists, trade unionists and Christian socialists, while being fully guided by the moral law, had to struggle, protest and stand up to change oppressive laws. The same tended to be true, in a slightly less extreme way, in the early days of unionization in the United States. It was all too easy then for people to use the moral law to reinforce a *status quo* which was badly in need of reform. So while, of course, all Christians would strongly stress the role of the moral law inwardly apprehended by the conscience, the role of this in society cannot be separated from the use to which it is being put by particular groups and sectional interests.

Novak is surely correct in taking sin into account. Here he has been influenced by his early mentor, Reinhold Niebuhr. Novak writes:

> Liberty begins in the sharp and reasoned awareness of human sinfulness and fallibility. In the very name of this Christian liberty, Christians (and others) must resist the premature enforcement of the Kingdom of God – the reign of social justice – upon earth. This is because some elite group of flawed and fallible human beings would in fact be trying to impose their own limited and sinful view on the consciousness of others.[13]

But it has to be stressed again that this is not the only form that sin takes and not the only expression of it that needs to be watched and guarded against. There is an inexorable tendency in capitalist society for the rich to get richer, the strong to get stronger and for those who begin disadvantaged to be crushed and go to the wall.

Novak argues that if we value personal liberty and a society which provides opportunity for that liberty to be exercised, there will inevitably and rightly be a great diversity of financial outcome. It will later be argued that freedom and equality are not so totally opposed to each other as some claim. From a religious point of view we are all of equal worth in the eyes of God. This is expressed in our society, in equality before the law, equality of voting power and so on. Many would want to go beyond this and argue that for a society to offer genuine equality of opportunity, positive measures must be taken in education, social welfare, housing and health. It is true that in any society like that of the United States there will always be a few outstanding individuals who can go from rags to riches. In the United States there may be a good number of such people. However, there are millions, blacks and Hispanics, for example, for whom help is needed, not simply to provide for basic necessities (which Novak champions) but in order to give genuine freedom of opportunity to a much wider range of people. This brings to the fore Novak's own personal vision of society. In speech and in print he is clearly moved by the fact that his family, who were once peasants in Central Europe, have, as a result of the American system, been able to make their way and enjoy many of the good things of life. He quotes one working-class girl who ended up working for CBS News and then in the White House, who wrote in a best-selling book: 'This is the fairest place there ever was, it's wide open, and no one has cause for bitterness.' Novak shares that American dream. It is not an ignoble one but it is certainly limited. By its nature some people fail to make it and are left behind, and when their numbers run into many millions questions must be asked. There is also the issue of the quality of life of those who are left behind, not just their material state but their emotional and spiritual condition. Some people who know poverty in both India and the United States argue that it is much more degrading in the United States. In India a poor person lives against a spiritual background in which poverty is not regarded as a disgrace and all human beings have a spiritual worth. In the United States, where now tourists trample over the poor in the streets of many main cities, the poor are simply failures, those who have not made it in a success-orientated society. There is also the question of what the American dream does to people who are not on the streets. The classic expression of this is in Arthur Miller's play *Death of a Salesman*. The play is a deeply moving story of someone caught up in the American dream, who cannot quite make it, and therefore lives a life of fantasy which destroys him and his family. The American dream is destructive because it fails to recognize that there are other values in human society besides success, and we all have to relate to one another as mutual failures, not just potential victors.

Novak wants to help the poor. He writes: 'Our aim must be to liberate the poor; that is, to enable them to appropriate their own liberty – to become independent, self-reliant, autonomous, free citizens.' But many of the poor, who live lives with one another that are a great deal richer than the lives of those who have made it in a success-orientated society, would say that this understanding of liberty is itself deeply flawed. To be free as a human being is to be part of a community, part of a network of relationships in which one is valued, relationships that are characterized by mutual giving and receiving. This includes personal responsibility but it also sees the self as essentially related to other selves, not as a self-reliant, autonomous being, who dips in and out of relationships when he or she chooses. Novak quite rightly rejects one view of helping others that sees 'a large set of clients, now marginalized, to whom goods must be delivered to bring them up to a level of relative equality with others'. He prefers another mental construction, the social task consisting of so arranging an abundance of opportunities that the poor can become the agents of their own development, personal and economic, and gain power over an ever-broader array of personal decisions of their own lives. 'The urgent question at the present time is how to liberate, and not make servile, the able-bodied poor.' This is a question continuously on the minds of all those in the development field as well as those concerned with social welfare, whom Novak would regard as socialist or left-wing. It is good that the broad goals would appear to have converged. The main question which arises, however, is why the advocates of a capitalist system never place this goal in the forefront of their objectives. Capitalism is seen as the system which best favours the interest of those who have the biggest material stake in society, those who own houses and shares. It may or may not be the best system for raising the standards of those at the bottom of society. But the claim that it is would be more convincing if it was clearly set out in the policies of those parties most committed to the free market system. If, as Novak writes, the urgent question at the present time is how to liberate the able-bodied poor, then why is this question not taken more seriously by the theorists and politicians most committed to the market economy?

The market economy is both congruous with and expressive of the high Christian evaluation of human freedom. It also allows people to share in the creativity of God, using their initiative and willingness to take risks for the common good. However, Christian defenders of the market economy, both in the past, such as Adam Smith, and in the present, have stressed that it must be set within a moral framework which is orientated towards the common good. This is not just a theoretical consideration. Actual practical and legal steps have to be taken to safeguard the common good. While there is much in the writings of Michael Novak that can be accepted, in particular his emphasis on the fact that the liberal free market tradition does have a concept of the common good, his analysis is in the end deeply flawed. It lacks a proper historical sense and in particular a realization that a market never works in isolation from particular interest groups and power groupings maintaining and strengthening their hold on society's resources. Although Novak is rightly suspicious of the idea of one group of people imposing their vision of the common good on society as a whole, he totally fails to take into account the effect of sin in allowing dominant groups in a market economy to maximize their own power at the expense of others. The state, through its elected government, has a proper duty not just to encourage a market economy but also to ensure that the market economy genuinely works for the common good by intervention when necessary. The fine pastoral letter of the United States Roman Catholic bishops, *Economic Justice for All*, stressed that 'the teachings of the Church insist that *Government has a moral function: protecting human rights and securing basic justice for all members of the Commonwealth'.* It then went on to note the principle of subsidiarity, by which decisions are always made by the smallest unit or community possible. This does not mean, however, 'that the government that governs least governs best'. Rather, it defines good government intervention as that which truly 'helps other social groups contribute to the common good by directing, urging, restraining, and regulating economically as "the occasion requires and the necessity demands"'.[14]

Ronald Preston judges that 'the ideology of the free market is un-Christian, as distinct from the market as an institution'.[15] This is an important distinction. The free market is in danger of becoming an ideology when it is invested with almost religious status. This certainly appeared to have happened at periods during the cold war, when capitalism and Marxism were regarded as competing religions. Nevertheless, as has been argued here, the market as an institution is not morally neutral. It both expresses and safeguards certain values. In a fallen world the way it does this is always flawed and it needs therefore to be subjected to searching critiques and corrections. It is only an awareness of the faults of the free market as we have it at the moment, and a willingness to work for built-in correctives, that can prevent the defence of the system from becoming an ideology. It has been argued here that the free market, despite its flaws, does genuinely express and safeguard the values of freedom and enterprise, both of which are prized from a Christian view of what it is to be a human being. Furthermore, although it makes use of self-interest and this self-interest can often become inordinate greed, self-interest, in a Christian view, is not in itself wrong. Moreover, while the justification of a commercial policy will usually be in terms of corporate interest, this does not mean to say that all who work for the corporation are only motivated by self-interest. On the contrary, many admirable motives, such as the desire to do a good job, loyalty and so on, will be present. Nevertheless, because of the effects of sin in every institution, leading to the unjust distribution of power and resources, positive action on behalf of those who start off disadvantaged will always be an essential element in a Christian approach to the market.

It will be argued in the next chapter that equality is as fundamental as freedom to the effective operation of a market economy. Although during the past 200 years the two values have worked against one another in the economic sphere, they do in fact belong together and can be held together. But this will mean a strengthening of those forces in capitalist societies which seek to mitigate the worst excesses of the market and which encourage affirmative action on behalf of those who seem to lose out as a result of it. This affirmative action, while it includes equality, in the sense of giving everyone an equal regard and concern, will also express the Christian commitment to the disadvantaged. It will strive not simply for equal opportunity but for those resources without which the idea of equal opportunity is a sham.

Ronald Preston sets out four requirements for avoiding the abuses of the free market.[16] The first is harnessing self-interest to the common good; for example, using the price mechanism to control pollution, that is allowing competitive bidding for the rights to pollute up to the limit thought advisable. The second is providing a strong welfare state. This will involve citizens' rights and responsibility. The third is ensuring that private centres of economic power do not become more powerful than the government. The fourth is taking participation in decision-making seriously in matters where vital interests of citizens are at stake. In short, markets are useful for risk-taking innovation. There is a major role for competition and the entrepreneur. There is no case for saying that markets work best if they are left alone. That is to erect a false social philosophy on the concept of the market. Much thought, therefore, needs to be given to the social framework within which markets operate. Can they serve more egalitarian ends?

The French Revolution took place in the name of *liberté, egalité, fraternité*. The horrors of the Revolution, particularly its aftermath, have given this combination of values a bad name, yet they sum up that moral framework within which the market economy must operate if it is to realize Christian and humane values. For fraternity is no less essential than freedom and equality and it is a value that is essential to the Christian life. Christians belong together in the one fellowship of Christ. Human beings belong together in the one fellowship of God's family, touched and drawn together by his one Spirit. Indeed it is only if this consciousness of fraternity is present that a free market can remain within the bounds of moral acceptability. For the market economy includes competition as one of its essential ingredients. In competition some are defeated, some go to the wall. It is a sense of fraternity which mitigates the worst effects of competition and which, together with a strong notion of equality, prevents the system becoming exploitative.

In short, the market is a sphere of operation in which millions of Christians are, quite properly, working out their vocation, meeting human need and increasing the resources of society. But, as with every other human endeavour, there will be an equally proper Christian suspicion, alert for ways in which organized self-interest is likely to work against the well-being of those least able to stand up for themselves.

NOTES

1 Frank Field, *Losing Out: the Emergence of Britain's Underclass* (Blackwell, 1989).
2 Denis Munby, *Christianity and Economic Problems* (Macmillan, 1956).
3 Andrew Phillips, 'Is the market mentality a licence for greed?', the Hibbert Lecture, *The Listener* (25 February 1988).
4 Ronald Preston, *Religion and the Persistence of Capitalism* (SCM, 1979), p. 47.
5 Gerard Hughes, 'Christianity and self-interest' in *Christianity and the Future of Social Democracy*, ed. Michael Taylor, (G. W. & A. Hesketh, Ormskirk, 1982), pp. 7–32.
6 Bishop Hall, 'Can we get as much as we can?' in *Buying and Selling: the Works of Joseph Hall, DD*, Vol. VII (Talboys, Oxford, 1837).
7 Adam Smith, *The Theory of Moral Sentiments*, ed. D. D. Raphael and A. L. Macfie (OUP, 1991).
8 Adam Smith, *The Wealth of Nations* (Penguin Classics, 1986), pp. 358, 359.
9 Peter Morgan, 'The Church and the enterprise culture', *Church of England Newspaper* (30 March 1990). It is also true that a modern market economy can only work where there is a general acceptance of honesty and trust. No one would buy shares in a company unless they were reasonably sure that the directors were honest and were going to pursue the business purpose set out in their articles of association. No one will go on trading with a person who cheats. Such honest practice and trust is not required to make a command economy work because people are provided with what the State has decided they shall have. Indeed, as Kenneth Adams points out, because the only way of getting more than your ration is to cheat, a command economy positively encourages dishonesty. This was well demonstrated in wartime.
10 Brian Griffiths, *Morality and the Market Place* (Hodder & Stoughton, 1980), p. 9.
11 Ibid., p. 36.
12 Michael Novak, *Free Persons and the Common Good* (Madison Books, 1989).
13 Michael Novak, *Morality, Capitalism and Democracy* (IEA Health and Welfare Unit, 1990).
14 *Economic Justice for All*, Pastoral Letter on Catholic Teaching and the US Economy (USCC, 1986), pp. 60–2.
15 Ronald Preston, 'Christian faith and capitalism', *The Ecumenical Review*, 40, no. 2 (April 1988).
16 Ronald Preston, *Religion and the Ambiguity of Capitalism* (SCM, 1991), p. 64.

8

For Those with Possessions

Equality

G. K. Chesterton once remarked that the English working man was less interested in the equality of human beings than he was in the inequality of racehorses. Matthew Arnold in the nineteenth century detected a rather more sinister situation, when he observed that in England inequality was almost a religion. One of the reasons that suggests there may still be some truth in Arnold's view is the extreme hostility shown by so many people to the whole concept of equality. Nevertheless, there are in fact real areas of agreement between egalitarians and their opponents. It can be readily conceded, for example, that human beings are differently endowed with brains, looks, drive and initiative. Such inequalities are marked and are unlikely to be eradicated. They are part of the variety of God's creation. So a belief in the equality of human beings does not imply that they are equally clever, beautiful, dynamic or strong.

Everyone in a liberal democracy in fact accepts equality as a basic principle over many areas of human life. It is basic to our system that everyone is equal before the law. A prince and a black teenager, both caught speeding, should be treated equally. Then, equality is basic to our democratic procedures. Everyone has one vote, not more and not less. One counts for one.

Furthermore, it can be readily conceded that communist societies have certainly not brought equality, rather the reverse. Many years ago Milovan Djilas drew attention to the emergence of the new class in communist societies, a class of people close to power who enjoyed all the appurtenances and perks of power.[1] Wage differentials in the former Soviet Union were often greater than in liberal democracies. So to defend equality is certainly not to be an admirer of the old Soviet system. Nor need a belief in inequality be based on envy. What W. B. Yeats described as a 'levelling, rancorous, rational sort of mind'[2] is to be avoided. The surroundings of the rich, a well-proportioned house and pleasant spacious gardens can be appreciated without necessarily wanting to possess them.

This said, how far does the Christian faith give support to the value and principle of equality, compared, for example, to that of freedom? One of the most interesting theological attacks on the notion of equality in recent years came from C. S. Lewis. He argued that hierarchy and obedience belong to our pure unfallen nature and that although equality is necessary in our world, it is essentially a concession. Our real hunger is for inequality, as shown, for example, by the appeal of right-wing dictatorships and in the desire of millions to create heroes and superstars. Indeed, unless we give hierarchy its proper place dangerous political movements, like the Nazis, will spring up. 'The man who has never wanted to kneel or to bow is a prosaic barbarian',[3] wrote Lewis. This desire to reverence and worship belongs to our essential unfallen nature. Nevertheless, because we live in a fallen world, we can never trust any one ruler or group with unbridled power. We need liberal democracy and the concept of equality that goes with it, in order to check potential tyranny. So equality is necessary in this world but 'there is no spiritual substance in flat equality'. We should recognize that 'under the necessary outer covering of legal equality, the whole hierarchical dance and harmony of our deep and joyously accepted spiritual inequalities should be alive'. It is good that C. S. Lewis admits the necessity of equality in this fallen world. But it is doubtful whether his championing of this value is strong enough. If there are indeed genuine spiritual inequalities, then in the name of these we may need to offer powerful protests against all other kinds of inequality, based on inheritance, the capacity to coerce or riches. C. S. Lewis says that 'there is no spiritual substance in flat equality'. But there is certainly spiritual substance in attempts to counteract the world's scale of values by positive action in the name of Christ's very different scale. We bow, kneel, reverence and worship the sublime humility of God incarnate. We reverence the holiness of God's true saints. Jesus taught that the last shall be first and the first shall be last. There will be a great reversal, when humility will be crowned in majesty and love will be clothed in splendour. Then indeed we shall prostrate ourselves in true worship. But the values revealed then are very different from those that the world tends to court and submit to, namely power and wealth. So, if Lewis's point is conceded, that there are spiritual inequalities, this should lead to a sense of revolt against the world's inequalities. The New Testament would suggest, therefore, affirmative action, or positive discrimination in favour of Christ's values and opposition to our usual inequalities based on money and power.

At the time of the French Revolution, it was assumed that liberty, equality and fraternity belonged together and that if one emerged the others would soon follow after. The French feudal system enforced legal inequalities. The revolutionaries believed that if these hierarchical restrictions were done away with and they were free, then financial equality would follow. So as R. H. Tawney put it: 'Liberty and equality, which later generations have sometimes held to be incompatible, appeared for a golden moment to walk hand in hand.'[4] It was only for a moment. The history of Europe and North America in the past 200 years has revealed new forms of inequality, based not on ancient custom and legal privilege but on new-found wealth. So it is that in the modern world freedom and equality are often opposed to one another in the minds of their respective champions. Yet here too there is some common ground. For the market economy is based not simply on the value of freedom but also, and perhaps more importantly, on the value of equality. The fundamental point about a market economy is that customers choose what goods they wish to purchase. Every customer has this choice. They are equal in this respect. This is in contrast to a system where a ruling elite or bureaucracy decides on their behalf what they shall purchase. As Ronald Dworkin has written:

> We are familiar with the anti-egalitarian consequences of free enterprise in practice; it may therefore seem paradoxical that the liberal as law giver should choose a market economy for reasons of equality rather than efficiency. But, under the special condition that people differ only in preferences for goods and activities, the market is more egalitarian than any alternative of comparable generality.[5]

The qualification of course is the reference to special conditions that people differ only in preferences for goods and activities. People differ in other ways: some are rich and others are poor, some are well endowed with brains and initiative, others are slower or more passive, some have a good home and education, others an unsatisfactory upbringing or a debilitating environment. Hence, the egalitarian will always argue that equality of opportunity is not enough. 'The existence of such opportunities in fact, and not merely in form, depends, not only upon an open road, but upon an equal start.' Or again, 'Equality of opportunity is fictitious without equality in the circumstances under which men have to develop and exercise their capacities.'[6]

In a recent attack on the notion of equality, Professor Antony Flew[7] draws a distinction between Good Samaritans and Procrustians. He argues that poverty is an evil and that we should be like the Good Samaritan, doing all that we can to relieve it, rather than the mythical Procrustes, stretching and chopping people to fit an inflexible standard. However, poverty is not necessarily related to inequality. Flew objects among other things to definitions of poverty which are related to the relative wealth of a particular society. This understanding of poverty, made familiar through the works of Professor Peter Townsend, comes from a belief that to be a human being involves more than simply keeping physically alive. It means sharing in the society of which one is a part. In order to do this one needs appropriate means. If people are so poor that they are never able to entertain friends or eat out, or go on holiday or visit places, they are being deprived of that which the majority of the society take for granted. So a person may be physically alive, with enough to keep the body going, but it is not a proper or fully human life. No doubt all definitions of poverty are to some extent arbitrary and it is not always easy to draw a line between absolute poverty and relative poverty. Nevertheless, there is clearly a difference between people starving to death in Ethiopia and a single parent with three children living on social security. There is a fundamental human obligation to meet the basic needs of both for food and shelter. In our society it is also legitimate to ask the question how far such a mother is able, with her children, to have a meaningful life. This will inevitably be to some extent relative. Here the inequalities of a society are a legitimate concern. So while it can readily be conceded that the duty to eliminate grinding poverty is fundamental and does not depend upon any view about inequality, nevertheless the concept of inequality is relevant to the reduction of some forms of poverty deprivation, particularly in advanced societies.

Flew quotes the Institutes of Justinian, that the mark of the just person is 'a constant and perpetual will to assign to each their own due' (*constans et perpetua voluntas ius suum cuique tribuere*). He then argues that justice demands not that equal conditions be imposed on all but they will all be subject to the same set of rules. It is unjust to treat two people who have committed exactly the same offence in two different ways and hence unequally. For a system in which offenders were treated in exactly the same way as non-offenders would contradict itself as a system of criminal justice. Applied to the market economy this presumably means that those who work should get paid and those who slack should not, and that people should get rewarded according to a system of supply and demand. However, there are different ways of understanding what is due to a person. From a Christian point of view what is due is what is required to meet their basic needs and help them to grow into the fullness of the person that God has in mind for them to be. From the fourth-century Fathers we derive the notion that this is due to all people, without exception. This does not mean to say that the ordinary rules of the market economy have no place. They do. Only, for a Christian, they certainly cannot be the only consideration and they are certainly not absolute. The nature of justice is illumined by our understanding of God's grace in Christ.

Flew argues, as do other writers from the Social Affairs Unit, that the poor are not necessarily impoverished by the rich being rich.[8] He argues, for example, that the view of Engels that Victorian capitalism in Manchester impoverished the working class cannot be sustained. For if there had been no capitalism their situation might have been worse still. The same argument is applied to the relationship between the developed and the developing world. Third World countries might have been even worse off without imperialism. Perhaps or perhaps not. Two points are, however, pertinent. In any capitalistic enterprise the workforce is indispensable. The labour of employees is no less essential for the profitability of a firm than the organizational power of its managers and the capital of its shareholders. If a company is highly profitable, then it is the workforce as much as anyone else that has contributed to this. It is not true, as Marx asserts, that they are inevitably exploited. It does mean, however, that vast differentials and gross disparities are an affront to our basic sense of fairness, that all those who contribute to the success of an enterprise should share in its rewards, if not with a flat rate equality (for we live with the market economy) at least in a way that recognizes the real value, indeed indispensability, of the employees. Furthermore, as was argued in the section on self-interest, there is always a tendency for firms to pay the minimum they can get away with while at the same time retaining the kind of workforce they want. If the workforce has few rights, as is the case in many parts of the world, then that minimum is low indeed, and workers are regarded as highly dispensable. So wider considerations of justice and equality are needed in order to counteract the tendency of capital to be a juggernaut. Though it is not inevitably true that a workforce is exploited, it is often true, and the tendency for it to be so exploited is always present.

Christians can agree that in one fundamental sense all human beings are equal. We are equally of value in the eyes of God. He has regard for, considers, the needs of each one of us. This equality is built into our society in many ways. We are all equal before the law, we have one vote, we ourselves choose what we shall buy. There remain, however, striking inequalities in the society in which we live, which have to do not simply with different personal characteristics, but different conditions and opportunities. On a Christian view of equality, we share in the work of God in helping everyone to develop the potential they have within them. This will properly mean a concern for the conditions which make this possible and a widening of opportunities which are available to all.

Jesus told a parable about some workers:

> For the kingdom of heaven is like a householder who went out early in the morning to hire labourers for his vineyard. After agreeing with the labourers for a denarius a day, he sent them into his vineyard. And going out about the third hour he saw others standing idle in the market place; and to them he said, 'You go into the vineyard too, and whatever is right I will give you.' So they went. Going out again about the sixth hour and the ninth hour, he did the same. And about the eleventh hour he went out and found others standing; and he said to them, 'Why do you stand here idle all day?' They said to him, 'Because no one has hired us.' He said to them, 'You go into the vineyard too.' And when evening came, the owner of the vineyard said to his steward, 'Call the labourers and pay them their wages, beginning with the last, up to the first.' And when those hired about the eleventh hour came, each of them received a denarius. Now when the first came, they thought they would receive more; but each of them also received a denarius. And on receiving it they grumbled at the householder, saying, 'These last worked only

one hour, and you have made them equal to us who have borne the burden of the day and the scorching heat.' But he replied to one of them, 'Friend, I am doing you no wrong; did you not agree with me for a denarius? Take what belongs to you, and go; I choose to give to this last as I give to you. Am I not allowed to do what I choose with what belongs to me? Or do you begrudge my generosity?' So the last will be first, and the first last. (Matthew 20.1–16)

The anti-egalitarian will understandably argue that it is not possible to run an economic system on those lines. The next day the labourers who worked all through the preceding one might very well hang around until the last moment hoping to be hired then and get away with only one hour's work. If people are going to be given a day's money for an hour's work, then there is no incentive for people to work all through the day. In order to work we need incentives and rewards that are commensurate with the effort put in. As long as this world continues all these are legitimate considerations. But Christians believe that the Kingdom of God has also broken in upon us. The King, recognizing the need of the labourers and their families, hires as many as he can and pays them all. The law of the market is not the only law. It lives under, is judged by, and is beckoned towards, the higher law of the Kingdom.

It is necessary to defend equality against anti-egalitarians. But it is clear from the foregoing that a Christian cannot remain content with a flat level notion of equality. Living with a sense of God's worth for every single human being will mean, in a great number of situations, not equality according to some abstract notion, but affirmative action, positive discrimination, in order to help the most vulnerable human beings attain their potential. This is for three reasons. First, capitalism, like all forms of organized self-interest, will if left to itself further the interests of the wealthy and powerful at the expense of the relatively poor and powerless. The poor and the powerless may participate in the prosperity created by capitalism, but never enough; and others will be simply used or, still in some places today, exploited. Secondly, the New Testament sets forth a reversal of values. The first shall be last and the last shall be first. Thirdly, the Christian notion of justice, rooted in God's grace towards us, is concerned with the full development of every single human being. A Christian understanding of personal growth is not identical with a humanist one. We are to grow into mature humanity measured by nothing less than 'the stature of the fullness of Christ' (Ephesians 4.13). This means that we look for growth even when there are human frustrations and limitations or when life is cut short, as in the case of Christ himself. But this does not detract from the obligation to help everyone develop their ordinary human potential as far as they can.

The British in particular have a built-in suspicion of equality. However, in practice, our society accepts the notion in many areas of our life. The attempt by C. S. Lewis to defend spiritual inequality on theological grounds leads to the conclusion that Christians should seek to oppose major inequalities of wealth and power. At the French Revolution it was assumed that if only legal inequalities could be done away with then financial equality would follow from the new-found freedom. This was not found to be the case. Political and legal equality has led to gross economic disparities. The New Right is vehemently opposed to the notion of equality but an examination of Antony Flew's position reveals it to be defective from a Christian point of view, in that it works with a secular rather than a Christian understanding of justice. A Christian understanding of justice is not simply concerned with treating people exactly the same in a mechanical way. The Christian understanding of justice, illuminated by God's relationship to us, is concerned with developing the full potential, human and spiritual, of every human being. In the light of God's love for them this is what is due to them by us. Other New Right thinkers argue on economic grounds that inequalities do not make for poverty; rather differentials allow all in due course to have their standard of living raised. It is not necessary to oppose all differentials and ensuing inequalities to know that there is a tendency to pursue one's own interest without fully taking into account the interest of others. At its worst this results in situations which can only be described as exploitative. Christians will not be concerned with a flat level notion of equality. Rather, they will be concerned with affirmative action on behalf of those who at present suffer from the way things are. This will mean opposing the inequalities which are built into the system. No doubt there will always be some degree of inequality. But we should be highly suspicious of those who seek to justify such inequalities rather than taking positive action on behalf of those most adversely affected by the system. This raises the whole question of ownership. For one of the most fundamental inequalities of the capitalist system as we have it at the moment is that in Britain, as in so many countries of the world, a tiny percentage of the population owns most of the wealth.

Ownership

The attempt to restore private property in the former Soviet Union and in those Eastern European countries which were until recently under communist rule raises the question of ownership in a very contemporary form. So does the attempt in Great Britain to privatize many industries which were until recently nationalized, such as water and electricity. This is a debate that the Church has engaged in down the centuries and to which it still has much that is distinctive to contribute.

Quotations from the fourth-century Fathers in Chapter 3 established the following points. First, they believed that God's intention in creation was a common ownership. As air and water are available to all so should everything else be. Secondly, private ownership exists because of human sinfulness.

What is not clear from a reading of the Fathers is how far they believed that in the world as it is now the institution of private property should to some extent be accepted and how far we should seek to abolish it altogether. Like the Stoics they look back to a golden age when all things were held in common. But what should we do now that the golden age has passed, in our fallen sinful world? The situation in relation to private property is similar to that in relation to the state. Some writers at the Reformation, like some in the fourth century, took the view that the state was not only an expression of human sinfulness but a means of keeping that sinfulness within bounds. In the Garden of Eden there was no need for a state. As Luther put it, God ruled the world by the moving of one finger. It is because of human sinfulness that we have coercive government. However, because of human sinfulness, that flashing sword is necessary. It acts as a dike against sin. Similarly, the institution of private property can be seen as both a result of sin and a remedy for sin. Without human sinfulness it would not be necessary. But given human sinfulness it performs a useful, indeed an essential, function in limiting human divisiveness. So in the world as we know it we have to accept, to some extent, that private property is necessary.

Other Fathers may have believed, however, and this is the way some modern theologians interpret them, that we should not simply put up with private ownership as we know it. We should protest against the whole idea and seek to re-establish the principle of common ownership, with the goods of the earth being freely made available to all.

It may be questioned whether the Fathers of the fourth century were correct in seeing private property simply in terms of human sinfulness. This is a point which will be returned to later. However, the prime principle to emerge from the fourth century is that there are no *absolute* property rights. This is clearly fully in accord with the biblical understanding of man as a steward of God's creation. It is also in sharp contrast to the notion that developed in the seventeenth century, particularly as a result of the influence of John Locke, about the sacredness of private property. There is a radicalism about the teaching of the fourth-century Fathers, with their emphasis upon the common good, that calls into question all the bourgeois notions that people in Europe and the United States have taken for granted during the past three centuries.

St Thomas Aquinas drew a distinction between procuring and distributing property on the one hand and using it on the other.[9] He regarded the right to procure and distribute property as entirely legitimate and gave three reasons for this. When something is our own or going to be our own we work better. If everything was held in common there would be a tendency to shirk. Secondly, it is good from the point of view of the ordering of society that everyone has something of their own to look after. Thirdly, the fact that property is divided, with different people owning different parts, makes for less quarrelling. If everything was held in common there would be even more disputes than there are now.

According to the view of Aquinas the natural law is that all things are common. Despite this he does not regard the institution of private property as contrary to natural law. He regards it as an addition to it by reason. However, the reasons which Aquinas adduces all reflect and appeal to humanity's fallen nature. He implies that we would not work for the common good as hard as we would work for our own good and we need private property to reduce quarrelling.

Although Aquinas believed that we have a legitimate right to procure and distribute property, he did not think that we have an absolute right to use it for ourselves. Here we are bidden to remember that property exists for the common good, and we have an obligation to minister to those in need. So in this regard he is as radical in his critique of private property as the fourth-century Fathers. As far as use is concerned possessions belong to those who have need of them, not simply to those who have possession of them. This led Aquinas to some startling conclusions. In contrast to St Augustine and the canonist Gratian, St Thomas maintained that a person in dire need could steal or other people could steal on his or her behalf. His argument is that human law cannot override divine and natural law and, according to these, material goods exist to supply human necessities. In the case of extreme necessity all things are common.

The followers of Calvin took a rather different attitude to stealing. It was from the commandment prohibiting theft that they derived the right to private property. People like Bullinger and Baxter, English puritans, maintained that private property was a legitimate right. They derived this right not from natural law but from the belief that the commandment against stealing implied it. For if everything was held in common then anyone who stole would only be stealing his or her own. The fact that people can steal implies that what they take belongs by right to someone else. Calvinists and Lutherans were to some extent reacting against the religious communities, whose way of life they regarded as a mistake and a failure. They were also reacting strongly against the Anabaptists. Peasants incited by Thomas Müntzer took over property and tried to set up communal ways of living. They circulated a document known as the 'twelve articles', which was mainly concerned with returning to the common man what had been appropriated from him. Martin Luther reacted strongly against this teaching. So did the authors of the Book of Common Prayer in England. Article 38 of the Thirty-nine Articles reads: 'The riches and goods of Christians are not common, as touching the right, title and possession of the same.' Nevertheless, in England in the seventeenth century the radical impulse reasserted itself. Left-wing elements in Cromwell's army, the Levellers and the Diggers, again argued for common ownership and sought in various ways to put this into practice. The

Diggers, for example, organized themselves along communist lines, trying to put common land and Crown property under spade and plough. Their democratic society excluded money, hire and the exploitation of labour.

Such radical movements did not succeed. The institution of private property prevailed and was justified. Nevertheless, all Christian teachers urged that we are stewards of God's gifts and these have to be used wisely. As Cromwell put it: 'If there be anyone that makes many poor to make a few rich, that suits not a commonwealth.'

At the end of the seventeenth century the new middle class found their most effective spokesman in John Locke.[10] He asked, if you pick up acorns or apples from under a tree, when do they begin to be yours? When you digest them or eat them or when? It was plain, he judged, that if the first gathering did not make them yours nothing could. It was that labour, picking them up, that gave you an inalienable right to them. This right antedates those of the state. Although human beings come together to make a kind of contract as a result of which we get the state, the state exists to protect the rights of private property. The state can make many laws to interfere with private convenience, it can make us march to war and so on, but nothing, however pressing, could overcome what has been described as 'the inherent sacredness of the breeches' pocket'.

Locke's view sounds sensible enough at a first hearing but it takes no account of the inequalities of distribution of private property that rapidly arise in any society. Ten men cultivate ten plots of land with their own labour. Each of those ten men has ten sons. If they leave their land to the elders, that leaves ten owners and ninety landless labourers. If the children fight it out among themselves, then some are likely to emerge with the lion's share and others with nothing. In theory, there could be an equitable distribution. But theory has rarely corresponded to practice.

Karl Marx saw the radical implications of John Locke's teaching. If a man has a right to the fruits of his labour, then this must be accepted in the only logical form, he has a right to the *whole* produce of his labour. Not surprisingly, many others besides or before Marx saw this. One of the Diggers put it this way:

> If a man have no help from his neighbours, he shall never get an estate of hundreds and thousands a year. If other men help him to work, then are those riches his neighbours' as well as his . . . rich men receive all they have from the labourer's hand, and when they give, they give away other men's labours not their own.

Marx argued, on the basis of the principle that a labourer has a right to the whole produce of his labour, that private appropriation is wrong. The only morally legitimate system is one in which the means of production are held in common. This view has now been discredited by the total failure of communism as we have known it in practice. It is also wrong in theory. Though private property is not an absolute and inalienable right, it does have, with qualifications, a moral and theological legitimacy.

Private property is not simply an expression of and a concession to human sinfulness. A limited amount of property is both natural and necessary. For possessions are necessary for the expression and development of our individual personality. Being a human being involves more than the existence of a naked soul. We exist as flesh and blood. We take up space in the world. Inevitably we express our personalities through the clothes we wear, the kind of paint we put on the walls, the seeds that we put in the garden or windowbox. The ancient Hebrews regarded a person's property almost as an extension of his or her personality and there is some truth in this idea. It could of course be argued that people can express themselves through communal property and that it is not necessary for them to own anything in order for this to be done. But if an amenity is owned by the community no one individual is able to stamp his or her particular personality on it. It will express what the community as a whole needs and wants. For a room to be an expression of a particular individual's personality, the person needs enough security of tenure to be able to paste up a particular kind of wallpaper or buy a certain set of chairs. People cannot express themselves in and through a room if there is uncertainty about someone else coming in at any moment and re-arranging the whole colour scheme. The same principle applies in the garden. One person wants a herbaceous border, the other wishes to grow vegetables. So each has an allotment and they express their personal preferences there.

This is not an argument for unlimited private property, nor from this point of view does it even need to be very extensive. It is simply that we all require a sphere, a space, a kind of extension of our personality in which we can have some assurance of being able to make choices that will hold for a predictable period of time. If I plant a rose I want some assurance that it will be there in two years' time. Of course, human existence is radically uncertain. The rose might die or someone might steal it. But the framework of custom, expectation and law should be such as to reinforce the predictability of human existence.

The most popular argument in favour of private property is that of St Thomas Aquinas, already mentioned, namely that we are more willing to work well for what we will acquire for ourselves. This is in part a concession to our fallen human condition. But it is also an expression of legitimate self-interest which, as was argued in a previous chapter, is part of our God-given human nature. The failure is our inability to take into account the interests of our neighbour. It is not a failure to want to acquire a home or look after it well.

This said, the biblical witness, together with that of the Fathers of the fourth century, makes it quite clear that there is no absolute right to all the property we might think we possess. We are stewards and the resources of the earth exist to meet the needs of all human beings. Such needs can be met in various ways, including voluntary and institutional enterprise. But the common mind, acting through the organs of the state, certainly has a right to curtail or redistribute private property in accord with the general need. It does not have the right totally to abolish the institution.

Recent decades have seen a switch away from the polarization between private and public ownership towards the concept of wider ownership. It would seem to be an idea very congruous with the main thrust of Christian social teaching on property. Wider ownership takes many forms, from the encouragement of millions of ordinary people to own shares to the sale of council houses. It includes many forms of hidden ownership; for example, the way pension funds now form such a major sector of the financial market. Millions of people, through their pensions, have a stake in this.

There remains the question raised by Karl Marx, about the alienation of the worker from his work when he has no stake in the means of production. Yet this alienation occurred on an even more devastating scale in state-controlled economies under communist rule. Alienation from work has to do with a range of factors, not simply ownership. People feel at ease with their work when the work is fulfilling, utilizing their talents and abilities; when they feel that it is making a useful contribution to society; and when they belong to a company or an organization that they feel is doing a good job of which they can feel proud. Sadly, by the last criterion, state-owned industries have often shown up so much worse than private enterprise. There is no inherent reason why this should be so, for the armed services are noticeably successful in encouraging a sense of pride in the ship or the regiment to which a particular serviceman belongs. Nevertheless, the negative point holds, namely that because an enterprise is run by the state it in no way follows that people who work for it will not feel alienated. Conversely, people who work for private businesses can feel that their work is integrated with their personality and the rest of their life.

Few would deny that there is a great deal of scope here for further experiment and development. Far too many people do still feel alienated from their work. Co-operatives, worker or management buy-outs, and other forms of employee participation are all to be encouraged. Some innovative firms, like the John Lewis Partnership, have been exceptionally successful, both in human terms and commercially. In the John Lewis Partnership, everyone who works within it is a partner, sharing in the profits and enjoying a wide range of benefits. Yet John Lewis has always been among the leading retailers.

Communal ownership operates at many levels. In a village where the village hall is owned by the village as a whole it is often very successful. Although a small trustee body is usually responsible for its running, the whole village will feel they have a stake in it and will try to maintain it well. Municipal services, such as public swimming pools or playing fields, can be equally well run, with the community as a whole feeling they have a part in it. In recent years, bodies like the National Trust, acting for the wider community but in a way that is independent of government, have made an invaluable contribution, not simply opening up houses to the public but saving long stretches of the coastline and areas of the country-side for common use.

Modern society is working its way towards a balance on the question of ownership, which, provided it is a genuine balance, would seem the healthiest way for society to proceed, and one which does justice to the various moral and Christian principles involved. Works of art are a good example. It is entirely proper that people should be able to acquire works of art, either modern or ancient. It is a natural and important way in which some people choose to express their basic preferences. Yet great works of art, like beautiful areas of the countryside, should be available to all. So we have museums and art galleries. The state has a duty to ensure that, within limits imposed by other claims, works of art are so available. Yet philanthropists, both in their lifetime and when they die, also like to make a contribution to the common good. So whole collections are sometimes given and a wider public enjoys them. There is, of course, scope for endless disputes about whether a particular painting should be acquired for the nation and, if so, how the money is to be raised. There will be no specifically Christian judgement in most instances. However, provided the basic principle that people have a right to acquire works of art for themselves is preserved, the thrust of the Christian tradition is to make available the good things of life to as many people as possible and this includes our cultural and artistic heritage as well as our natural scenery.

In line with a policy of expanding ownership rather than abolishing it, it would seem appropriate for Christians to support the move to wider share ownership. The major contribution towards wealth creation in the population as a whole is made by home ownership and building up pension rights. The payments for these together dominate the capital market in Britain. Already in Britain 62 per cent of listed company shares are owned by pension and insurance funds. Yet in addition to this, there is major scope for employee ownership of shares.

George Copeman has argued that one of the main reasons for the disparity between rich and poor in capitalist societies is not exploitation, as Marxists maintain, but that those who own shares are able, at certain moments, to acquire wealth rapidly through an expanding market. Further-more, in an expanding market, people who already own shares in fact have many tax concessions, because they are investing now in companies whose profits will be in the future.

At the end of 1989 there were 4,199 approved executive share option plans, 879 approved profit-sharing share ownership plans and 869 approved savings-related share option plans (some of these latter two types both occurring in the same company). There are four different UK employee approved share plans at the moment and clearly there are opportunities here for more companies to participate in them.

Even if the economy is relatively stagnant certain companies can suddenly grow rapidly. For example, Tim Waterstone, from £16,000, mostly borrowed, investment in one bookshop in 1982, built up a chain of thirty bookshops. These were sold within seven years for £42,000,000.

> Because a steady but high rate of profitability produces a geometric rate of growth and the profits are spent on growth, owners face a potential conflict if their employees are excluded from participation in the capital growth. At Waterstone's they did participate. But suppose the employees had been excluded, and demanded in lieu higher pay than the market rates? Meeting such demands could absorb all the high profits, and how would the growth come then?[11]

Employees who own shares can participate in what George Copeman calls the 'spurt factor'. Their participation may also help to make the company more profitable. It was found that during the eight-year period 1978–85 the performance of profit-sharing companies was over 78 per cent better than the performance of non-profit-sharers.

It has been argued here that the ownership of property is not simply a concession to the sinfulness of the human condition, but is a natural expression of human nature in an unfallen state; through our possessions we make our choices and express our personality. Nevertheless, property rights are not absolute. We are stewards of God's bounty, in the last analysis trustees rather than owners. We have a leasehold, not a freehold. This point is quite clear not only from the biblical material, but from the witness of the fourth-century Fathers and the teaching of St Thomas Aquinas, to mention just a few of those who have reflected on this from within the Christian tradition.

The question of how much property is not a question that can receive any precise answer. That there will be differences, inequalities, is inevitable. The aim, obviously, is for an increasing prosperity in which all share to some extent or another. Virginia Woolf said that all she wanted was a competence of £300 a year and a room of her own. To some at that time this would have seemed a fortune. To others, hardly adequate. We have different needs and we make different choices. Nevertheless, the move to wider ownership, in the form of homes and shares, particularly shares owned by employees, is to be encouraged. Not only will this allow a wider range of people to participate in any prosperity that is around (and also any recession) but ownership conveys security and power. A person able to buy a council house or flat has that much greater dignity. A worker who owns some shares in the firm has a stake in it and is less likely to be alienated from the work. It is easy to scorn this notion as humdrum or petit-bourgeois. But from what height is that scorn emitted? Sometimes it comes from those who themselves certainly have a competence or more, or who through education have been able to participate in many of the best things which this life affords.

Wider ownership does not have all the glamour of fabulous wealth allegedly held out by an unbridled capitalism nor the apocalyptic vision of the end of all private property put forward by anarchists and Marxists. But to those who have little or nothing it holds out the prospect of a desirable stake in society and an affirmation of dignity for their families. Earlier in this chapter it was argued that Christians will be sympathetic to the idea of equality, at least in being suspicious of those who justify inequalities, and by themselves taking positive action on behalf of those who are adversely affected by present inequalities. This affirmative action will take the form of creating conditions for everyone to have a financial stake in society, for example through home and share ownership. While some Christians will sit so light to possessions that they can virtually do without them altogether, it is important that what they choose for themselves should not be urged on others as an obligation. A society in which everyone had a home they could call their own and a financial stake in the enterprise for which they worked would not be the Kingdom of God. But it would be a great deal fairer and more desirable than what we have at the moment.

NOTES

1 Milovan Djilas, *The New Class* (Thames & Hudson, 1957).
2 W. B. Yeats, 'The Seven Sages': *The Poems of W. B. Yeats*, ed. Richard J. Finneran (Macmillan, 1983), pp. 241–2.
3 C. S. Lewis, 'Equality', reprinted in the Canadian *C. S. Lewis Journal* (Summer 1990). It originally appeared in *The Spectator* in 1943.
4 R. H. Tawney, *Equality* (Allen & Unwin, 1964), p. 95.
5 Ronald Dworkin, 'Liberalism' in *Public and Private Morality*, ed. Stuart Hampshire (CUP, 1978), p. 131.
6 Tawney, *Equality*, p. 106.
7 Antony Flew, *The Philosophy of Poverty* (The Social Affairs Unit, 1985).
8 For a thoughtful attack on the notion of equality see David G. Green, *Equalising People* (IEA Health and Welfare Unit, 1990).
9 Thomas Aquinas, *Summa Theologica* II. 2, qu. 66, 2 and 6, qu. 32, 7.
10 John Locke, *An Essay concerning the true, original, extent and end of civil government*, ch. 5, 'A property': *Two Treatises of Government* (Everyman, 1984).
11 George Copeman, *Exploding Wealth for All* (Centre for Policy Studies, 1990).

9

For Shareholders, Employees and the Rest of Us

I argued in previous chapters that the market economy, whose goal is to increase the quality of life for all by maximizing society's resources, has a moral basis and a moral purpose. It is only because the whole enterprise can quite legitimately be seen in ethical terms that we can have a concern about the morality of its constituent activities. Conversely, because it can and should be seen in moral terms, the various activities which go into its make-up must be evaluated in a moral light.

The old cliché that 'business is business' is less often heard nowadays. It implied that business occupied its own, autonomous sphere, free of values. This is simply not true. Like everything else in life business presupposes and expresses values. People sometimes make the same mistake in relation to the arts, judging that they occupy a neutral sphere. This is nonsense. Every work of art, whether it is a novel, a painting or a poem, is imbued with the passion and outlook of the creator. There is a very sharp distinction to be drawn between propaganda and genuine works of art. The former is trying to convey a point of view at the expense, for example, of the reality of the characters or the plot. But a genuine work of art is not value-free. It too presupposes and expresses a feel for life, which is inevitably rooted in a set of values and a perspective of belief or disbelief.

Another parallel can be drawn with education. In recent years there have been criticisms that the syllabus and courses of certain polytechnics have reflected a left-wing bias. In reaction to this people have called for the traditional educational ideals of respect for the facts, truth for its own sake and education rather than propaganda. But these educational ideals are also rooted in particular moral values, as well as in political ones. The alternative to left-wing or right-wing bias is not neutrality, for there is no such thing. The educational system in this country has been based upon values that are at once educational, moral and political, in that they are integrally linked to the values that inhere in a liberal democratic society.

Another mistake that is sometimes made is to think of morality or ethics only in negative terms. I once helped to convene a conference on 'Values and Soap Operas', where producers, writers and critics of soap operas came together. Though it was stimulating, it was not easy to get people to focus on the main theme because of the extreme suspicion in which many held the word 'value'. They associated it only with negative attitudes, in particular negative attitudes towards sex and violence. In fact, however, the works of some writers who were most suspicious of the word were often the most deeply imbued with a profoundly humane set of values.

Nothing is value-free, whether it is art, education or business. What is important is being aware of the presuppositions, assumptions and implicit values of the organizations for which we work or the activities in which we engage, and being reflective about them. The alternative is to leave business associated only with the negative image that it has in the minds of a good number, who see it as essentially hostile to humane values. In this regard there is an important parallel with the conference on 'Values and Soap Operas'. Because of a narrow connotation of the concept of value, one that leaves a good number of business people feeling uneasy or threatened, there is a temptation not to engage and a danger of leaving the whole area unexplored.

Businessmen are moral beings. Like the rest of us, the vast majority like to see and justify what they do in terms that they can live with, in other words in the light of their own values. Despite the negative image that business has sometimes acquired and the scandals which day by day rock the financial world, there is a high level of integrity in most business organizations. Indeed, clergy who have worked in business will often be the first to maintain that the level of integrity in the business world is in many respects as high as or higher than that of the organized churches. Unfortunately, some business people still feel threatened and therefore defensive about the whole subject. I sometimes speak to business groups on the subject of business and values, trying to help them examine their presuppositions and making it quite clear that this is in no way an attack on business. Sadly, sometimes, as soon as the introductory talk is over, one participant will launch into an attack on the Church. I am the first to acknowledge the validity of much of such criticism. But it will be unrelated to the main theme of the discussion and is the expression of minds that are highly defensive on the whole subject of values. When the subject of values is raised, still more the subject of morality, people immediately feel they are being 'got at'. But with many organizations there is that about which they can feel proud as well as, perhaps, that which they want to examine more critically.

It is maintained here that the values of a business will be formed by its response to five main claims. These are the claims of shareholders, customers, employees, business associates and the wider community. Today these claims will almost always have a legal component and some will argue that this is all that is either necessary or possible. It is the law that matters, the moral dimension is neither here nor there. It is indeed true that in almost every country now relationships with shareholders, customers, employees, business associations and the wider community are governed by complex laws. This has been most obviously so in recent years in relation to pollution and the wider community. During the earlier years of this century it was most obviously true in relation to the claims of employees. The law is not, however, the end of the matter. For the law itself is grounded in morality and the obligation to obey the law is itself a moral claim. Take, for example, the enormous amount of legislation relating to how employees are to be treated. Despite this legislation, few would say that the treatment of employees is a purely legal matter. Most would recognize a moral claim to treat employees fairly in a way that may or may not be fully safeguarded by a particular law. There might be some disagreement about what constitutes fairness in a particular instance, but there would be a common appeal to what is fair.

The law comes into the matter because people with moral insight and perseverance have recognized a wrong and have worked to bring about legislation to safeguard a particular group of people. The law is a recognition of what has been achieved, a basic minimum universally or at least nationally acknowledged. But that law may need improving in the light of moral insight developed in relation to its application in fresh situations. Or there might need to be new laws. A. B. Cleaver, Chief Executive of IBM, has written:

> In some areas, there may yet be no legal framework, but our own experience may lead us to believe that standards are necessary. So, for example, I.B.M. had clearly defined guidelines on the use of data well before the introduction of the Data Protection Act in this country . . . Operating as we do, in dozens of countries, with varying, and sometimes conflicting, national legislation and political persuasions, such situations are by no means unusual.[1]

It is not uncommon now for organizations that acknowledge such claims to justify this in terms of self-interest. A. B. Cleaver concluded his lecture on 'the social responsibilities of business' with the words 'it is possible to demonstrate that business does indeed have social responsibilities. Equally, I have suggested that they are no more than enlightened self-interest.' At the beginning of the lecture, while saying that he believed personally that moral principles and Christian values apply to business, he said 'I also believe ethics are not central to my main thesis.' These are deep philosophical waters and it is understandable that they should become somewhat dark. But, first, it must be made clear that enlightened self-interest is also a form of morality, indeed, some moral philosophers would maintain, the best basis for morality. Secondly, we cannot drive a wedge between personal morals and corporate responsibilities, in the way that A. B. Cleaver seems to be implying. There is only one morality. The obligation, for example, to be truthful with a potential customer about the product impinges upon people in their personal morality as well as in their roles as employees of the company.

It is very understandable that company chairmen should want to justify their activities, even the benevolent ones, in terms of enlightened self-interest. It is certainly more appealing to shareholders and no doubt they judge that it carries more conviction with a wider public than simply talking about morality. Furthermore, as was suggested in Chapter 5, a justification in terms of enlightened self-interest does not preclude an altruistic motivation in those who work for the firm. Nevertheless, as was also suggested, in practice enlightened self-interest can lead to an unacceptable minimum: wages that are far too low in a poor country, for example.

More basically, although enlightened self-interest is one form of morality, and probably an aspect of every morality, it is not the whole of morality. It is in the interests of a firm to treat employees well, particularly if they are highly trained. But most people would say that it is right to treat people well for their own sake. Morality is about recognizing the value of human beings as human beings and reacting accordingly. The vast majority of people who work for an organization will indeed hold this view, at least in some areas of their life. As human beings they will want to be appreciated for their own sake, not simply treated well as a means to making higher profits for the firm. So although the five claims which impinge upon any organization do indeed have a very great deal to do with enlightened self-interest, this is not the sum of the matter. The obligations on the shareholder, the customer, the employee, the business associate and the wider community are valid in their own right. Meeting these claims is in the long-term interest of the organization. But even if it was not in the interest of the organization the claims impinge upon us, for we are moral beings and the organizations for which we work, however much geared up to their own success, are composed of moral beings.

The first claim upon a company to be considered is that of the shareholders. In the past this was usually judged to be the only or in all instances overriding claim. So the first point that needs to be made is that a company is faced with five claims, not one. It cannot be assumed that priority should always be given to the shareholders when claims conflict. As has already been mentioned, the claims of customers, employees, business associates and the wider community are now all enshrined in law. This legislation presupposes and expresses a moral claim. Unfortunately, in some quarters there is still an assumption that a company belongs to the shareholders and the shareholders can do what they like with their own. They cannot. The law hedges them about. There are five sets of claims to be balanced one against another. From a specifically Christian point of view, the idea that one claim must in every circumstance be the overriding one is rejected on the grounds of potential idolatry. Only God is ultimate. In a finite world, a variety of moral principles have to be taken into account. Balances have to be struck and compromises made. To elevate one principle or one set of claims above all others in every circumstance is to usurp the position of God.

Nevertheless, it is obvious that shareholders not only have a claim but have the greatest power in order to ensure that that claim is recognized and met. Shares fall and management can be sacked. Shares rise and the firm can be sold. Takeovers take place, with many of the former employees being made redundant.

One of the main pleas of modern management is that shareholders be educated to take more than a short-term view. Rapidly developing technology in so many fields requires companies, those who wish to stay in business, to invest in research and development; it requires them continually to keep ahead of the game by altering, sometimes radically, their processes or what they produce. This is not always shown in terms of short-term profits but is essential for the future. So, as Lord Laing has put it,

> Whilst earnings per share growth must be a very important criterion by which a company's performance is judged, at least as important is the underlying long-term strength and competitiveness of the business on which those earnings depend. If a company's first concern is to maximise short-term profits in order to keep its earnings per share growing at the fastest possible rate, it is unlikely to be assigning sufficient investment to the long-term development and future security of the business – its technology, its market share and its people . . . The main justification for the capitalist system is that it provides the best climate for innovation and risk taking. But if the managers of a business are discouraged from taking risks, from undertaking research or from investment in innovation and an increasing market share, capitalism itself is called in question.[2]

In short, he writes, 'I am seeking to encourage a change in the climate of opinion in which the institutional owners of British companies accept the responsibility of "ownership" and take a rational, informed and reasonably long-term proprietorial view of the assets in which they have invested.'

The next claim to be considered is that of the customer. According to the basic philosophy of a market economy the customer is king. It is what the customer buys in the supermarket or dress shop that triggers the process which in the end decides what is produced. This is of course a gross oversimplification. We do not live in a phantom world of naked choices before an unlimited range of goods equally available to all. Choices are made by people, subject to pressures of various kinds and limited in what they are able to purchase by the means at their disposal. It is the perennial thrust of business to persuade people to choose one set of goods rather than another.

This raises major questions about the enormous power of advertising and the money that is spent persuading people to make particular choices. It is not only the money but the talent. An enormous amount of sheer ability goes into the advertising industry, together with its related arms of market research and PR. Many of the advertisements which appear on television are highly sophisticated, amusing and successful in that they remain in people's conscious and perhaps also their sub-conscious minds. Inevitably these advertisements are highly expensive and they utilize much human creativity. All this raises major questions. Can we really say that the customer is king if those who produce and sell the goods also have the resources to pay for the advertising to persuade people to buy those particular goods? Then there are the vast inequalities in people's spending power and the consequent curtailment of choice for millions of potential customers.

These are large questions beyond the scope of this chapter. However, they do press home the point for the individual Christian, about the worthwhileness of the products made or sold by the firm for which he or she works. Are they really worthwhile? Are they really worth trying to persuade other people to buy them?

Below the big political questions there is a further range of major legal concerns. If the customer is king then monopolies and price-fixing rings need to be outlawed. Yet here again the matter is not easy. If a company today is to operate in international markets it needs to be large enough to compete. It might be large enough to compete only if it has the lion's share of the home market. Nevertheless, any government committed to genuine freedom of choice will always be vigilant for what Adam Smith called a conspiracy of business people against society as a whole.

Within a particular firm there are certain standards that are pretty obvious even if they are not always observed: a commitment to the highest quality of product, accuracy of information about what the product can and cannot do, a prohibition on bribes or substantial gifts and so on. It is most obviously in relation to the customer that ethics and enlightened self-interest converge. It is in the interest of a business to retain its customers. So the customers must genuinely trust that they are receiving products of a high quality and good service. With the advent of sophisticated technology, requiring continuing innovation and adaptation, the relationship between customer and firm these days is very often a long-term one. So trust is basic to the relationship, and trust can only be built upon mutual honesty.

Traditionally and to some extent still it is the moral claims made by employees that place the greatest strains on the value system of an organization. In the more sophisticated industries enlightened self-interest demands that employees are well looked after. They are highly trained people whose skill and experience constitute a major investment in the firm. It is highly important to retain their services. Similar care is not always taken over the office cleaner or the casual labourer.

Although women have traditionally been discriminated against and still earn less and have less prospects of promotion, the shrinking labour market will in the next few years enhance their prospects. With fewer school-leavers available with the necessary expertise, companies will be actively recruiting women and ensuring that it is worth their while to stay with the firm. More crèches will be provided, more flexible working hours will be encouraged and women will be more likely to rise to positions of senior management.

The way that enlightened self-interest seems to work varies from one culture to another. American, Japanese and British companies appear to ask rather different commitments of their employees. American companies tend to demand more, drive harder, including giving shorter holidays, while at the same time giving greater financial rewards. Japanese compan-ies, while looking after their employees well, appear to swallow up their whole lives, seeking a lifetime's loyal and total commitment. In return there is a great sense of security and belonging. Asking all, they offer all. In some Japanese companies new employees are greeted by the directors, who begin by cleaning their shoes for them.

The law, too, plays an important part in relation to employees. Not only are there laws on unfair dismissal and the rights of those made redundant, large companies are required to employ a certain number of handicapped people. But how far should a firm go in retaining the services of someone whose performance has fallen below scratch, perhaps someone who has given sterling service in years past? One priest who exercises a non-stipendiary ministry works as a research scientist in a large international organization. What he finds most difficult is the way the organization judges people entirely in terms of their performance. As a Christian and as a human being he wants to treat other people as being of value in themselves. Yet a firm needs to operate efficiently and economically and simply cannot afford to carry passengers. On the other hand, if a firm is characterized by a continuous sense of anxiety that people are about to lose their jobs, this is hardly conducive to an effective operation.

Jobs are important to people. They are not simply the means whereby we make a living. It is through our jobs that most of us define ourselves, make our contribution to society and find our place in the community. Loss of a job means not only loss of income but loss of dignity. An organization that works on the philosophy of draining everything out of people up to the age of 45 and then kicking them out is treating human beings as economic units. Anyone with a sense of humane values would resist this.

It is morality and not just the law that operates in this area, as can be seen in Arthur Miller's play *Death of a Salesman* and the reaction to it in America when it was first produced. The play, already referred to in an earlier chapter, has as its background the American dream, the idea that anyone with ambition and hard work can make good. It also presupposes

American business practice, at least of a previous generation, whereby people can quickly become expendable. The central character is a salesman who is failing to sell all that his superiors require of him but who keeps up a fantasy world of big talk. When *Death of a Salesman* was first performed in the United States many were deeply moved. Arthur Miller describes the reaction in these words:

> As sometimes happened later on during the run, there was no applause at the final curtain of the first performance. Strange things began to go on in the audience. With the curtain down, some people stood to put their coats on and then sat again, some, especially men, were bent forward covering their faces, and others were openly weeping. People crossed the theatre to stand quietly talking with one another. I was standing at the back and saw a distinguished-looking elderly man being led up the aisle: he was talking excitedly into the ear of what seemed to be his male secretary or assistant. This, I learnt, was Bernard Gimbel, Head of the Department store chain, who that night gave an order that no one in his stores was to be fired for being over-age.[3]

Human considerations include not only age and performance but also the kind of pressure put on family life. How far is it right to ask a person to commute across the Atlantic twice a week? Once again, moral considerations cannot be totally divorced from economic ones. A man or a woman whose marriage is breaking up, at least in part because of the pressures of an over-demanding job and lack of time together, is hardly likely to be a person in a fit state of mind to make sound business decisions. Domestic life and business life cannot be totally separated from one another. The person who works will as likely as not also be a spouse and a parent. To view people simply as an isolated economic unit is so artificial that it is likely to fail not only morally but economically. On the other hand, the economic performance of the company is not simply an economic issue. On its success depend the jobs of the whole company and its contribution to the well-being of the wider community. So it is not a question of impersonal economic forces being pitted against humane values. It is the value of an effective organization, upon which everyone depends, being held in tension against the particular needs and values of every individual who works for it.

Inevitably there are sharp clashes and hard decisions to be made. A friend of mine who was at that time a non-stipendiary priest in the City of London and ran a major company found himself in the uncomfortable position of having officiated at the marriage of one of his employees and then shortly afterwards having to tell that person that he would have to leave the company because he simply did not have the aptitude for a particularly demanding kind of job. Successful organizations take care of their employees. When closures are necessary they take every step possible to try to offer a job elsewhere in the company, honouring all responsibilities and demonstrating to other employees a willingness to preserve employment in the face of major change.

In developed societies there is now a great deal of legislation that protects the rights of employees. Certain classes of people, however, remain vulnerable, not least members of ethnic minorities. There is clear evidence of racial discrimination in the employment of black and Asian people. On the continent of Europe immigrant workers are especially subject to fluctuating unemployment.[4] In Germany, for example, the number of migrant workers employed has shrunk from 2.5 million to 1.5 million in the past sixteen years. However, between 1973 and 1986 the total population of foreign workers increased from 3.9 million to about 4.5 million. With the decreasing number of wage earners, unemployment and poverty have become a serious problem. Similarly, in the Netherlands migrant workers are the first to be thrown out of work when industry restructures. It has been estimated that 60–75 per cent unemployment exists among these people, and that women are especially hard hit.

In the developing world the situation is even more serious. With millions of unemployed, it is much easier for international firms to operate a 'hire and fire' policy. Huge lay-offs can take place with no compensation for those who suddenly find themselves unemployed. Wages can be low and nearly always are, particularly for women. The unions of the kind that have safeguarded basic rights in industrial democracies may not be in existence or may find themselves relatively powerless.

The shareholder of a multinational company in the United States, Europe or another part of the developed world, who is a professed Christian, cannot distance him or herself from such concerns. Nor can the Christian who works for international companies, where there is disquiet about labour practices. It must be emphasized that the record of multinationals is often an excellent one. Even when their presence in a country such as South Africa has been unhelpful from the point of view of abolishing apartheid, and for this reason I have campaigned against them, they have, within the limits provided by the system, done what they can to improve conditions, raise wages and promote black, Indian and so-called Coloured South Africans.

Another category of person who remains to be considered is the business associate. This includes both suppliers of the main firm and those who act as its dealers or retailers. The larger firms are conscious that they have considerable power as a purchaser and try not to use this power unscrupulously. Some firms endeavour not to achieve a position whereby a supplier is so dependent on one business that withdrawal of support would cause the collapse of his own business. So strict limits on the proportion of any supplier's output that would be purchased are imposed.

Finally, there is the wider community, both people and the environment as a whole. A few years ago the majority of companies would have denied that there was any significant obligation to the wider community. Now this is being increasingly recognized. Pollution is the obvious example. Increasingly tight legislation on pollution is being enacted. Most now acknowledge that this is a moral obligation and not simply a legal one. Major companies now have members of staff concerned particularly or solely with environment issues.

A good number of businesses are now contributing to the wider community, particularly the generation of business in neglected inner-city areas. Firms are often willing to help in training people, in developing the necessary skills to start a small business: management skills, training skills and sometimes specific technical skills. Courses for people from voluntary organizations which aim to introduce some of the techniques of business management are put on. Sometimes employees are seconded to organizations in disadvantaged areas.

Sometimes commercial organizations like to gain some short-term recognition for this work and their names are attached to particular projects. There is certainly nothing wrong with this. Some, however, see such activities as a long-term investment. For the success of industry and commerce depends in the end upon a flourishing wider community. So as A. B. Cleaver puts it:

> Business is the wealth creator in society, but to do so it needs a healthy and flourishing environment in which to operate. *To assist in the creation of a prosperous and balanced society is not only good for society, it is good for the long-term future of industry and commerce . . .* There are very sound commercial reasons for the exercise of social responsibility [italics in original].

As such a quotation makes clear, the tone of business is markedly different from what it was even ten years ago. They wish to convince themselves and the wider public that they are taking their moral and social responsibilities seriously. How much of this is just whitewashing and how far is it a reality? A conference of the European Business Ethics Network, which was held in Spain towards the end of 1989, criticized companies for ducking the more difficult ethical issues and for the way codes were not in fact always enforced. The President of Nestlé's Spanish off-shoot raised eyebrows by making a speech on 'ethics in the corporation', which failed even to mention his parent company's much-criticized promotion of powdered baby milk in developing countries suffering from contaminated water supplies.[5]

The inadequacies of many corporate codes of ethics in the face of real business situations came through strongly. For example, it was reported that a quarter of European countries with codes failed to circulate them to external interest groups and even to all employees. Many companies lack effective mechanisms to enforce their codes. Many codes give little, if any, guidance about how to behave in markets in countries where corruption or other malpractice is the norm. In short, many codes were seen as little more than window dressing.

More and more European companies are introducing their own codes although Europe is still behind the United States. There, about 75 per cent of companies have them. In the UK, France and Germany about 40 per cent are believed to have had them by 1988. This is a rise compared with the 14 per cent who had them in 1984. However, there is still a major gap between their existence and their effectiveness in many spheres.

There has been a dramatic change from the days when some industrial magnate or business tycoon regarded his company as entirely his own possession with which he could do what he liked. Ownership is now usually shared among many shareholders. At the same time it has become increasingly recognized that the shareholder is just one group among others, all of whom have a vital stake in the success of the business. We have moved from shareholders to stakeholders, the five main stakeholders being the shareholder, the customer, the employee, the business associate and the wider community. This is increasingly recognized in theory. The practice still has a long way to go in order to match up to the stated policy.

A major conference of industrialists, academics and politicians from Europe and the United States welcomed the new emphasis upon business ethics but was not sanguine about the prospects of any early recovery in business morality.

> They saw the new emphasis on ethics of business schools as a necessary but insufficient move in the right direction. Scepticism about the effectiveness of self-regulations was also marked, especially among the Americans present.

Some companies still take the attitude expressed by Milton Friedman that 'the one and only social responsibility of business is to increase its profits'. However, an encouragingly large number of vanguard companies do now take the stakeholder approach, summed up in a quotation from the constitution of Dayton Hudson, an American retailing group:

> The business of business is serving society, not just making money. Profit is our reward for serving society well. Indeed, profit is the means and measure of our service – not an end in itself.

This conference also brought out the vital connection between morality and law. Once anti-social practices become illegal, executives can no longer make the excuse that they have to engage in them for their business to remain competitive.[6]

In recent years there has been a great deal of disquiet about the alleged fall in moral standards in the City of London. One experienced City solicitor alleges that there is a thin red line of solicitors holding the ground against a massed army of accountants. Others maintain that the City's traditional reputation for integrity and financial probity, though severely shaken by a number of scandals, remains essentially intact. All are agreed that regulations are necessary.[7] But though essential, they are not by themselves enough. A participant at a conference on 'Ethics and the City'[8] argued that 'legislation could never be as effective as a standard of conduct so firmly ingrained in the corporate identity that it becomes almost unthinkable for any employee of that company to break it'. He quoted the example of Unilever's company policy of not bribing, even in cultures which consider bribes as a normal part of business life. Furthermore, as another participant emphasized, the mere presence of a corporate culture, though essential, is not sufficient. 'Once a company, like any other social group, has reached a certain size, complexity, and turnover of personnel, there must be ways and means of transmitting that culture.'

In the past, professional bodies, with their codes of conduct, have been important transmitters of moral values. In our own society, increasingly polarized between state action on the one hand and isolated individualism on the other, the role of intermediate communities of all kinds in preserving and shaping a moral outlook is increasingly crucial. Major companies, with their vast power and increasing influence, have a major role to play in maintaining and transmitting high standards of business practice. Many Christians are already active in this field. So, too, are some Jews and Muslims, for both Judaism and Islam have a long tradition of business ethics.[9] As business ethics is an expression of natural law morality, building on those values which people of all faiths and none have in common, the co-operation of businessmen from different religious traditions is a highly possible and worthwhile endeavour, with ramifications far outside the business sphere itself.

Transnational corporations (TNCs), on which there has been a great deal written in recent years, pose special problems. They are a relatively recent phenomenon, really emerging only after the Second World War, and their sheer size is staggering. Between 80 and 90 per cent of the exports of the United States and the United Kingdom are associated with TNCs. The combined sales of the top 200 TNCs in 1986 were equivalent to around 31 per cent of the non-socialist world's gross national product. Between three and six TNCs account for 90 per cent of total world exports of wheat, corn, coffee, fresh pineapples, forest products, cotton, tobacco, jute and iron ore. Because of what has been described as a merger and takeover mania many of these vast TNCs are getting bigger still. As just one example, by no means the most extreme, in 1985 Nestlé offered $4,000 million for the British confectionery company Rowntree, which was more than the gross domestic product (GDP) of Paraguay, Costa Rica or Bolivia.[10]

It is wrong to demonize transnational corporations, as some tend to. But their economic muscle, which is often vast in relation to the poor countries in which they operate, needs to have the same checks and balances as any power anywhere. Because these companies are transnational, capable of moving their paper assets swiftly from one country to another, they are that much more difficult to regulate. Transnational corporations are so vast they provide a culture in themselves. As has been stressed, this can provide high standards for employees. Yet, as the World

Council of Churches study on transnational corporations emphasized, there are often assumptions and presuppositions in this corporate culture that need to be brought out and subjected to a critical examination. For example, there is a presupposition that there is a basic natural harmony between the goals of industry and the interests of society as a whole. Many Christians who work for transnational corporations can play their part with others in creating and sustaining a corporate culture in which moral integrity in the business sphere is regarded as the norm. They can also do their part in refusing to accept uncritically all the assumptions and presuppositions of TNCs. In particular, they will want to look at their effect on the economies and environments of the poorest countries in the world.[11]

Since the advent of the Industrial Revolution a good number of Christians, of all denominations, have been active both theoretically and practically in trying to devise forms of industrial life that are less divisive and harmful than we have had so far. Most recently, Professor Charles Handy, giving due acknowledgement to George Goyder,[12] has argued that we need legal recognition that a company is a community of people, which exists in its own right, and which can therefore plan for its future on a long-term basis.[13] While recognizing that profits are essential, he criticizes the concept on which he was brought up in American Business School, that the aim of business is always to maximize profits. Profits are a yardstick but profits exist for something else. Like others, he is concerned about short-termism, the way investors buy and sell shares without any consideration of what is needed by way of investment for the long-term profitability of the company.[14] He also notes the large number of takeovers in British industry. During the ten years 1972–82 one-third of the biggest 730 quoted companies in Britain changed ownership. The comparable figure for Japan was under 8 per cent and in Germany of the 450 companies quoted on the stock exchange only 30 or so are actively traded. Professor Handy would like to see the development of the 'existential corporation'. By this he means the corporation whose principal purpose is to fulfil itself, to grow and develop to the best that it can be. 'It is not a piece of property, inhabited by humans, it is a community, which itself has property.' In short, instead of shareholders owning the company, with certain limited rights to others involved, the company itself needs to be recognized as a legal entity, with shareholders having a rather more restricted role. This would necessitate some kind of board of trustees, as well as directors. Professor Handy, like others, looks to some Japanese and German companies which are able to engender a high degree of employee loyalty and to plan seriously for a long-term future. He also argues that stakeholder interests will not count unless they can be counted seriously. More work needs to be done here in order to ensure that that is the case.

Japanese companies suffer from stereotypes which many British people find instinctively antipathetic. However, those who go to Japan to investigate Japanese companies at first hand are often highly impressed. No doubt there is a very great deal that British business can learn from them. The problem, however, lies elsewhere. First, in Japan those who do not belong to one of the major companies as part of their core workforce, such as day labourers, have a very hard time. Furthermore, within Japanese society certain classes of people, such as the Koreans, are marginalized and oppressed.[15] Secondly, however admirable a transnational corporation might be for its employees, there remain wider questions in relation to society as a whole and the impact of that company on that society.

The way that companies in recent years have moved towards the concept of stakeholders, rather than simply shareholders, many of them adopting admirable mission statements, is encouraging. It is also encouraging that many Christians in the business world are challenging traditional ways of doing things and seeking to bring about changes in the nature of companies, which not only could lead to greater prosperity but which are in greater accord with principles of natural justice.[16] These are technical matters, into which no pretence is made of entering here. The point is that many changes have taken place and are taking place, partly as a result of the efforts of Christian businessmen. Such people have not confined their Christianity to the sphere of personal relationships. They have sought to make company structures and the business environment as a whole conform more nearly to the standards of God's Kingdom. They have sought to work out their Christian discipleship in corporate and financial terms, as well as inward and personal ones. Jesus Christ is Lord of public limited companies and transnational corporations as well as of states and persons. Serving him in these spheres means trying to make the company ethos and the financial environment genuinely serve human ends both for those within the company and for those in the society where the company is set. Today that society is worldwide and includes the unborn generations, who must also be borne in mind.

NOTES

1 A. B. Cleaver, *The Social Responsibilities of Business* (IBM, 1987).
2 Sir Hector Laing (now Lord Laing), *The Balance of Responsibility* (United Biscuits, 1987). See also *Ethics and Operating Principles* (United Biscuits, 1987).
3 Arthur Miller, *Time Bends: a Life* (Methuen, 1987), p. 191.
4 The Ecumenical Committee for Corporate Responsibility, *Churches, Companies and Share Ownership* (1989).
5 *Financial Times* (13 November 1989).
6 Tony Thomas, 'Market pressures', *The Tablet* (3 December 1988). This was one of five articles in a series on 'A moral agenda for business'.
7 Jack Mahoney, 'Christian perspectives on business ethics', *Studies in Christian*

Ethics, 2, no. 1 (T. & T. Clark, 1989). Frank McHugh, 'A bibliography of business ethics', ibid.

8 *Ethics and the City*, St Catherine's Conference Report no. 23, available from Cumberland Lodge, The Great Park, Windsor, Berkshire SL4 2HP.

9 For example see Sir Monty Finniston, 'The Jewish business ethic', a lecture given to Muslims, Christians and Jews at St George's House, Windsor, in 1987.

10 Rob van Drimmelen, 'The gospel of big business', *The Christian Action Journal* (Winter 1990).

11 Ronald Preston, admitting that he holds no particular brief for transnational corporations, writes that 'Their public accountability is a major question of concern. Shareholders can have little effective control; only Governments are in a position to exercise checks on their powers, and in certain circumstances they can be more powerful than Governments. Some form of international supervision is needed. The evidence on what they do is mixed. There are good and bad points, and there is little agreement among those, Christians included, who investigate them on the verdict to be passed. Those in the Third World are apt to find them a scapegoat for all their woes. Yet four fifths of the Third World is beyond the scope of their activities (their impact is mainly in cities) and most of their trade is within the First World': *Christianity and the Ambiguity of Capitalism* (SCM, 1991), p. 166.

12 George Goyder, *The Just Enterprise* (André Deutsch, 1987).

13 Charles Handy, 'What is a company for?', *RSA Journal* (March 1991).

14 Michael Novak, *Free Persons and the Common Good* (Madison Books, 1989).

15 Report of a visit by the Revd Canon Ron Mitchinson, Oxford Diocesan Industrial Missioner, to Japan at the end of 1990.

16 Kenneth Adams argues that the whole question of limited liability needs to be looked at afresh. Before the nineteenth century unlimited liability was normal, as it still is for partnerships and members of Lloyds. Limited liability was a great privilege granted by the community in the nineteenth century to those who chose to invest in shares in limited liability companies. It meant that the worst that could happen to them was to lose the current value of their shares. Limited liability leads to limited responsibility on the part of those who own a company, i.e. the shareholders, and this may be a factor in creating the 'irresponsible shareholder'. Those who are granted special privileges, as are those with limited liability, are normally required to accept special responsibilities.

10

For Investors

The traditional ban on usury

People sometimes accuse the Church of having or having had a negative attitude towards sex. But its hostility to usury has been often more pronounced. For 1,700 years, among both Catholics and Protestants, usury was singled out for particular condemnation. All this has now gone. Lending money on interest is taken for granted as one of the basic procedures of the world economy. It raises the question: why was the Church so fierce in its denunciation of usury over such a long period? Was it all based on a misunderstanding, or is there some important ethical insight that we should be recovering today?

There is no doubt that the Church's traditional condemnation of usury was in significant measure based on a mistake or, to be more exact, two mistakes, one philosophical and the other in biblical interpretation.

Underlying much of the Church's hostility to usury right through at least until Calvin, in the Protestant Churches and even later in the Roman Catholic Church, is the view of Aristotle, whom the Church, at least after Aquinas, took to be the philosophical guide. Aristotle reflected on nature and noted how everything had the capacity to reproduce itself.[1] Trees put forth buds and leaves, sheep gave birth to lambs, hens laid eggs and so on. In contrast to this, money left to itself produced nothing. It was sterile, barren. Its sole function was as a medium of exchange. For this reason, a mere passage of time did not add to the value of money. Passage of time enabled cows to give birth to calves and plants to scatter seed. They multiplied. But nothing happened to money. It was worth no more at the end of a period than at the beginning. So Shylock in Shakespeare's *Merchant of Venice* refers to that 'breed of barren metal'.[2] For the theologians of the early and mediaeval Church, therefore, simply lending money to someone could not entail interest. All lenders could do was ask for the same sum back at the end that they had lent in the beginning.

Aristotle's comparison is clearly an inappropriate one. Of course money does not reproduce itself in the way that living organisms can. However, money can be productive. It enables people to buy a farm or farm implements. It enables people to begin a business, invest in machinery, hire skilled labour. Money has the capacity to get things done, it is a form of power, it is potentially productive. Nevertheless, Aristotle's negative attitude to lending money on interest prevailed and drastically influenced Christian thinking on this subject over the centuries.

There is no doubt that the Hebrew scriptures condemn some kinds of lending money and goods on interest. Just a few of the key texts are:

> If you lend money to any of my people with you who is poor, you shall not be to him as a creditor, and you shall not exact interest from him. If ever you take your neighbour's garment in pledge, you shall restore it to him before the sun goes down; for that is his only covering, it is his mantle for his body; in what else shall he sleep? And if he cries to me, I will hear, for I am compassionate. (Exodus 22.25–27)

> You shall not lend upon interest to your brother, interest on money, interest on victuals, interest on anything that is lent for interest. To a foreigner you may lend upon interest, but to your brother you shall not lend upon interest; that the Lord your God may bless you in all that you undertake in the land which you are entering to take possession of it. (Deuteronomy 23.19–20)

> And if your brother becomes poor, and cannot maintain himself with you, you shall maintain him; as a stranger and a sojourner he shall live with you. Take no interest from him or increase, but fear your God; that your brother may live beside you. You shall not lend him your money at interest, nor give him your food for profit. I am the Lord your God, who brought you forth out of the land of Egypt to give you the land of Canaan, and to be your God. (Leviticus 25.35–38. See also Nehemiah 5.7, 10; Psalm 15.5; Proverbs 28.8; Ezekiel 18.8; etc.)

These sayings are set against the background of a predominantly agricultural economy. What they have in mind is the poor man who has to borrow out of dire necessity. It may be that he has to borrow simply to keep alive or in order to purchase seed for next year's crops. In any case, interest would come as one more burden for him to bear. It is this that is forbidden. The situation is totally different from that of a modern company, wanting to expand its business, and therefore borrowing from a bank on terms that are totally agreeable to both partners. The partners meet as equals, there is no question of any individual being crushed and the money is borrowed not in order to keep alive but to bring enhanced prosperity all around.

Unfortunately, moral theologians, canonists and Church councils, in condemning usury on the basis of these texts, failed to take into account the context in which the teaching was given. That teaching is as relevant today as it was then. However, it is not universally applicable to totally different situations. With the rise of a mercantile society in the Roman, Byzantine and mediaeval European world, people wanted to borrow for business reasons, not only out of dire necessity. It is hardly surprising, then, that when the Church went on repeating its traditional condemnation of usury throughout the sixteenth, seventeenth, eighteenth centuries and even part of the nineteenth century, in some places, at a time when lending money on interest was absolutely basic to the newly emergent capitalism, that teaching should quickly have fallen into disrepute and have been forgotten.

There still remains the question of whether, despite the mistaken philosophical basis and the mis-reading of scripture, there are any fundamental insights in the Church's traditional teaching on usury that need to be recovered for today. Most obviously what the Hebrew scriptures had to say about not lending on interest to the poor is directly applicable to the situation of so many underdeveloped countries today, crippled as they are by debt. This point is considered further in the next chapter. More generally, however, another point emerges. There need to be good reasons for lending money on interest. We are stewards of the resources that God has given us, and money constitutes power to get things done. We cannot simply do what we like with what we mistakenly think of as our own. There need to be sound reasons for doing what we do.

Although the Church fiercely condemned usury, people did of course go on lending money on interest and the Church found various ways of justifying this. Some of these will now be considered. The implication behind them all is that there needs to be a good, moral reason to back up what we do with our money.

The early Fathers were unanimous in their condemnation of usury, as were the early ecclesiastical legislators, the first canonical prohibition coming from the Council of Elvira in the year 306. In the beginning this prohibition applied only to clerics but by the ninth century it was forbidden to all.[3]

In the twelfth century there was an economic revival which required money to be in circulation. Lending went on with great vigour, disguised under one of the extrinsic titles, as they were called. Eventually three main titles emerged. The first was *Damnum Emergens* (literally 'injury appearing'). This referred to the actual monetary loss incurred through making a loan, though this had to be proved. Compensation had to be paid from the first day of the loan, before the delay was actually experienced, provided it could be shown that the loss was clearly established. This form of compensation was never seriously questioned by scholastic moralists. The second was *Lucrum Cessans* (literally 'gain ceasing'), which referred to the profit forgone. Scholastic moralists were much slower to give their assent to this and Aquinas did not approve of it. There was, thirdly, *Periculum Sortis* ('risk of chance'). The receipt of a surplus in excess of the capital was also justified if the lender risked the loss of part or all his original sum. In this way, loans on interest could be made to owners of ships.

In 1462 the Franciscans in Orvieto inaugurated the Monti di Pietà, whereby funds were collected to provide credit facilities for the poor. Eventually they had to charge a sum to borrowers to defray the expenses of the operation. This was attacked by the Dominicans but eventually allowed by the Fifth Lateran Council, which gave as the definition of usury, 'when gain is sought from the use of a thing not fruitful in itself (as a flock or a field), without labour, expense or risk on the part of the lender'. Thus fierce condemnations of usury, together with sophisticated justifications for lending money on interest under certain circumstances, continued together.

At the Reformation the whole subject was opened up again. Luther's thinking went through various stages. Calvin's was more consistent, as well as being more radical by the standards of the time.[4] Calvin wrote: 'If we wholly condemn usury we impose tighter fetters on the conscience than God himself.' Scriptures forbid only biting usury, usury taken from the defenceless poor. In Deuteronomy 23.19, God had no other object in view: 'Except that mutual and brotherly affection should prevail amongst the Israelites'. The precept to lend without usury was for the Israelites and not a universal spiritual law, or else God would not have allowed the Jews to lend at usury to Gentiles. God has permitted many things that are in themselves not good, and therefore he did not mean to legitimize the taking of usury from strangers. He merely left it unpunished. Among themselves the Jews were to relate in fraternal brotherhood without usury. In relating to the Gentile world they could operate the same standards as prevailed in that world, namely taking interest on money.

In applying the teaching of the Hebrew scriptures to Christians today, in their very different circumstances, Calvin argued, first, that the specific teaching for the Jewish people having been abrogated, there remained the basic rules of charity, equity and justice out of which the specific concern for the needy comes.

> The Law of Moses (Deuteronomy 23.19) is political, and does not obligate us beyond what equity and the reason for humanity suggest. Surely, it should be desirable if usuries were driven from the whole world, indeed that the word be unknown. But since that is impossible, we must make concession to the common utility.

Although other texts in the Bible seem to condemn usury as such and not simply harsh usury directed against the poor, usury does not in fact conflict with the law of God in every case. On the other hand, it must not be assumed that usury can be allowed indiscriminately at all times, under all forms for everybody; one who takes usury constantly has no place in the Church of God and interest taken from the poor is always prohibited. In short, it is important to cling to the rule: usury is permissible if it is not injurious to one's brother.

In facing the objection that usury should be outlawed among Christians for the same reason that it was forbidden to Jews, 'because among us there is a fraternal union', Calvin's reply is of great consequence:

> There is a difference in the political union, for the situation in which God placed the Jews and many other circumstances permitted them to trade conveniently among themselves without usuries. Our union is entirely different. Therefore I do not feel that usuries were forbidden to us simply, except in so far as they are opposed to equity or charity.

Again:

> Usury is not now unlawful, except insofar as it contravenes equity and brotherly union. Let each one, then, place himself before God's judgement seat, and not do to his neighbour what he would not have done to himself, from whence a sure and infallible decision may be come to. To exercise the trade of usury, since heathen writers counted it amongst disgraceful and base modes of gain, is much less tolerable among the children of God; but in what cases, and how far it may be lawful to receive usury upon loans, the law of equity will better prescribe than any lengthened discussion.

So although Calvin still had a traditional distaste for the full-time professional usurer, he recognized that taking interest on a loan in the course of business could be perfectly in accord with the will of God. The cardinal principle for Calvin was that it should not offend equity, charity and brotherly union. It should not be injurious to our brothers.

In England usury permitting 10 per cent interest on loans was legalized by an Act of Parliament of 1545, an Act repealed in 1552. But a fresh Act in 1751 made a distinction between interest above and below 10 per cent. In short, the distinction between what was allowable and what was not became one of degree, not kind, a change of attitude that R. H. Tawney regarded as momentous.

In the seventeenth century, the group of moral thinkers known as the Caroline Divines were much exercised by usury. Bishop Joseph Hall of Norwich, for example, argued that we should give to the very poor, lend freely to the poor, but that when a rich person was borrowing for his own advantage there was no reason why he should make a profit at someone else's expense. Hall preferred a voluntary agreement between the borrower and the lender rather than adherence to a system of set interest, though if there was some risk involved in the loan then the set interest was allowable. Distancing himself from the view of Aristotle, he believed that money was a commodity, in some respects like any other, and profits are made on commodities when they are bought and sold.

Despite all this, Hall still wanted to make a sharp distinction between usury and legitimate lending of money. Usury is unlawful 'both by law natural and positive, both divine and human'. But it is legitimate to lend money for interest in order to compensate for the loss sustained or any gains that are missed — a clear reference to *Damnum Emergens* and *Lucrum Cessans*. The rule is charity: 'Whatsoever is not a violation of charity cannot be unlawful; and whatsoever is not agreeable to charity can be no other than sinful. And as charity must be your rule, so yourself must be the rule of your charity.'[5] We must do as we would be done by. It is charity that enables us to distinguish loans that are legitimate from usury, though we must beware of self-indulgence, injustice and hypocrisy, of which there is much in this area.

Sanderson, another Caroline Divine, also regarded usury as odious. He distinguished it from legitimate lending money on interest but admitted that this was a fine distinction which only circumstances could reveal. There is legitimate interest when the money might be put to good use elsewhere and if there is kindness, in which case it is both lawful and an act of charity. Usury occurs when a person intends to live upon the money, making a fixed rate and considering only how much is coming in. Yet even here he admitted that it was justified for those who are ill and who cannot work. He advised the purchase of annuities instead but admitted that there was not much difference from receiving interest on a loan.

Sanderson argued that we should give away some money, lend some freely and only then lend some with interest. We should go for a moderate return, less than the law allows, the return depending on how safe the money is. It might seem similar to usury but lending money on interest in this way is less obnoxious to the lender and the manner of payment will be made easier.

When lending to great merchants we only need to see that we do them no harm. However, we need to examine ourselves to make sure we are not lending to them out of greed instead of lending to those with whom we have nearer obligations. He gives as an example young tradesmen, who might need a loan to begin or expand their business. Lending to them is a greater act of charity than lending to a great merchant.[6]

The dislike of usury has gone deep into Christian consciousness. In 1822 a penitent in Lyons who had been refused absolution for receiving interest on invested property appealed to Rome and the case was decided by the Holy Office against the confessor. Thirteen similar decisions were made in the course of the nineteenth century. However, the general theme of these was that if the faithful lend money for a moderate interest lay people are 'not to be disturbed'. The general theoretical question of usury was left unresolved. Canons that deal with the subject in the twentieth century have been interpreted in various ways.

The fierce hostility of the Churches to usury, coupled with all kinds of sophisticated qualifications to allow lending on interest in practice, has been unhelpful from the point of view of the credibility of the Churches in this sphere. It all seemed too remote, too complex and too like unnecessary hair-splitting for the average businessman. Nevertheless, something was being preserved by this tradition. It is that the money we have is given us by God to do good. Who then, we might say, is a usurer? Someone whose sole concern is to find the maximum return on his money so that he can live idly off the fat of the land for the rest of his days. In contrast to this, someone trying to be obedient to Christ will regard his money as a trust. As both Joseph Hall and Sanderson taught: he will give some away. He will consider lending some without interest to those in real need. Because, like most people today, he will need money to live on in retirement, he will lend at ordinary rates of interest. But this too will be done in charity, with equity. There may be businesses that need support, where there is some element of risk. Receiving a return on his money will be part of a balanced, responsible and Christian approach to the use of his resources, bearing in mind the needs not only of himself and his dependents but of others as well.

Ethical investment

The almost universally prevailing attitude towards the economic order in our own time is to regard it as a morally neutral sphere in which there is money to be made or lost. This attitude, the culmination of a movement which began in the seventeenth century, if not earlier, would have been quite unthinkable to the majority of Christians in previous ages. Now, however, there are just the beginnings of a welcome return to considering investment in other than purely financial terms. Ethical investment is an idea whose time is beginning to come. Its origin can be traced to the ferment in America during the 1970s, though the University of Yale had pioneered the issue earlier. First raised in 1968, it was examined thoroughly at a university seminar which went on through 1969 and 1970. Conclusions of the seminar were incorporated into a book, *The Ethical Investor*, and were later adopted by the University's governing body. Dissatisfaction with the Vietnam War and the role of the military–industrial complex, the impact of Rachel Carson's book *Silent Spring*, describing the damage to the environment caused by the chemical industry, the critical study by Ralph Nader on automobile safety, and the civil rights movement as it related to employment practices were but some of the many influences which served to shape this new climate. Public interest groups began to spring up, American churches and universities and trade unions began to scrutinize their investments, and the first ethical funds were launched in response to demand from discriminating investors.

In 1983 EIRIS (the Ethical Investment Research and Information Service) was founded in Britain.[7] There had previously been a great deal of thought as to what kind of service this should be, and whether it should be located in the Churches or not, but eventually it was founded as an entirely independent, self-financing research service. Since then it has gone from strength to strength. During the 1980s a number of new ethical investment trusts were founded and now a new one seems to appear every few months. Some are governed by negative criteria, such as no involvement in South Africa, the nuclear arms industry, tobacco, alcohol or research involving animals. More recently, trusts have been founded which emphasize a positive contribution to the environment and conservation.

The present tendency is for ethical investment trusts (EITs), both old and new, to stress both negative and positive criteria. Findings indicate that this is what people want. A natural question for people to ask is whether investing in portfolios with ethical considerations will result in a lower yield or return. Indeed, some seem to have a vested interest in suggesting that this will be so. But a growing body of research indicates that investment in portfolios with ethical criteria stands up to financial scrutiny. EIRIS, for example, examined the record of eight index portfolios for a period of five years up to October 1988. During this period the yield on the FT all-share index was 4.36 per cent and the cumulative return on the portfolio over the five years 161.1. Some EITs did slightly worse than this. At least two did better. Portfolio 1, for example, which excluded all company groups which had any subsidiary or associate interest in South Africa (i.e. held more than 10 per cent of the equity of any company registered in South Africa), had a slightly lower yield at 4.08 per cent, but a higher cumulative return at 166.2. Portfolio 8, which had criteria relating to South Africa, nuclear weapons and tobacco, had a yield of 4.38 per cent and a return over the five years of 169.2, higher in both instances. In 1989 the Christian Ethical Investment Group (CEIG) was founded to support a stronger ethical investment policy in the Church.[8]

The Christian basis for ethical investment is both simple and sure. The money we have been given is to do good with. This includes good to our families and ourselves. But it also includes good for the wider community. We have this money on trust from God to further his purposes. Furthermore, money is power, and through our money we can actually change things for the better as well as avoid making matters worse. Many champions of the market economy are now arguing that it needs a moral basis. Part of that moral basis must include ethical criteria in investment. It is therefore somewhat surprising that neither Brian Griffiths nor Donald Hay discusses the subject, despite the fact that morality is basic to their approach. Yet there is here an untapped market, as shown by the *Which?* survey in February 1989 on ethical trusts. This revealed that 51 per cent of those interviewed strongly disagreed with investing in firms with any connection with nuclear weapons, 40 per cent in companies involved in tobacco products, 39 per cent in companies with associations with South Africa and so on. In short, there exists a large gap between the percentage of the market occupied by ethical investment trusts and those who say that they have very strong ethical feelings about certain areas. Friends Provident Stewardship Trust (the eighteenth largest of a total of 204 funds) grew by 14 per cent in the six months to 1 January 1990 compared to a 6 per cent decline in the section overall. In the United States of America since the mid-1970s ethical investment has been a growing area. Now all the major universities and church bodies take it for granted that ethical considerations will be taken into account in investments. In the seventeenth century there was a swing from one extreme in which usury was officially banned to the other when financial considerations were the only ones that mattered. It may now be that at long last the pendulum will begin to swing back towards the middle and we can have a more discriminating ethical approach.[9]

Inevitably in a free democratic society people care about different issues. One American stockbroker that specializes in socially responsive investing gives the following list of issues which are monitored in relation to corporations that have shares on the stock exchange.[10]

Corporate citizenship
Formal code of ethical conduct
Charitable contributions
Community outreach programmes
Facilities in underprivileged areas
Loans to underprivileged neighbourhoods

Environment
Corporate committee to monitor and reduce company impact on environment
Air and water pollution control
Proper hazardous waste disposal
Effects of company or products on ozone layer

Disclosure
Company willing to disclose information on social issues
Company has a formal social responsibility statement

Labour practices
Women on board of directors and in professional and upper management
Minorities on board of directors and in professional and upper management
Complies with affirmative action
Positive labour relations
Good safety record
Good employee benefits
Plant closings notification
Retraining and consulting for employees laid off

Military involvement
Top 100 defence contractors
Involvement with Strategic Defense Initiative (Star Wars)
Nuclear weapons production
Chemical or biological weapon production

Nuclear power
No more than 20 per cent in nuclear power production, on line or planned
Manufacturer of equipment used in nuclear energy

Contractor or subcontractor building nuclear plants

Northern Ireland
Follows MacBride principles or equivalent standards

Product categories
Birth control
Gambling services
Infant formula abuse
Liquor
Pornography
Tobacco
Toys promoting violence

South Africa
Direct investment
Indirect investment
Licensing agreements

This particular broker obtains its information on companies in relation to these issues from the Investor Responsibility Research Center.[11] In Britain EIRIS supplies a similar research service.

Portfolio managers with this American broker work directly with their clients first of all to review and discuss their moral and social criteria and then to obtain policy and portfolio guidelines for social criteria and financial goals, which are developed jointly. Clearly the situation is more complex for institutional investors. An individual will know what his or her own ethical convictions are. Within an institution or trustee body, there may very well be a variety of convictions. Nevertheless, this should not stop any corporate body taking ethical considerations into account. As they have to come to a corporate mind on a number of issues so they can and must on the ethical principles which should guide their investment policy.

A further complication arises with the possibility of a less advantageous return if certain sections of the stock market are eschewed or others are emphasized. An individual investor is fully entitled to receive a lower return on his or her money if he or she so wishes. A corporate body is not in the same position. Here the law enters in. Does the law require a charitable body, for example, always to strive for the maximum financial return? From the moral point of view it seems quite clear that if ethical principles are to be followed at all there may very well come a time when following them will incur some financial penalty. This has to be faced.

What the law allows or forbids will depend upon the legislation in different countries. In Great Britain there was a famous case concerning the pension fund of the Miners' Union. In *Cowan* v. *Scargill*, Sir Robert Megarry ruled that there was 'a duty of undivided loyalty to the beneficiaries', i.e. the pensioners of the fund. However, even in the case of pension funds, this is not likely to be the last word on the subject. In November 1989 in the case *Martin* v. *City of Edinburgh District Council*, Lord Murray argued that trustees should not simply rubber stamp the advice of their professional advisers. 'I cannot conceive that trustees have an unqualified duty . . . simply to invest Trust Funds in the most profitable investment available. To accept that without qualification would, in my view, involve substituting the discretion of financial advisers for the discretion of trustees.' In short, when trustees have received all the financial advice they need they still have to make their own judgement about the relationship between financial advantage and the overall interests of the body of which they are trustees.

Charitable bodies are not the same, legally speaking, as pension funds. A charitable body has a specific, non-financial purpose; for example, a temperance society exists in order to promote temperance, a cancer research society to promote cancer research, and so on. The 1987 report of the Charity Commissioners stated that the trustees of charitable bodies not only can but must take into account the purpose for which their charity was founded. 'We agree that, unlike a private trust, the purpose of which is solely to generate funds for its beneficiaries, a charity has a public purpose and object . . . charity trustees should not invest in companies pursuing activities which are directly contrary to the purposes or trusts of their charity, and they should have the discretion to decline to invest in companies pursuing activities which are inimical to its purposes.' In short, whereas the trustees of a pension fund or private trust have a duty of undivided loyalty to the beneficiaries, the trustees of a charitable trust owe a duty of undivided loyalty to the charitable purposes which their trust funds are there to promote or achieve, as Timothy Lloyd, QC, has put it. Even a moment's reflection reveals the truth of this. A temperance society, for example, must legally be able to avoid investing in the drinks industry, even if this means that it receives less than the maximum financial return. A cancer research organization must legally be able to avoid investing in tobacco, even if tobacco investments are highly profitable and more profitable than other forms of investment. In the case of charities there must be no discongruity, no contradiction between the central purpose of the charity and the area where it invests its funds.

In 1991 there was an important case in relation to the Church Commissioners. Over a number of years the General Synod of the Church of England called upon the Church Commissioners to disinvest from companies with a stake in the South African economy. The Church Commissioners responded by withdrawing its investments from companies that in their judgement had a major stake in South Africa, but refused to disinvest totally on the grounds that this would have restricted too much the number of companies from which they could receive a return. They have argued that to limit the market in which they could invest in this way would lead to unacceptably low financial returns. Furthermore, they have argued that they must by law follow 'a policy where financial considerations are paramount', as their 1985 Report puts it.

The Church Commissioners do already pursue an ethical investment policy. They do not, for example, invest in tobacco, drinks, newspapers or arms. They maintain that they are able to pursue this ethical policy without any financial loss. However, they judge that if they further restricted the area of the market where they could invest, their returns would fall and they are legally obliged to maximize their returns.

The purpose of the case was not to turn the Church Commissioners into a general charitable fund. They do indeed exist to raise money for the stipends and pensions of the clergy of the Church of England, so that the overall purpose of the Church of England might be promoted, a purpose that the Church Commissioners also have. But raising money to pay stipends and pensions is a means towards an end. For a charity, and especially a Christian charity, there must be no disjunction between the means and the end; the purpose and the means by which that purpose is effected must be all of a piece.

The case sought to determine whether the Church Commissioners are more akin to a private trust fund or a charitable body and whether, if they are the latter, an ethical investment policy in accord with the mind of the Church of England can be followed, even if it means a lower financial return than a policy that is not governed by such ethical considerations.[12]

This chapter has argued that though the traditional ban on usury was misconceived, there lies behind it an important principle, namely that our money is held in trust from God to do good with, good not only to ourselves and our immediate family, but for the wider community. Ethical investment, that is, investment that refuses to support financially companies that are harmful in one way or another and positively supports companies that take social, moral and environmental factors into consideration, is a proper form of Christian obedience in the use of our money.[13] It involves discrimination for both the private investor and a corporate body. But this is part of the maturity of judgement to which God is calling us. Corporate bodies are bound by the law but, it is argued, the law does not always oblige them to go for the maximum financial return. It is quite proper to take into account the overall purpose for which the body exists and to try to ensure that as far as possible there is no contradiction between that purpose and the activities of the companies from whom it derives its dividends.

NOTES

1 Aristotle, *The Politics*, ch. 1, 10.
2 *Merchant of Venice*, Act I, Scene 3.

3 For the history of the Church's attitude to usury see B. Nelson, *The Idea of Usury* (University of Chicago Press, 1969), and Thomas Divine, *Interest* (Marquette University, 1958).

4 For a discussion of the relevant texts in Calvin, see Nelson, ibid., pp. 75ff.

5 Bishop Joseph Hall, *Economics*, pp. 372–91: *The Works of Joseph Hall, DD*, Vol. VII (Talboys, Oxford, 1837).

6 *The Works of Robert Sanderson, DD*, Vol. V (OUP, 1954), pp. 127–36.

7 EIRIS (Ethical Investment Research and Information Service), 4.01 Bondway Business Centre, 71 Bondway, London SW8 1SQ.

8 Christian Ethical Investment Group. Secretary, Canon Bill Whiffen, 90 Booker Avenue, Bradwell Common, Milton Keynes, Bucks MK13 8EF.

9 'Ethical investment: an idea whose time has come', report of seminar (January 1991) available from EIRIS.

10 Scudder, Stevens and Clark, Inc., 345 Park Avenue, New York, NY 10154-0010.

11 Investor Responsibility Research Center, 1755 Massachusetts Avenue, NW, Suite 600, Washington, DC 20036.

12 Although the judge did not make the declarations requested by the plaintiffs, some significant points in favour of an ethical investment policy were made in the judgement. First, the judge agreed that there would be some cases, comparatively rare, which would conflict with the aims of the charity. If, in such instances, 'trustees were satisfied that investing in a company engaged in a particular type of business would conflict with the very object their charities were seeking to achieve, they should not so invest'. Secondly, a particular investment 'might hamper a charity's work, either by making potential recipients of aid unwilling to be helped because of the source of the charity's money, or by alienating some of those who support the charity financially'. Thirdly, trustees must not bring their charity into disrepute. They must act as responsible landlords and shareholders.

13 For a Jewish approach, Aaron Levine, *Economics and Jewish Law* (Yorkshire UP, NY, 1987), ch. 7. For an Islamic approach, Dr Muhammed Nejatullah Siddigi, *Rationale of Islamic Banking* (Oxford Centre for Islamic Studies, 1981).

11

The Cry of the Desperately Poor

The figures for desperate poverty in the world remain horrifying. The World Bank Report for 1990, the first that it has issued on the world's poor since 1980, reveals a situation which is quite appalling and getting worse. In 1985 more than one billion people, about a third of the population of the developing world, were living on less than US$370 (£216) a year, which is how the World Bank defines the poverty line. What these stark figures mean is suffering and death for millions. Life expectancy in sub-Saharan Africa is 50 years, while in Japan it is 80. Mortality among children under five in South Asia exceeds 170 deaths per thousand people, while in Sweden it is fewer than ten. Some 250,000 small children die from starvation or easily preventable illness every week.

The World Bank believes that with the right policies in place the number of poor could fall by some 300 million by the year 2000, to 825 million. But even if this target is achieved, 700 million people would still be living in abject poverty at the start of the twenty-first century.

In my files I have cuttings of various reports on world poverty over the years. They make gloomy reading. *The Times* on Monday, 25 August 1975 led on its front page with the headline 'Chilling figures of growing world poverty given by Bank'. On 17 August 1978 *The Times* headlined an article 'The growing legions of the world's poor'. On 30 December 1979 *The Observer* headlined its survey 'Decade of despair for earth's poor', quoting statistics from the Worldwatch Institute of the United Nations. It described how more than 40 Third World nations were ending the decade with lower per capita incomes than in 1980. The examples could be multiplied a thousand times.

In fact, it isn't all doom and gloom. Evidence points to some progress in reducing poverty, especially in the 1960s and 1970s. But in the 1980s, sometimes called 'the lost decade of the poor', the picture was mixed. The debt crisis and the international recession bore very heavily on some countries. Yet the situation in others did improve, especially in Asia, which saw sustained growth during the decade. In Latin America, sub-Saharan

Africa and Eastern Europe, on the other hand, poverty increased. The average Latin American's income has dropped by 9 per cent since 1980, the average African's by 25 per cent. One in every three Peruvian children is stunted because of malnutrition. Child deaths from hunger doubled in Zambia in the first half of the 1980s, while life expectancy fell in nine African countries. Poverty in Brazil increased sharply between 1981 and 1987.

All the Churches, together with the aid agencies, many of which are strongly supported by the Churches, have struggled to keep world poverty on the agenda. Both World Council of Churches and Roman Catholic statements have been highly critical of the world economic order and its failure to alleviate this terrible burden of human suffering, in some cases allowing it to become worse. The Churches themselves, however, have been criticized either for having a too simplistic view of complex matters or for having a totally false understanding of the causes of this poverty. One of the most astringent critics has been Professor Peter Bauer (now Lord Bauer).[1] He believes that Church statements, particularly Roman Catholic and papal ones, have promulgated four myths that are totally untrue. Those alleged myths will be considered. First, poverty is the result of injustice. 'Poor countries are poor because rich countries are rich.' This is not true, maintains Bauer. Similarly, the view that 'in Latin America the prosperity of the landowners, industrialists and merchants has been achieved at the expense of the poor' is totally misleading.

It must certainly be agreed, with Bauer and others, that the causes of poverty are various. Geography and climate are obvious factors. So too are natural resources and the political organization of the society. Sometimes whole areas are kept in abject poverty because of civil strife or war. There is also the cultural factor. Bauer's favourite example is the Chinese of Malaysia, who, despite being discriminated against, have always been more prosperous than the Malays themselves, because of their ambition and drive.

Brian Griffiths wants to stress the cultural and therefore also the underlying religious factors which make for a prosperous society. This is a point that should not be overlooked. In fairness though, if it is to be asserted that certain cultural characteristics lead to a materially prosperous society it may also be true that other factors lead to a more harmonious and balanced way of life. Behind the emphasis on injustice as the cause of continuing poverty in the Third World, Brian Griffiths sees lurking the influence of Lenin, who maintained that the relationship between the colonial or post-colonial world and its dependencies was bound to be exploitative. Griffiths argues that the international order, characterized by the opportunity for every nation to trade, is in essence fair.

The standpoint of this present book is that the market economy, both nationally and internationally, can indeed be underpinned by Christian values and that, whatever its faults, it is 'the worst system we've got –

except for all the others'. Furthermore, Marxism is fundamentally flawed from a Christian point of view, as has been exposed in numerous books, not so much because it is atheistic but on account of its fallacious view of human beings and the nature of the state. Nevertheless, certain aspects of Marxist analysis are not only valuable, they are essential. For Marxism reveals one way in which sin expresses itself in the economic order. According to the Christian faith, we live in a fallen world, in which every human operation is to some extent flawed. This is true not just of individual life but of government and of all forms of inter-group relationship. Such relationships are characterized not just by self-preservation and healthy competition but by aggrandizement and the will to power. One way in which Marxism went wrong was in thinking that everything is reducible to economic power. This is not so. It is the will to power which is basic, economic power being, in most situations, the dominant one. Nor can we ignore the reality of class. So it is necessary at one and the same time both to affirm the market economy as expressive of certain Christian values and to be sharply critical of the way that, without checks and balances, it will inevitably express a certain class or group interest at the expense of others.

One of the failures of Edward Norman,[2] in his critiques of Church thinking, is that he uses some Marxist analysis in order to reveal unacknowledged presuppositions and assumptions, but does not recognize that the values that are championed might at the same time have validity. For example, it is notorious that the value of freedom has served the interests of the rising bourgeoisie ever since the seventeenth century. It enabled them to free themselves from the shackles of medievalism and feudalism and to create a commercial society in which those who were free to initiate, invest and work would be suitably rewarded. Yet, however much it is true that the clarion call of freedom serves the interests of the middle classes, it remains a vital value for all classes. Marxist analysis, like any other sociological analysis, should enable us to be more aware of the element of self-interest or group interest in the values we espouse. But those values may remain utterly valid. The work of Reinhold Niebuhr is instructive and of abiding importance in this sphere. In *Moral Man and Immoral Society*[3] and numerous other writings he was able to have a more realistic, many thought cynical, view of the human factors at work, whether psychological, sociological, economic or political. At the same time, he robustly defended, none more so, the fundamental values expressed in Western liberal democracies.

In theory everything may operate according to the principles of a free market. A Latin American country grows a cash crop, say coffee, which it wants to sell and North America wants to buy. Banks are involved in lending money, commodity markets are involved in fixing prices, transnational corporations work with local businesses and land owners. These in their turn are enmeshed with the political ruling class. In this web of interactions the power of finance, international and national, linked in with the land-owning and political elite, means that the several hundred workers or so who work on a particular estate are relatively powerless, a human spar floating on the surface of strong economic and political currents. This means that without a whole series of most rigorous checks and safeguards and without concerted action, national and international, those who actually produce the crop are likely to be used by the system, perhaps even misused and certainly not properly taken into account.

So while on paper the system of international trading and finance might conform to the notion of a free market economy, in practice it has worked and is working, at least in some countries, to the disadvantage of the most disadvantaged. Surprisingly for one who stands in the tradition of reformed Christianity, Lord Griffiths has failed to take into account the factor of human sin. Markets are not impersonal mechanisms. They are operated by people, people with a will to power and an incipient drive to exploit.

The second myth that Lord Bauer seeks to uncover is that 'governments always act for the common good'. He quotes, or purports to quote, *Octagesimo Adveniens* of Pope Paul VI from 1971. In this encyclical the Pope sets out the proper vocation and responsibility of government. It does not imply that government always lives up to its ideal. Paragraph 46.1, from which Professor Bauer quotes, begins 'Political power . . . must have as its aim the achievement of the common good.' The paragraph goes on to affirm points with which Professor Bauer would wholeheartedly agree, such as the responsibility of individuals and groups within society to work for the common good, and how government is to respect their proper task. Nevertheless, government does have a task, which is proper to it. It is true that the style of papal encyclicals is sometimes in the indicative rather than the imperative mood. But it is quite clear from the context that what is being talked about is the proper vocation of government. It is perverse and absurd of Professor Bauer to misread this and attribute to the Pope the idea that government always perfectly fulfils its vocation of working for the common good. Nevertheless, government does have a proper vocation, one set out in the papal encyclicals. It is to look after the interests of the whole. In any society the powerful can be relied on to look after their own interests. So government quite properly will have a concern for those who are least able to look after themselves.

The third myth that Professor Bauer seeks to expose is that income distribution is always necessary, both nationally and internationally. He argues that most income distribution helps not the poor but the government, their immediate supporters and the middle class.

There is clearly some truth in this criticism of the way aid has been used in recent years. Too little has really helped the most destitute. But the aid agencies and the Churches have been among the foremost critics of the way that development has been approached in the past three decades. The development debate has been unceasing, with many changes of emphasis and fresh insights. But it is highly doubtful whether development can take place without money. The question at issue is how and where money should be applied. Nor, of course, is money all that is needed. But money, that is money redistributed from the wealthier parts of the world to the poorer parts and from the rich to the poor in a particular country, has potential for bringing about change, getting things done. Money is power. Aid is no substitute for improved terms of trade and a reformed economic order, but it can relieve immediate need and get worthwhile projects off the ground.

The fourth myth Professor Bauer locates is that land distribution is crucial. This is not so, he thinks. There is plenty of unused land available and prosperity does not depend on resources. Countries like Switzerland, with very few resources, are enormously prosperous. Economic strength varies with personal and cultural differences.

Again, there is some truth in this. But in predominantly poor rural communities, where the emphasis is quite properly agricultural, the ideal of every family having their own small farm, rather than being part of a collective or large estate owned by a single family, would seem to accord with the most elementary principles of economic justice, principles fully espoused, for example, in the Conservative government's policy of council house sales. G. K. Chesterton's ideal of every man with a plot of land and a cow is not an ignoble one. In a post-colonial situation, government action is inevitable if such an ideal is to be realized. In Brazil there are more than six million landless peasants. Without land they will simply make their way to the cities to add to the millions already squatting on the rubbish dumps. They do not have land because most of it is owned by a tiny minority.

A Christian approach to the desperate poverty of the world can begin by accepting, with whatever reservations, the economic framework in which we all now live. It is the one we have got for the foreseeable future so we have to make the best of it. As has been argued here, it also expresses and safeguards certain fundamental values. Nevertheless, a Christian approach will always seek to be alert to the way the most vulnerable are affected. Writing about the international economic system, Professor Griffiths writes: 'Within this framework exploitation is certainly possible but it depends on the evidence and not on the assumptions'.[4] It does indeed look to the evidence. But one Christian assumption, human sinfulness, means that unless steps are taken to counteract it, exploitation will inevitably creep into the system in one way or another.

The early Church was characterized by a generous sharing of resources. Without such sharing today no individual or church deserves the name Christian. But the point at issue is whether this sharing should be done simply at an individual level, through the aid agencies, or whether there should be concerted government and international action. Here, the Bible and Christian tradition combine to suggest that such action is not only necessary but obligatory. First of all, there is the teaching of the fourth-century Fathers that God created the goods of the earth for humanity as a whole. To give to someone in need is not to bestow charity but to meet an obligation, to render what is due to the person within the providence of God. Secondly, taxes, from which the money comes to fund aid programmes, should, provided there is no governmental waste, be welcomed. Taxes exist to bridge the gap between what we want in our best moments and the much lower standards that we habitually observe. In our best moments we want to feed the hungry and alleviate the terrible suffering of those experiencing malnutrition and disease. Yet the pressure of other interests usually leads us to respond less than wholeheartedly. Taxes ensure that what we want in our best moments is in fact carried through even if we become personally indifferent.[5] So money raised for development work by governments is not an unfair imposition. For our surplus is owed to the poor and in our best moments we recognize that we both want and ought to do all we can to help them.

The most crippling burden for many developing countries is not lack of resources, geography, climate, war or cultural inertia but the huge foreign debts. In 1988 Brazil owed 115 billion dollars, despite the fact that 176 billion dollars had been paid to service the debt in the previous sixteen years, from 1972 to 1988. The cost of servicing the debt in 1988 was 17 billion dollars. In human terms this means that interest payments on the debt in 1988 were approximately equal to the value of 266 million minimum wages, or 81,700 classrooms for 60 million pupils, or 7.7 million houses, sufficient to house 30 million people.

Everyone accepts that there is a prima facie obligation to pay back a loan and honour a debt. Furthermore, everyone can see that it is common prudence to do so. If debts are defaulted on, there will be little likelihood of further loans. Furthermore, defaulting can bring disaster on the debtor country itself. However, the debt for Brazil and so many other countries is in no way normal. We need to ask who took on the debt and for what purpose. What mandate did the government have and on what did they spend the money? The fact is that many of the regimes that have incurred huge debts have been corrupt. Sometimes they have been military dictatorships, at other times totally unrepresentative elites. Too often the money has been spent on prestige projects. Too little has been used to meet the real needs of the poorest sections of society.

In the case of a family with an alcoholic father who has got in debt, there is in most people a desire to help the children, to stop the children suffering even more as a result of their father. It is above all the children who are suffering in so many developing countries. In Brazil it has been reckoned that about 55 per cent of children below the age of five are suffering from malnutrition. The cause of death for 69 per cent of children who died below the age of five was again malnutrition. In 1987 there were approximately sixteen million abandoned children. The children are

suffering and whatever our ordinary sense of obligation suggests and prudence advises, their crying need must override other considerations. As
Julius Nyerere put it: 'If you can pay debt, pay: it is honourable to pay
debt. If you cannot afford, it is a sin to pay. It is immoral to repay loans
and leave children starving.'

Responsibility for the vast debts incurred by the developing countries is
not simply that of the countries themselves. The whole international economic system has worked against the developing world and this is primarily
the responsibility of the developed nations. Furthermore, those nations
have had a vested interest, over a long period, in lending as much money
as possible to whoever they could persuade to borrow it.

At the end of the Second World War 44 leading countries came together
in order to agree certain financial measures to prevent the kind of spiralling
devaluation that led to inflation and prepared the way for the Nazis.[6] This
Bretton Woods Agreement, as it was known, had a number of pillars, such
as fixed currency in relation to gold or the dollar, and the emphasis on
free trade brought about in 1948 by the GATT (General Agreement on
Tariffs and Trade). However, in the 1960s matters began to go badly
wrong. The huge cost of the Vietnam War was financed not by taxes but
by huge budget deficits. This led to inflation and interest rates were pushed
up. President Nixon abandoned the gold/dollar exchange. The dollar fell
and all Western currencies were also allowed to fall. Many developing
countries lost out on this. However, the OPEC countries (Organization of
Petroleum Exporting Countries) took steps to counteract the fall by raising
the price of oil in 1973 from eight to seventeen dollars a barrel. This was
a severe blow to the international economy. But it meant that the oil-
producing countries had a great deal of money to lend. With the second
oil price shock in 1979 this was even more so. From 1975 to 1982 banks
were desperately looking for borrowers and they bombarded developing
countries with offers of loans. At the same time, oil prices in the West
pushed up prices. Inflation took off and governments responded by tight
controls on the money supply which pushed the world economy ever deeper
into recession.

This is only part of the story but it is enough to show how vast economic
forces, triggered off by decisions in the developed world and the oil producing countries, increased the problem of malnutrition, disease and death
among children in so many countries of the world.

The Christian tradition suggests a number of considerations which need
to be borne in mind when this debt is considered. First of all, there is the
fundamental principle running through the Hebrew scriptures that the
earth belongs to the Lord and we are his stewards. One of the most
dramatic expressions of this was the year of Jubilee described in Leviticus
25. According to this teaching, every 50 years land which had accumulated
was to be returned to its original owners, so that everyone had a share.

The land shall not be sold in perpetuity, for the land is mine; for you are strangers and sojourners with me. And in all the country you possess, you shall grant a redemption of the land. (Leviticus 25.23–24)

But if he [the poor person] has not sufficient means to get it back for himself, then what he sold shall remain in the hand of him who bought it until the year of Jubilee; in the Jubilee it shall be released, and he shall return to his property (Leviticus 25.28)

Economic structures exist for people and not the other way round. The Christian faith asserts the supreme value of the person. It is people, in particular the millions of children, who have priority in relation to any other obligations there might be. The whole of the Bible witnesses to the paramount value of people, particularly those in need. This is not to deny that claims often conflict and hard decisions have to be made. Nor is it to deny that sometimes an impersonal order or structure will result in the short-term suffering for some as a price to be paid for the long-term benefit of the whole. But when human suffering is on such a vast scale, when what is intended to benefit has clearly not benefited but made matters worse, the overriding priority of human beings in pain must be asserted. The system exists to serve them and if it is failing to do that, indeed is making their pain more intense, then there is something wrong with the system.

Thirdly, and most crucially, there is the Church's traditional prohibition of usury. As was shown in a previous chapter, the Church made a mistake in applying what originally referred to the poor to ordinary commercial transactions between equals. It had a two-fold deleterious effect. It made the Church's teaching in the rising world of capitalism out of date. Secondly, and no less important, it has led to the neglect of the original purpose of the prohibition of usury, namely the protection of the poor. The Hebrew scriptures are absolutely clear that the poor person is not to be burdened with debt. Leviticus 25 again makes the point:

And if your brother becomes poor, and cannot maintain himself with you, you shall maintain him; as a stranger and a sojourner he shall live with you. Take no interest from him or increase, but fear your God; that your brother may live beside you. You shall not lend him your money at interest, nor give him your food for profit. I am the Lord your God, who brought you forth out of the land of Egypt to give you the Land of Canaan, and to be your God. (Leviticus 25.35–38)

The developing countries who are in debt dislike the phrase 'debt forgiveness'. In their view, they have repaid the debt many times over. A powerful message to the Churches by a seminar of Churches in Brazil argued that:

Obligation to Pay is a *myth* which our creditors would like us to believe . . . The debt has been already paid several times over. In 1973 we owned 9.5 billion dollars. From that year until 1985 we paid 121 billion dollars in interest and in amortization. . . . Today we owe more than ten times the amount owned in 1973 or 120 billion dollars.

The message to the Churches went on to argue that much of the loans, around 18 to 20 per cent, never entered the country and what did took the form of private loans by transnationals to their branches in Brazil. Furthermore, Brazilian economic policies are dictated by the major international economic organizations with the result that the country has to follow an export policy which contributes to the impoverishment of the people and a policy of recession with all its social consequences.

> All the data demonstrates that the external debt of Brazil and of other countries is today one of the most efficient means of shortening life and causing death. It is an instrument of collective sin and usurps the sovereignty of God. . . . We cannot ask forgiveness for debts already paid; what is possible is that the oppressors and their allies recognize their sins and offences, they repent and humble themselves before God so that they may be forgiven and still live.

The huge amounts paid in interest, many times the original loan, and all the consequences of this in terms of human suffering, point up the absurdity and moral perversity of the whole exercise.[7] When normal commercial loans are lent, it is on the basis that there is a business which is going to produce reasonable profits for all concerned, so that the interest can be met and the loan eventually repaid. Perhaps some loans to developing countries can legitimately be seen in those terms. But, as the latest World Bank report emphasizes, the real need is for investment in primary health care, schools and all those aspects of community life which will raise the quality of life for the community as a whole. These are not going to produce any short-term returns for either shareholders or governments. The attempt to make them appear as commercial loans has meant the sending abroad of money that should be used for internal development, and internal policies dictated by the IMF which require strict financial control rather than community development, and which require an emphasis upon crops or goods which can raise hard currency rather than those which actually meet the needs of the people. Commercial loans should be on a proper commercial basis, with proper constraints to ensure that the borrower does not take on more debts than can be repaid. Other money should be given for social development or lent with no interest, as the seventeenth-century Anglican divines suggested in their discussions on usury.

Blame for the present burden of suffering imposed upon the poor of developing countries cannot be laid only at the door of Western nations or the economic order. The governments of the developing nations themselves must take a large share of the responsibility. For some of these countries are surprisingly prosperous on paper, despite the fact that the majority of their population is characterized by dire poverty. Brazil, for example, is eighth in the world league of GNP. It is the world's fourth biggest exporter of food, the fifth biggest of weapons and the sixth biggest of vehicles. Communications are good and the cities, leaving aside the shanty towns which surround them, are modern. Yet of the 145 million population, 50 million live in misery. One feature of the internal aspect of this injustice is the flight of capital abroad. In Brazil there was a net outflow of capital of $50.4 billion between 1980 and 1987.

A necessary first step is for developing countries themselves to introduce measures to discourage the flight of capital. This would probably necessitate an international agreement requiring disclosure of private and corporate bank deposits and investments of non-residents above a certain level. Although this violates the principle of confidentiality in the banking system, such confidentiality is also a cloak for much illegal activity and has resulted in considerable injustice. IMF sources give a figure of $150–200 billion capital which left the developing world for private bank accounts in Switzerland and the USA from 1974 to 1985. Some $30 billion of this was from Africa.

It cannot be asserted too strongly that seriously to tackle these problems means addressing economic and political realities. For, as at present organized, they have become 'structures of sin'. Sin, which is a basic word of the religious vocabulary, an expression of our freedom in relation to God and our fellow human beings, is inseparable from personal responsibility. Nevertheless, we all belong to and are caught up in societies and systems of various kinds, which perpetuate personal characteristics, for ill as well as for good. Pope John Paul II, while condemning social sins, has emphasized that these are always 'the result of the accumulation of concentration of many *personal sins*'.[8] Structures of sin 'are rooted in personal sin, and thus always linked to the *concrete acts* of individuals who introduce these structures, consolidate them and make them difficult to remove. And thus they grow stronger, spread, and become a source of other sins, and so influence people's behaviour.'[9]

As a result of these personal sins, structures are set up characterized by an all-consuming desire for profit and a thirst for power, both attitudes carrying with them the further characteristic 'at any price'. In the light of this, it is necessary to develop attitudes and structures of a consciously different kind, based on solidarity with those in need and an option or love of preference for the poor.

The necessity of reckoning with structures of sin was borne in upon Paul Vallely, the writer on developmental issues for *The Times*, who went with Bob Geldof to Africa. Like so many others, being moved by the plight of the starving and wanting to do something about it, he was struck by how little seems to change despite the goodwill of many. For example, the First World gives in aid less than half what it takes from the Third World in terms of tariffs and duties imposed on raw materials. Debt and interest repayments from the Third World are three times more than all the aid they currently receive. Aid by itself is simply not enough. So in a vivid extension of the parable of the Good Samaritan Vallely suggests that the person lying in the road injured has been robbed and knocked down by the agents of the Good Samaritan. Furthermore, the money which the Good Samaritan uses to look after the injured person is money that was stolen from him in the first place. The structures of sin that he locates are the fact that aid is not really aid but too often something else in disguise, neo-colonialist exploitation and protectionism. To sell fresh pineapples within the European Community, for example, a Third World producer must pay a tariff of 9 per cent. To sell tinned pineapples it must pay 32 per cent and to sell pineapple juice 42 per cent, the effective rate of protection on pineapple juice being equivalent to a tax of more than 75 per cent. The rapacity of the transnationals and the apparent impotence of the international monetary institutions to do anything about the situation are other structures of sin that Vallely discusses. As in this book, he argues that capitalism must be made to work better for the benefit of poor people. He quotes Tawney: 'To convert efficiency from an instrument to a primary object is to destroy efficiency itself.' He also argues that 'Even if we accept that capitalism can never work at its maximum efficiency in creating wealth within the context of a welfare state, that is not a sufficient argument against such provision for social justice. Maximum efficiency cannot be a Christian virtue if it is achieved at the expense of the full humanity of a billion people.' There is a need for a wider moral framework and Christian vision which will temper capitalism and tap its resources for those most in need.

To sum up then, words can hardly describe the plight of the world's poor. And this appalling situation is becoming even worse.

In recent decades the Christian Churches and the aid agencies struggled to keep this issue on the world's political agenda. Now, however, exponents of the so-called New Right politics argue that previous attempts to alleviate world poverty have been misconceived. So some of the arguments of the New Right were looked at and found to be fallacious. Nevertheless, the Christian *qua* Christian is not rigidly committed to any doctrinaire solution to this problem. The priority is to find a solution, wherever it comes from. If the New Right are able to show that the policies which have achieved some success in their beloved Taiwan are equally applicable in Africa and Latin America and these policies can be shown to actually work there, we will all rejoice. Meanwhile, the New Right would be more convincing in their attacks on developmental policies if they could show that the plight of the world's poor was high on the agenda of governments following New Right policies. If champions of unbridled capitalism went to the polls with a policy for the poor as the No. 1 priority, with a readiness to measure the success of their programme by the effect that it has on the poor, their negative criticisms of existing programmes would carry more weight.

The Christian Churches as Churches offer no particular technical expertise in this area, although very many Christians as individuals do. What the Churches can do is bring to bear certain fundamental principles. First, the goods of the earth are given by God for the benefit of all. This theme of the fourth-century Fathers is constantly reiterated in modern papal encyclicals.

> It is necessary to state once more the characteristic principle of Christian social doctrine: the goods of this world are *originally meant for all*. The right to private property is valid and necessary, but it does not nullify the value of this principle. Private property, in fact, is under a 'social mortgage', which means that it has an intrinsically social function, based upon and justified precisely by the principle of a universal destination of goods.[10]

Secondly, Christian insight into human sinfulness alerts us to the way in which the developed nations themselves have been in significant measure responsible for the inability of so many underdeveloped countries to clamber out of their poverty. The international economic order may not in theory be exploitative but in practice it is.

Thirdly, the scriptures, both Old and New Testaments, teach us to put the needs of the poor before other considerations. In this chapter, I looked at the principle of the Jubilee year, in which all debts were remitted. Even more crucial, it was argued that we need to recover the original purpose behind the Church's traditional ban on usury, namely protection of the poor from burdensome and oppressive debts. Whatever technical considerations there might be we cannot continue with a situation that is literally forcing millions of children into starvation and death.

Considerations such as this can overwhelm us with a combination of anguish, guilt and a sense of our own powerlessness. What, if anything, can we actually do? We can share in the work of the aid agencies, not only their humanitarian projects, but their educational and political work. We can try to ensure that when the next election comes developmental issues are taken seriously by all Parliamentary candidates. One of the sad features of British public life is that, as is often said, there are no votes in overseas aid. The Churches can make a significant contribution by insisting that both locally and nationally the parties not only consider these issues but put them higher on their own political agenda. Indeed, it might be salutary for all churches to unite in urging their members to vote for the political party which takes world development issues most seriously.

At the personal, vocational level, there will be Christians in positions of responsibility in commercial banks, the World Bank and working for the International Monetary Fund. There will be other Christians concerned with these issues as civil servants, diplomats or professional politicians. On such people a great responsibility rests. There are no simple answers and there are certainly no quick fixes. But the least we can ask is that our brothers and sisters in Christ approach these complex, technical questions with some of the principles outlined in this chapter. I once preached at a famous public school on world poverty. I indicated that this did not mean that everyone had to join an aid agency or go abroad. It was no less important to have people in merchant banking or the Foreign Office who carried this burden in their hearts. Afterwards two boys sauntered up to me and remarked, 'That was very interesting, sir – but of course we don't think like that here.' That is the trouble. There is a total divorce in so many people's minds between the world of economics and politics on the one hand and the Christian vocation to be in solidarity with the poor on the other. But Christ calls the whole world to be transformed in the light of the standards of the Kingdom he came to bring. This includes such matters as loans, terms of trade and access to markets, which so vitally affect the well-being of the most needy human beings.

The problem is so immense and complex that it is easy to feel that nothing can be done about it. So it is important to note that steps have been taken, are being taken and can be taken to overcome the problem. First of all, in relation to the poorest countries in the world, who owe most of their debts to governments, the British government has cancelled £1 billion of old aid loans. Furthermore, Mr Major, when Chancellor of the Exchequer, put forward proposals in September 1990 which, if generally accepted, would substantially increase relief to these countries. He proposed that when an eligible country seeks rescheduling of its debt to government creditors, this debt should be reduced by two-thirds. The remainder should be rescheduled over 25 years with no payments at all in the first five years. If this proposal is agreed by other creditors it could lead to a reduction of some 18 billion dollars in the debt of the poorest countries.[11]

The major debt burden is borne by middle-income countries, however, and this is a mixture of official and private debt, both mainly at market-related interest rates. The Baker initiative of 1985 sought to deal with this problem by proposing that the private creditors should agree to both rescheduling of debt and the supply of new credit. Private creditors showed themselves unwilling to respond to this initiative, not least because they did not see why they should make concessions when the official creditors were not prepared to match their efforts.

The Brady initiative of 1989 attempted to deal with the shortcomings of the Baker plan, in particular by making it possible for debtors to obtain new credit at the same time as private debt reduction, financed in part by the use of official funds supplied by the IMF, the World Bank or Japan. But it made no provision for public debt reduction and has failed in other ways.

The experts most concerned in this field, distinguished bankers and heads of aid agencies, believe that a new initiative is called for in relation to the middle-income countries. This would involve the acceptance by official creditors of the same responsibilities for debt reduction as are sought from private creditors. There would also be a specific element designed to enable the debtors, after a restructuring of their debt, to obtain new commercial credit.

The technicalities of this initiative do not concern us here. However, two points need to be made. First, despite a number of initiatives in recent years, involving rescheduling of loans, debt equity buyouts, reductions and so on, the burden of debt is still as heavy as ever for many countries and new, more radical initiatives are needed. Before the G7 (the seven largest economies) meeting in June 1990 there was some expectation that a new initiative by Mr Major would make a significant contribution to debt reduction. However, the advent of the crisis in the Soviet Union and other matters, as well as a failure to find significant agreement, has resulted in a disappearance of this. It is a characteristic feature of the debt issue that it so quickly gets pushed off centre stage. This makes it all the more imperative for the Churches as well as the aid agencies to keep the urgency of this issue before the public and politicians.

Secondly, there are people, bankers and politicians, who recognize the crucial importance of solving this problem and who are prepared to work at it with fresh proposals. Given public will and support there is no reason why they should not succeed. Communism in the Soviet Union and Eastern Europe looked as though it would last for many more decades. But the spirit of the people refused to be broken and in the end it was their spirit and will which brought the Berlin Wall tumbling down and ensured the triumph of Boris Yeltsin over the Communist Party. When the Gulf War was over and the Kurds were fleeing in their millions from Saddam Hussein's murderous designs, President Bush appeared to have washed his hands of the whole business. It was a sense of moral outrage in Britain and the United States, together with John Major's persistence, that forced President Bush to set up sanctuaries for the Kurds. Public opinion does still count, for good as well as ill. And where there is a political will changes can indeed be brought about. The story is told of an Anglican diocese which wished to pull down a parish church in order to build a new cathedral. Inadvertently one of the appeal letters went to the local Roman Catholic bishop. He replied 'Neither my faith nor my office allows me to support the building of an Anglican cathedral, but I have pleasure in enclosing a cheque for a thousand dollars to pull down the parish church!' Where there is a will there is a way. This chapter has tried to show that from a biblical point of view there is every reason urgently to find that way. At the end of the Second World War the United States wrote off the massive debts of its allies and gave huge sums towards the rebuilding of Europe. The crisis in the developing world is no less than that of Europe after the Second World War. We who benefited by having our debts written off are now in a position to show a similar realism and magnanimity to those being crushed by present debts.

NOTES

1 Peter Bauer, 'Ecclesiastical economics of the Third World: envy legitimised' in *The Kindness that Kills*, ed. Digby Anderson (SPCK, 1984), pp. 34ff.
2 Edward Norman, *Christianity and the World Order* (OUP, 1979).
3 Reinhold Niebuhr, *Moral Man and Immoral Society* (Scribners, 1932).
4 Brian Griffiths, *Morality in the Market Place* (Hodder & Stoughton, 1980), p. 131.
5 A defence of taxes and the question of whether it is ever right to refuse to pay them has been written by Stanley Booth-Clibborn, the Bishop of Manchester, *Taxes: Burden or Blessing?* (Arthur James, 1991).
6 There are many accounts of the debt crisis and how it arose. A useful short account is *Proclaim Jubilee: Debt and Poverty*, CAFOD, 2 Garden Close, Stockwell Road, London SW9 9TY. A more extended but thoroughly readable account of how the debt arose and the structural factors involved in trying to lift it is Paul Vallely's *Bad Samaritans* (Hodder & Stoughton, 1990).
7 In 'The ethics of international debt' in *Finance and Ethics* (Centre for Theology and Public Issues, New College, Edinburgh, 1987), Charles Elliott argues that some countries might now have no alternative to dedicating a manageable proportion of their foreign exchange earnings to debt service, irrespective of what proportion of their total obligation that meets.
8 *Reconciliatio et Paenitentia*, 16.
9 *Sollicitudo Rei Socialis*, 36.
10 *Sollicitudo Rei Socialis*, 42.
11 Mr Major unilaterally cancelled £500 million of debt, but the USA has yet to follow his lead.

12

Transformation of Us and All Things

The good news of God's love in Christ always comes as the possibility of transformation now by that presence and power who in the end will transfigure and irradiate all things. Clearly, then, we can only hear and receive that good news if we are aware of the need for change, liberation and transformation either in ourselves or in the world as a whole, or more realistically in both areas. As was suggested in Chapter 2, the starting point for most people will be an awareness of their own needs. We come to God conscious of our own emotional, moral or spiritual bankruptcy. We hold out our hands empty to God. The Welsh priest and poet R. S. Thomas puts this well in a recent poem.

> When we are weak, we are
> Strong. When our eyes close
> On the world, then somewhere
> Within us the bush
>
> Burns. When we are poor
> And aware of the inadequacy
> Of our table, it is to that
> Uninvited the guest comes.[1]

Classically this is an approach which Christians have summed up in the prayer of St Thomas Aquinas before receiving Holy Communion.

> Almighty and everlasting God,
> Behold we approach the sacrament of thy only-begotten Son,
> Our Lord Jesus Christ.
> Sick, we come to the physician of life:
> As unclean, to the fountain of mercy:
> As blind, to the light of eternal splendour:

As needy, to the Lord of heaven and earth:
As naked, to the King of Glory.

This book has been primarily concerned with material wealth. However, it is also important to note that there are other forms of riches which can encourage a false pride and self-sufficiency and which preclude that poverty of spirit which opens us up to the riches of Christ. H. A. Williams, writing on the text 'How hardly shall they that have riches enter into the Kingdom of God', takes his readers to an art gallery in Florence:

> Most of the visitors are trying frantically to accumulate riches. Clutching the
> *guide bleu* with grim determination, they are attempting to make capital for
> themselves out of the masterpieces they see. They hope that when they emerge,
> they will possess so much the more culture, so much the more conversation,
> so much the more cosmopolitanism. What a relief to find in the Uffizi that
> the last bay is unexpectedly a bar. For making this sort of money is terribly
> exhausting work. And the sad joke is that the money is worthless. For the
> masterpieces by means of which they inflate their own egos have shown them
> nothing and told them nothing, have sent them in fact empty away. Because
> they have treated the art galleries as a sort of aesthetic stock market, its real
> treasure is denied them. Their pitiable, laughable riches have excluded them
> from the Kingdom of God.[2]

Father Williams then develops this theme in relation to our attitude to work and our attitude to our friends. In both cases instead of appreciating something or someone for their own sake, we try to make capital out of them. Even more destructive, according to him, are religious riches. When we trust a particular attitude to the Bible or the Church or scholarship, or trust our own feelings, whether a sense of sin or ecstasy, instead of turning to God aware of the bankruptcy of all attempts to play these kind of games, we pile up those riches which cut us off from God.

There is only one Gospel, for rich and poor alike. What prevents us from hearing it is any form of complacency, smugness and self-righteousness. So, as experience proves, it is often when people are going through a bad patch, a bereavement, a sickness or a marriage break-up, that they really discover the depth of human existence and God's presence with them in it. Too easily, when things are going well, we slip back into taking things for granted. With an endearing honesty, General Sir Anthony Farrar-Hockley describes his own spiritual biography.[3] When he was a captive during the Korean War he suffered from malaria. The padre laid his hand on his head and the fever left immediately. However, afterwards Farrar-Hockley wondered whether this was simply a sort of conditioned reflex.

> Then, during a period of torture and solitary confinement, I prayed intensely
> and was often conscious that God was listening and responding. . . . Alone in
> a cell, I reflected on what I believed in, and concluded that my life was
> changed thereby.

When he was released life went back to normal. His faith slipped into the background.

> Then my first wife became ill with cancer, and died. I had breezily supposed that after a few serious prayers, her brave struggle would be successful. It became apparent to me that I presumed a knowledge of God's mind. During this most painful period of my life, the reflections in a captive cell returned to me, sparing me some of the confusion of bereavement.

His recent escape from an IRA bomb once again brought home to him the reality of God's mercy. And on this, as he says, 'I hope to build an indestructible faith'.

This does not mean that we have to wait for a personal knock before coming to our senses. On the contrary and as stated at the beginning of this book gratitude is no less strong a basis for religious faith than personal need. But as Sir Anthony Farrar-Hockley's experience so vividly illustrates, there is a tendency in all of us to slip back into self-sufficiency.

An awareness of our own need is a legitimate way into faith. It cannot, however, remain a resting place. One of the indispensable insights we all need to take from the liberation theologians, who were discussed in Chapter 5, is a consciousness of the context in which our faith is set and the social and political effects of such a faith. People in the industrialized world begin to find life somewhat empty and meaningless. As they reflect on existence they begin to discover a religious faith and their life takes on a new dimension. Such a faith can be entirely authentic. But it is important to realize that such a way into faith is different from that of someone whose prayer is an anguished cry for daily bread and sheer survival. Furthermore, it is vital to be aware of the kind of social, economic and political attitudes which will spring from such a faith. Will they be such as to enlarge our sympathy for the poor and deepen our commitment on their behalf? Will such a faith lead to action?

A faith that originates with a sense of personal need does not begin by being inauthentic. But it can become so if it confines its understanding of faith to what goes on inside our hearts and minds and between people in interpersonal relations. There is a disturbing element of blindness about all forms of pietism which fail to take into account the social, economic and political matrix within which faith arises and which refuse to ask hard questions about the political effects of belief.

The way to transformation is: first, a willingness to come before God with our own personal needs; secondly, a willingness to subject our understanding of faith to a critique about its context and effects;[4] thirdly, the development of a sense of spiritual solidarity with all those in need of different kinds. Sometimes it is only a bitter experience which brings about that solidarity, as was the case for King Lear. King Lear gave away his kingdom to his daughters. When powerless, he found himself treated with ignominy. Goneril and Regan subjected him to scorn and stripped him of even that little which he had left. Caught in a storm he tells his Fool to seek shelter and says 'I'll pray, and then I'll sleep.' The Fool leaves him alone and his prayer takes the form of a meditation on those who are in a similar plight to himself and his own previous thoughtlessness for them.

> Poor naked wretches, whereso'er you are,
> That bide the pelting of this pitiless storm,
> How shall your houseless heads and unfed sides,
> Your loop'd and window'd raggedness defend you
> From seasons such as these? O! I have ta'en
> Too little care of this! Take physic, pomp!
> Expose thyself to feel what wretches feel,
> That thou mayst shake the superflux to them,
> And show the heavens more just.[5]

It was Lear's own pitiful plight that made him aware of other poor wretches. He realized that he had given too little thought to them, that his pomp needed medicine and that the medicine was to feel something of what they feel. Nor was this just a matter of feeling. The hope expressed in Lear's meditation is that the world's surplus might go to those who need it and the heavens thereby be shown to be more just.

It was adverse experience which brought about a new awareness in King Lear. But we are asked to develop this awareness whether things are going well or badly for us personally. It is in this sense of spiritual solidarity that our action is to be rooted. As the Vatican discussion of liberation theology brought out so clearly, solidarity with the poor is an essential characteristic of a truly Christian life and community.

The fourth element in the way of transformation is a passionate sharing in the longing of the dispossessed for a different world. Running through the Hebrew scriptures is the ardent prayer that God will act to put right everything that is wrong in the world. People longed for the time when his Kingly rule would be apparent in human affairs and the whole of human existence would be transparent to his glory. Jesus announced that this kingdom of love, this new order of peace and justice, was breaking into the world and he invited people to live in a radically new way under God's Kingly rule. It was those who had been most knocked about by life, either through physical suffering or through their sense of being rejected by society, that welcomed him with alacrity. They longed for this new state of affairs with all their being and recognized its presence in Christ. So, in every age, it has always been the poor who have composed the vast majority of Christian people. It is only if others can to some extent share the longing for God's Kingdom that they can receive the message about it.

In Luke's version of the Beatitudes we read: 'Blessed are you that hunger now, for you shall be satisfied' (Luke 6.21). A few verses further on comes the corresponding woe: 'Woe to you that are full now, for you shall hunger' (Luke 6.25). It is quite clear that Luke is referring to physical hunger.

Matthew puts the matter differently. He records: 'Blessed are those who hunger and thirst for righteousness, for they shall be satisfied' (Matthew 5.6). Yet are the two Beatitudes so totally opposed? Or is it possible that to hunger and thirst for righteousness, really to hunger and thirst for a different world, is to be in profound solidarity with those who starve? The playwright Tennessee Williams once said:

> I have always regarded myself as an incomplete person. . . . To tell you the truth, I am not sure I have ever met a complete person. I have met many people that seemed well-adjusted but I am not sure that to be well-adjusted to things as they are is to be desired. . . . I am not sure I would want to be well-adjusted to things as they are. I would prefer to be racked by desire for things better than they are, even for things which are unattainable, than to be satisfied with things as they are.[6]

A person may have everything material that they want and life may be going marvellously for them. However, if they share something of that sense of Tennessee Williams they are still capable of hearing the good news of God's Kingdom. When this desire is present, not only emotionally but spiritually, practically and politically, we have the hunger and thirst that is blessed.

Fifthly, in order that this longing might be more than a pious hope or fantasy it is important for there to be actual personal contact with people who are in one way or another marginalized. One of the great insights of the liberation theologians is that true theology emerges out of communities of committed poor struggling for a different world. Yet few Christians in the developed world will have real opportunity for prolonged contact with the base communities, as they are called, which have sprung up in Latin America, Sri Lanka and elsewhere. Instead of romanticizing about what is happening in far distant lands it is more realistic as well as more costly to try to link one's life with people locally who in one way or another are suffering. One theologian whom I greatly admire has always made a point of keeping a close relationship going with a prisoner or tramp in order that his theology might be rooted in lives where the knocks are hardest. Even if we are not theologians, it is a good principle. There are many categories of people, fashionable and unfashionable, not many blocks away to whom we can relate our lives and with whom we can share the struggle for a different, better world. These might be groups of homeless, the mentally ill, single parents and so on. But what is desirable is not only one-to-one relationships but the attempt to create communities taking responsibility for their own lives and seeking to change things for the better. Every priest and every Christian could be a catalyst for some such group of people.

Sixthly, there will be a developing sense of how much we have to receive from those who have little of this world's goods. One parish priest tells me that since he began to minister seriously to mentally handicapped people his whole ministry has been transformed. He realized how much he had to receive from the mentally handicapped and from this came a totally different approach to others, in terms of a greater patience and sense of receptivity to what they had to offer.

The New Testament gives us a picture of the Church as a community characterized by mutual sharing. In the early centuries this was a living reality, and the fourth-century Fathers continually stressed how much the Church as a whole had to receive from the poor. On a recent trip to Brazil, the group I was with visited a group of 32 poor families who had just, after a bitter struggle, managed to acquire some land. They lived in makeshift shelters, covered only with old thatch and plastic. They had virtually nothing. Yet what struck us so forcibly was not just their material poverty but their dignity. The earth floor was swept clean, the saucepans were polished, the children's clothes were washed. The spokesperson for this group of families was a young mother. She emphasized that the family looked after one another. Recently one hut had burnt down with a loss of all possessions. The others had rallied round, each providing some piece of clothing or food. Nor did this group of families, because they had managed to acquire some land, adopt an 'I'm all right Jack' attitude. Quite the contrary, she emphasized that they were in solidarity with all the six million landless people in Brazil. There was one struggle for a decent life, of which they were all a part.

As we approached the families they came to meet us singing popular songs, many of them with words of faith. They presented us with small bunches of wild flowers picked from the fields and each of us was given a tiny handmade card with the words written on it in Portuguese: 'In these small gifts there is the presence of God.'

We knew that we had something to give to these people. Indeed, the representatives from the developed countries immediately pledged to raise the money to build 32 small houses, a well and a meeting hall for them. We also knew that we could not separate giving to those families from the wider political struggle to ensure basic living conditions for the millions of impoverished people in Brazil and elsewhere. Yet at the same time, we knew we had received and would continue to receive much from the people we had met. Their dignity, their faith, their sense of sharing, their courage, their strong sense of corporate solidarity with one another and all the rural poor was both a challenge and an encouragement. It presented a strong contrast to the selfish, individualistic striving of so much life in the so-called developed world.

Seventhly, there is the need to confront in our own situation those social, economic and political factors which bear most hardly upon the poor, whether in our own country or abroad. In his book *Comfortable Compassion*, Charles Elliott surveys the various approaches that have been adopted towards development in recent decades and highlights their inadequacies. One fundamental flaw, present in conscientization/liberation models as much as modernization ones, is that they situate the most effective point of engagement for those who wish to help in the developing countries themselves. Elliott argues that there will always be an imbalance between rich and poor, that the rich will always try to exploit the poor, and the root of this is not capitalism as such but human nature. Some forms of economic organization are of course better than others but none is definitive.

> What is definitive is the *level and nature of the consciousness that informs the actions of the rich and powerful in their dealings with the relatively poor and relatively powerless.*
>
> It is the creation of an *alternative* consciousness, which in the spirit of the Magnificat and Beatitudes puts the poor and the powerless at its centre, that is the true task of the Church in development. This alternative consciousness is not paternalistic or condescending; it is a consciousness that turns upside down the priorities and assumptions of twentieth-century industrialized, secularized acquisitiveness (whether capitalist or socialist) and judges relationships, structures, and economic ties not by what profit it brings to the dominant partner but by how much it enlarges the life chances of the subordinate partner. That means the judgements have to be made by the subordinate partner – which in turn means that the subordination is ended. The interests of the poor and powerless, as formulated and expressed by themselves, thus become definitive of the alternative consciousness. The rich and powerful, in other words, have to learn to use their wealth and power not for their own aggrandizement, but for the goals set by the poor and powerless.[7]

How do we develop this alternative consciousness? By experiencing at first hand some aspect of the world's poverty; by responding to the call of God to do something about it; and by learning to receive from, as well as to give to, those we are wanting to help. As Elliott points out, the parable of the Good Samaritan is as much about receiving as giving. The Orthodox Jew received from the despised Samaritan. Then we can face the institutional powers with the effects of their policies — the debt burden, commodity prices, the international monetary system. Who is responsible for all this? We are all caught in a web of value systems and explanations that 'justify' the present arrangements. We need to counteract this by developing strategies whereby many countries of the world are systematically confronted with the consequences of their own existence. The parables of Jesus provide a model for doing just this, Elliott thinks. So he writes:

> Here we have, I believe, a vital clue to the question of how we begin to open the structures of injustice to the redeeming love of Christ. We have to confront them, not in a spirit of condemnation and anger – which would itself merely reveal how little progress we had made on our own inward journey – but in a way that achieves the following objectives:
>
> (a)   reveals the effects of those structures on the poor and vulnerable,
> (b)   places us alongside those who suffer those effects,
> (c)   raises questions about the system, the structure, rather than about its agents.
> (d)   looks for total transformation, not ameliorative reform,

(e) accepts that the consequences of such a challenge will often be unpleasant,

(f) accepts that the process of confrontation does not, of itself, transform structures. It may challenge them, educate them, shock them into a deeper awareness of what their essence looks like from the bottom. In the end, however, transformation is the work of the spirit,

(g) sees, therefore, the process of structural transformation as a gift, a gift we all, both individually and corporately, need to share. For we are all engaged on the same (or perhaps a similar) journey.

In short, we truly help the poor, and at the same time become the poor who are blessed, not so much by action, in their situations (though that may be part of it) as by standing with them *in our own* situation and confronting the institutions and organizations and attitudes which maintain a system of impoverishment. The Church will be a centre of resistance, or a multicellular structure made up of a number of centres of resistance. So what is called for is an alternative consciousness that finds expression in the creation and sustenance of these centres of resistance – resistance to the powers that threaten human possibilities.

One of the key points made by Charles Elliott in his helpful analysis is that if we really want to help the powerless we have to confront the institutions that make them powerless in our own situation. This may be much more costly than simply offering direct help, though that is necessary also. One way in which many Christians have done this in recent years is by raising questions at the annual general meetings of transnational companies. This has been done in relation to environmental issues, particularly in Latin America. It has also been done in relation to companies which, by their very presence in South Africa, helped to give legitimacy to apartheid. It is not a particularly pleasant experience to rise at an AGM, a powerful board of directors sitting on a raised dais ahead, and surrounded by sober-suited city folk. As soon as the words 'South Africa' are mentioned, there is the sound of hissing and a chorus of disapproval. The embarrassment caused to those who try to protest, in however small a way, at such meetings is nothing compared to the suffering and humiliation undergone by fellow Christians in South Africa or elsewhere. However, it is a genuine act of solidarity, and like all such brings those who share this spirit up against the powers that be. For the financial forces of the world do not welcome the raising of basic questions about their operations.

In Chapter 2 of this book, when the question of who are the poor and why are they blessed was discussed, certain conclusions were reached. It was argued that the poor referred to in the Beatitudes, like the poor who are so often the subject of the psalms, cannot be regarded as exclusively either a social or a religious category. They certainly form a religious category, in that they pray to God out of their distress, look to him to put right everything that is wrong in the world and continue, despite everything, to put their trust in him. Yet they also constitute a social category, in the sense that in one way or another they lose out in the world as it is at present organized. Sometimes they lose out through material poverty but other forms of harassment and oppression are often referred to in the psalms. People with some degree of power, influence and wealth who stand alongside the poor in confronting policies that work against the poor are themselves likely to experience some of the ill effects of this. This has certainly been so in Latin America when Church leaders have challenged the status quo. It is not only Archbishop Oscar Romero who has lost his life. Dom Helder Câmara's statement, 'When I give food to the poor they call me a saint. When I ask why the poor have no food they call me a communist', is often quoted. It indicates that those who ask awkward questions about systems and institutions will always find themselves unpopular.

This is of crucial significance for our theme. For it means that those who are asking questions in their own situation about the effects of policies on those least able to stand up for themselves will experience something of what it is to be brushed aside. In short, imaginative, spiritual and personal solidarity with the poor suddenly becomes very real. And here is cause for great joy. For if we believe that the more we come before Christ conscious of our own emptiness the better able we are to receive the riches of his life-giving presence and grace, then this actual, practical and political solidarity with the poor in our own situation opens us up as nothing else to receive the fullness of God himself.

In Australia the Roman Catholic and Anglican Archbishops of Melbourne made a public appeal for virtue in public life. They called for a raising of the standard of personal morality, in business, commerce and politics. This was welcomed by a leading newspaper. In its leader column it commented

> Too many modern churchmen, perhaps despairing of the unregenerate ever being called to an account in this world, have preferred to assail institutional vices. At its most ridiculous, this tendency could be seen in the liberation theologist's doctrine of 'Structural Sin'. Capitalism, that diverse enterprise, was said to be stained with sin, but how could it repent, let alone attain paradise?[8]

The standard of personal morality does indeed need to be raised the world over. And perhaps structural injustice is a better phrase than structural sin, in that sin implies personal accountability. But the concept of structural injustice is not an invention of the liberation theologians. It is firmly there in the most authoritative Vatican pronouncements. Systems are not neutral. They inevitably reflect the interests and power configurations of fallen humanity. It is an essential aspect of Christian discipleship to be aware of this and to struggle against the results.

For it is the common conviction, not just of liberation theologians, but also of those who stand in the tradition of evangelical social ethics, that the fight is not just against personal sin but against systemic, structural flaws. As already mentioned, Paul Vallely went to Africa with Bob Geldof and wrote up his story. Like others, he was appalled at what he saw and wanted to do. As time went by and he discovered that charitable giving was not enough, he began to look more deeply into the causes of poverty in the world. Time and again he came up against structural injustice, that is, systems set in their ways, which tend to reinforce oppressive poverty, and about which a single individual seems to be able to do very little. The great challenge today is to do something about that system, to make it serve the needs of humanity as a whole.

In the famous parable a Samaritan finds a man knifed and robbed in the street. He takes him to a hotel and pays for his keep and medical care, then goes on his way. Following Paul Vallely's lead, we could develop the parable along these lines: The street is a dangerous one, so the inhabitants petition the authorities to police it better, which they do. Some of the criminals are caught. They turn out to be desperate people, with nothing to lose, so the charitable instinct of good people works for their reform and rehabilitation. Workshops are set up and new homes built. The Samaritan is still abroad, but he receives an appeal letter and responds most generously. Eventually, he comes by that way again, to visit his businesses and estates, and goes into one of these rehabilitation projects to encourage the good work which he is financially supporting. He talks to some of those being helped. He is appalled to discover that they are people who have been forced off his own lands, put out of work by his own businesses or been unable to survive on the minimum wage of $39 a month that they were being paid.

Faced with this situation the Samaritan, that is, any human being in a position to help, knows that the economic and political system itself needs changing. Personal generosity and institutional charity are essential indicators of our individual commitment but by themselves they are not enough.

This book has been written in the conviction that Christians can and should be fully active in the capitalist world on the basis of two principles. First, there is a fundamental compatibility between many aspects of a market economy and the Christian faith, which makes it legitimate for Christians to participate. Secondly, because of human sin, we will need to be continuously on the alert for the way the system gets skewed to further the interests of the powerful against the powerless. In recent decades the debate has often been polarized between those who reject the capitalist system lock, stock and barrel and those who work within it uncritically. My plea is for Christians to work within it with a conscience that is at once both easier and more troubled. That troubled aspect of our conscience will lead us to ask awkward questions and so share something of the disparagement experienced by millions of marginalized people.

Personal discipline and efforts to work out the economic and political consequences of our faith are not alternatives. They belong together as an integral whole. Without the discipline of personal prayer and generous giving political action can be a sham. On the other hand, discipleship confined to the personal sphere alone, in today's world, is simply escapism, bad faith and sentimentality.

Personal giving is an essential part of Christian discipleship. While many bodies, such as the Mormons or the house churches, put mainstream Christians to shame with their regular sacrificial giving, many Anglicans are also beginning to rediscover the liberation of tithing, that is, giving a regular 10 per cent of one's income to the work of God. This is not a substitute for political action but an essential prelude to it. Redmond Mullin, who argues that we need a radical transformation of our economic and political systems, and that this must be undertaken primarily by lay people, argues that personal Christian giving

> is neither the end nor the main process; it is one condition which makes the real process possible. The reason why the churches have failed to create a radical, Christian revolution in economic systems and behaviour, is partly attributable to their failure in the kind of elementary re-education just considered, which is a pre-condition for such a revolution.[9]

Metropolitan Anthony Bloom, who was trained as a doctor, once said:

> When I was a professional man, we made a decision with my mother never to live beyond the minimum which we need for shelter and food because we thought and I still think, that whatever you spend above that, it is stolen from someone else who needs it while you don't need it. It doesn't make you sinister, it gives you a sense of joy and sharing, and in giving and receiving. But I do feel that as long as there is one person who is hungry, excess of happiness — excess of amenities — is a theft.[10]

The language, as we might expect from an Orthodox, echoes that of the Fathers. It is a duty, not an optional extra, to try to meet the needs of the needy in as effective a way as possible, a way that gets to the heart of the matter. In responding we will be able both to hear the good news of God's love and to receive that love most fully and joyfully.

Because all things are possible for God, we cannot rule out hope of the rich entering the Kingdom of God. But we still need to view the prospect with a gospel set of values. Evelyn Waugh brings this out well, with his characteristic irony: which is also the divine irony? In his novel about Helena, the mother of the Emperor Constantine, Helena meditates at one point on the three kings who came to worship the infant Christ.

> How laboriously you came, taking sights and calculating, where the shepherds had run barefoot! How odd you looked on the road, attended by what outlandish liveries, laden with such preposterous gifts! . . . Yet you came, and were not turned away. You too found room before the manger, your gifts were not needed, but they were accepted and put carefully by, for they were bought with love. In that new order of charity that had just come to life, there was room for you, too. You were not lower in the eyes of the Holy Family than the ox or the ass.[11]

Helena then prays for all those with different kinds of riches: 'All who are confused with knowledge and speculation, of all who through politeness make themselves partners in guilt, of all who stand in danger by reason of their talents.'

> For his sake who did not reject your curious gifts, pray always for all the learned, the oblique, the delicate. Let them not be quite forgotten at the throne of God when the simple come into their kingdom.

If the good news of God's love in Christ always comes with the possibility of transformation now by that presence and power who in the end will transfigure and irradiate all things, then we can begin to experience that change now both in our own personal lives and in the setting where God has put us to work. This transformation begins with us but includes all people and all the social, economic and political forces which shape human life and destiny. To sum up. First, an awareness of our own personal need will be the way into faith for many and an aspect of faith for all believers. Secondly, though this may be the beginning of faith it must not end there. It needs to be subjected to the critique of the liberation theologians. Thirdly, this faith, if authentic, will lead to a developing sense of spiritual solidarity with all those in need of any kind. Fourthly, this solidarity will express itself in an active, shared longing for a different, better world. Fifthly, in order to avoid false romanticizing and fantasy it will be necessary to have direct personal contact and involvement with some people who are relatively powerless and vulnerable. Sixthly, we will be conscious of what we have to receive from such people as well as what we have to give in partnership with them. Seventhly, we will tackle the forces in our own situation which adversely affect the poor elsewhere. In so doing we may very well find ourselves in a very real way losing out and experiencing more intensely that blessedness which belongs to God's poor.

This requires commitment to the personal disciplines of the Christian life, including the use of our own money. It will also have as an essential component a properly Christian approach to the economic order. This is one that takes into account the necessity of increasing the resources of society in order to improve the quality of life for all; which does not disparage growth but asks for growth in the right areas; which supports the market economy, while at the same time works against its exploitative tendencies; that believes in ownership, but ownership much more widely diffused than we have at present; which believes in companies, even trans-national corporations, but believes that the concept of stakeholder needs strengthening and that companies themselves need to develop more of a corporate existence; which believes that the terrible burden of Third World debt can and must be lifted. In short, we need a new vision of capitalism existing for all God's children. Such a vision and the determination to bring it about is the work of Christian discipleship in the social, economic and political spheres. The risen Lord, whom Christians seek to serve, calls us to follow him not only in our personal lives but by denying ourselves, taking up our cross and following him into the companies, markets, exchanges and parliaments of the world. If we do this we are bound to come up against vested interests, and deeply ingrained forces of institutional self-interest as well as personal selfishness. But in suffering with Christ on behalf of the poor we will enter more fully into the joy of the resurrected life.

NOTES

1 R. S. Thomas, *Counterpoint* (Bloodaxe Books, 1990), p. 62.
2 H. A. Williams, *The True Wilderness* (Penguin, 1986), p. 55.
3 'The door', *The Diocese of Oxford Reporter* (November 1990).
4 This is especially important for the way in which we read and interpret the Bible. Too often we read the Bible to quieten our consciences rather than to allow it to question and challenge us. Christopher Rowlands and Mark Carver in *Liberating Exegesis* (SPCK, 1990) compare some traditional interpretations with those of poor people. They discuss, for example, the parable of Dives and Lazarus (Luke 16.19–31; on pp. 26–31).
5 *King Lear*, Act III, Scene 4.
6 Programme note, 1988 National Theatre production of *Cat on a Hot Tin Roof*.
7 Charles Elliott, *Comfortable Compassion* (Hodder & Stoughton, 1987), pp. 117–18.
8 *The Australian* (29 July 1991).
9 Redmond Mullin, *The Wealth of Christians* (Paternoster Press, 1983), p. 197.
10 Anthony Bloom, *God and Man* (Darton, Longman & Todd, 1971), p. 16.
11 Evelyn Waugh, *Helena* (Penguin, 1950), p. 239.

A ND they were exceedingly astonished, and said to him,
'Then who can be saved?'
Jesus looked at them and said,
'With men it is impossible, but not with God;

FOR ALL THINGS ARE POSSIBLE WITH GOD.'

(Mark 10.26–27)

Risen, ascended, glorified Lord,
Grant that I may be in such solidarity with those who
lose out now
That I too may be one of the poor whom you pronounce
blessed;
And grant that I may so stand against the forces that
crush the powerless,
Looking and working for your new order of love,
Trusting in you,
That even now I may be filled with the richness of your
presence
and know the glory of your kingdom.

Index